Invested

Invested

How Warren Buffett and Charlie Munger

Taught Me to Master My Mind, My Emotions, and

My Money (with a Little Help from My Dad)

Danielle Town
with Phil Town

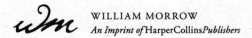

WILLIAM MORROW
An Imprint of HarperCollins*Publishers*

This book is designed to provide readers with a general overview of investment models and financial markets and how they work. It is not designed to be a definitive investment guide or to take the place of advice from a qualified financial planner or other professional. While the method of investment described in this book is believed to be effective, there is no guarantee that the method will be profitable in specific applications, owing to the risk that is involved in investing of almost any kind. Thus, neither the publisher nor the author assume liability of any kind for any losses that may be sustained as a result of applying the methods suggested in this book, and any such liability is hereby expressly disclaimed. In some instances, we have changed the date of an event or combined events for purposes of the story, but it does not affect anything substantively.

HarperCollins books may be purchased for educational, business, or sales promotional use. For information please e-mail the Special Markets Department at SPsales@harpercollins.com.

FIRST EDITION

Designed by William Ruoto

Library of Congress Cataloging-in-Publication Data has been applied for.

ISBN 978-0-06-267265-0

18 19 20 21 22 LSC 10 9 8 7 6

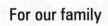

For our family

CONTENTS

Contents

Contents

IF YOU'VE BEEN THE PERFECT PARENT, FEEL FREE TO CAST THE FIRST stone. Otherwise, have a little empathy when I tell you that this book came about because I failed to teach my own daughter how to do what I do for a living. You know the old stories about the cobbler's kid who had no shoes or the farmer's kid who had no milk? Well, this book is about, in part, the investor's kid who had no investments.

Come on, now; it isn't my fault. I've been trying to get my daughter, Danielle, to learn to invest since she was old enough to do the math—like, fourth grade—because I've been investing since 1980 and I've been teaching investing ever since I wrote my first book, *Rule #1,* in 2006. It's simple: I want Danielle to be happy, and having enough money to do what she wants is part of happiness.

I knew I had to teach her myself because real investing isn't taught as a viable strategy anywhere except in occasional books and classes, and by me. Diversify and hold is commonly thought of as investing, but that strategy is really just a cleverly disguised form of speculation that provides $100 billion a year in fees and commissions to Wall Street sharks and sycophant financial advisers. Buying stocks and bonds that you don't understand isn't investing. Warren Buffett says investing is buying an asset that produces cash flow for substantially less than it's worth, like buying a $10 bill for $5. In other words, real investing is about having a high degree of certainty that you're going to make money because of the difference between what you paid and the cash flow value you bought; everything else is speculating.

I also wanted Danielle to learn to change a tire for equally obvious reasons. She didn't want to learn to do either one.

That changed when she graduated with her fourth degree and got a job and a condo. Suddenly she was faced with taxes and student loans and mortgage payments and the shocking discovery that even for an attorney working in a good law firm and making really good money by anybody's standards, accumulating wealth was hard. She finally did the math and discovered that unless she was willing to be a wage slave for her whole life, accumulating enough money to have choices was nearly impossible without investing.

She asked me what she should do. I gave her my two books to read. She read them, sort of, and told me those books were for people who were already interested in learning to invest. She didn't want to learn to invest. She just wanted the problem to go away. And thus began her journey that is this book.

She thought about it for a few weeks and decided that if she could get interested in investing and actually learn it, anyone could. She suggested that we do a podcast of our conversations about investing, and she would be the guinea pig. I was pretty sure it was going to be a train wreck. Who wants to listen to a podcast about investing in which the mentor's ideas get blown up on a regular basis by his very smart and skeptical daughter? Well, surprisingly, lots of people. Our podcast has consistently been at the top of the business and investing charts, and we get e-mails from people who are listening to the recordings over and over.

Clearly, many people instinctively relate to Danielle's classic heroine's journey in which she pushed forward into an unfamiliar and topsy-turvy world where down was often up and allies might be enemies. As much as I wanted to, I couldn't make her like investing; she had to find her own passion for it by "voting" for her values through investing as a conscious capitalist. Fear of making a mistake and losing money was a much bigger deal for her than I ever thought; because I have never felt much fear when it comes to investing, for the first time I took that fear personally. As a Vietnam War veteran, I've always had the perspective of "Nobody's shooting at me, so how scary can this be?" It took me a while to believe that fear was truly what was stopping her from investing. Once I understood that, it opened my eyes to the predicament of thousands of potential investors who are as desperate for a solution to managing their financial future as Danielle was. Danielle had to find her own way to face her fears, defeat the bad guys, and return with a message of hope and a plan for victory.

It is the right time for victory. This is not only the right time for the message of voting your values with your money, it is also the right time to stop being afraid of losing money by learning to prepare for a stock market crash. In spite of the rocketing stock market, some economists and investors, including me, think the United States may soon enter into another recession and market decline. Unlike what most people think, this situation could actually create a great opportunity to buy wonderful companies at attractive prices. It is my mission to educate people on the realities of today's market and how to acquire the skills to reap enormous financial rewards regardless of what the stock market is doing, what war is raging, what president is in office, or what the media and investing gurus say people should and should not do.

This book is our solution. The investor's kid now has investments and is prepared for her future. I still need to teach her to change a tire.

—PHIL TOWN

I AM A RELUCTANT INVESTOR.

When I hear "personal finance and investing," in my mind I see a long, dark path of thick, swirling gray fog filled with numbers and balance sheets floating in the turmoil. Some lucky people seem to be able to easily find a path through that fog. Long ago, I stopped trying to learn to be one of them. I was never one for numbers. They swim in my mind and, though I can usually catch them and force them into submission, it's never pleasant. And yet . . . this book is about my personal journey from financial illiteracy to becoming an educated investor. No one is more surprised than I am that I wrote a book about succeeding in personal finance and investing.

If I can do it, then truly, anyone can.

I learned how to invest on my own. I have learned what is called "Rule #1 investing" from my father, and from the wisdom of Charlie Munger and Warren Buffett, who originally coined the phrase. I've learned the theory, strategy, and practice of investing. And to all that, I've added what might be the most crucial element to keep me sticking with it after the novelty wears off: investing my money so it will make an impact on a Mission I support.

Allocating your money according to your own values, and supporting companies worthy of your investment, is reason enough to learn this practice and this method of investing. It's a way to vote with your money for the future you want. I realized that if I wanted to vote my personal values with my personal money, I was going to have to overcome my inertia and my fear and do it myself.

A lot of this book is about fear: how I deal with it, and how other people investing in the stock market act on it. Voting for a Mission with my money made me feel passionate about investing, but I still felt afraid of stepping into that gray fog. Many economists and investors, including my dad, think the United States is imminently headed for another recession and market decline. But crucially, I've learned to use my own fear to identify when other investors are scared so I might capitalize on their fear in the markets. In these chapters, I will implore you not to overlook what fear can tell you—being cautious is not a bad thing. But, equally, I implore you not to overlook the power fear gives you.

For example, I experienced the panic around the market crash of 2008, and it made me terrified of investing. But I've learned that a market crash is a natural part of the economic cycle that is going to happen whether I want it to or not. Regular market declines are inevitable. I also learned that even though it may seem counterintuitive, a crash is our best chance to leapfrog into financial freedom by buying wonderful companies on sale at bargain-basement prices. It's the investment equivalent of getting designer clothes for half of what they would have cost at the department store. These are the kinds of lessons that have given me power and understanding over my fear and allowed me to transform my life financially.

My dad and I have created an Investing Practice that anyone can do, no matter your age, income, job, or inherent math skills, which is set forth month by month. Each month of the year has a focus, along with detailed actions and exercises that support it. Most of the specific monthly tasks will take very little time, while others, such as the months practicing research, will take more diligence. Your time is limited and valuable, just like mine. This practice is meant to fit into the lives of all of us working full-time and struggling to manage everything that has to be done outside of work, and I know it's a lot. This Investing Practice is designed to integrate into your life, not detract from it. Remember that this is your practice and you should adjust it to do what works for you.

This is my experience alone. What happened to me is unique to me and my circumstances, just as your Investing Practice and what happens to you will be unique to you and yours. Practice makes perfect—but nobody's perfect. There is beauty in how our practices differ. Noticing and honoring what is easy for you and what is difficult will support your own Investing Practice much better than blindly following exactly what I did.

My experience gives you a barometer by which to gauge your own financial situation, along with the investing resources of the calculations, checklists, and worksheets provided throughout this book. Once you have your bearings, take your practice where you want it to go. Make the practice of investing your own, and you will have something that stays with you your entire life, a powerful skill that no one and nothing can take from you. I hope it compels you to think about your finances differently—not as a means to an end but instead as a source of happiness and freedom.

"Happiness doesn't always feel happy," Gretchen Rubin wrote in *The Happiness Project* about small goals like flossing daily or decluttering shelves. When it comes to something as life changing as financial freedom, I think differently. My practice of investing has created the deep happiness that comes from my authentically making the life I want, and that happiness feels passionate, big, and free. May your Investing Practice be successful beyond your wildest dreams. That kind of happiness always feels happy.

Let's begin.

CHAPTER 1

Becoming Brave

| January

This Month

▶ Warren Buffett and Value Investing
▶ Rule #1 Investing
▶ Inflation
▶ My Investing Practice

IT HAD BEEN ONE OF THOSE EXTREMELY LONG WEEKS, AND ONE FRIDAY night's sleep had only smoothed out the rough edges of how tired I was. I wasn't sure how many months it had been since I had really looked up from my desk, and that morning, I finally had a moment to remember that there was a world outside my office.

I was a low-level lawyer in the Boulder, Colorado, office of an international law firm, and as many other law firm associates have, I thought going to college, grad school, and law school and working hard at a law firm were the "smart" decisions for my financial future. After graduating from New York University School of Law, I had intentionally ignored the workhouse law firms of New York and gone back home to the Rocky Mountains and the "lifestyle oriented" law firms of Colorado. I had gotten my dream job doing venture capital and startup law in the deeply innovative Boulder entrepreneurial community, but still wanting to work at a sophisticated legal practice, I had ended up at a large firm with New York work hours anyway. I learned a great deal, and paying my dues with the stress from eighty-hour workweeks had been an acceptable trade-off.

However, as I observed the lifestyles of the people ahead of me in their careers, it slowly dawned on me that the only reward awaiting me was working more hours, internalizing more stress, and continuing to be salary dependent with no end in sight. I thought I had invested in myself, but really, I had invested in a lifelong treadmill.

The money was just not worth it. Yes, I could make enough money as an attorney to live well, but I had no time to actually live well. I wanted to feel passionate about my life. I wanted to wake up and be excited about the day. I thought of the partners in my firm, who were still on that treadmill despite years of experience, and realized: I don't want this life.

Striving for happiness through my law career wasn't working, but I knew that pursuing happiness without any regard for money was unrealistic. The truth is, there is a special kind of happiness money can buy. It can buy liberation from a lawyer's 6:00 A.M.-to-midnight grind. It can buy a house in a good school district. It can buy a permanent end to waking up at night anxious about medical bills, student loans, or a mortgage. And it can literally buy time and experiences and choices in life, like, say, a Porsche 911 and time to race it. The ability to do what you want feels like more than just happiness—it feels like joy. It feels like pure freedom.

Looking out the cold window that morning, I did not feel joy. As much as I adored the people around me and my legal practice, there is a tipping point at which the pain caused by overwork makes the experience and salary of a job not worth it.

I was ill. I hadn't been able to properly digest food for about two years and I had begun vomiting randomly. I would get a high, twenty-four-hour fever out of the blue, or leave the office with a dizzy feeling like I had been hit in the head. I got tonsillitis, then got it again, and again, and again. I hid my symptoms from my coworkers as well as I could, which wasn't very well. When I went on medication to control the vomiting, my doctor gently suggested that my illness was caused by stress. "I don't feel stressed, I feel normal," I promised her, and I meant it. I didn't get that my "normal" was skewed.

I should have seen that my body's reaction was a warning from the universe that I had slipped away from doing what I was meant to do in my life—what ancient Indian texts call "living in dharma." Being in your dharma should feel as smooth as floating in the current in a calm river. The river always flows in a straight line until it is forced to turn, which means you often are pointing in a different direction than your ultimate destination. And like that, zigging and zagging to try to find the current, we all make our way through life.

I wasn't zigging or zagging, though. I was toiling in the choppy waves, being slammed against the riverbank by the water, struggling to breathe and stay afloat, and I couldn't remember that there was a smooth current right next to me if only I would zag.

I had been down so long, it looked like up. My lack of work–life balance was particularly bad, but most of my friends, also in their mid-thirties, had the same types of jobs and similar stress. One lawyer friend had a mini-stroke on an airplane when flying overseas for work after months of almost no sleep. Another "burnt out" after months of intense work hours when he started seeing spots in front of his eyes and was unable to remember how to get home. Another had stress-related stomach problems so severe she was hospitalized twice. I knew at least three people who depended on weekly acupuncture appointments to function at work. It wasn't only my generation. A friend's father, a high-level manager at a well-known technology company, was the only person at his level to make it until his stock options vested—every other manager left for health reasons or passed away. When my friend told me about it, she said he was "the only one who lived."

Of course, work isn't the only part of life that causes life-altering stress. One couple I knew were juggling kids and jobs and were so sleep deprived that they barely spoke to each other anymore, to avoid starting an inevitable argument. Another friend's fiancé broke up with her, and she lost her love, her future, and her home in one day and had to scramble to find a place she could afford on her own and move in quickly. Money alone can't solve these problems, but it certainly can buy some literal help—childcare, movers, security deposits—and create peace of mind.

We are all exhausted and think it's normal to feel that way because it's so common. "Leaning in" to our work is considered *the* virtue—even though Sheryl Sandberg herself recently said she had not really understood how hard it is to succeed at work when you are overwhelmed at home.* We keep running on the treadmill because the challenge feeds our ambition, and if we stop, there sometimes aren't any other treadmills to get on that will pay student loans.

Still, I had been certain I could push through. It wasn't all bad. Supporting my innovative clients was my favorite part of the job, and working with my whip-smart, pragmatic, and kind colleagues was a pleasure. However, when my family started to suffer too, that became more than I could bear.

I had canceled plans with my dad, mom, and sister—and worked through Christmas—so many times that they stopped expecting me to show up; eventually, they stopped making plans with me because there was no point—we all knew I wouldn't make it. Hard work and ambition are prized in my family, and they understood, but there was a tone of concern that had been growing strongly, and lately they had started making pointed comments about how this wasn't going to work in the long term, and no job was worth the damage to my health. That January morning, thinking it over, I realized I needed to protect them, not hurt them.

But I couldn't get off the treadmill because I had student loans and a mortgage, and I loved a great deal about my work.

---

* Sheryl Sandberg, Facebook post, May 6, 2016.

I called one of my best friends from college, Kamala. "I don't know what to do anymore, Kam. I don't know how much longer I can keep this up."

She sighed. "Me too. I write every morning before work, but I hate what I write." Kamala is an extraordinary writer and novelist who was getting up at 5:00 A.M. each day to write her second book, while working a day job in marketing. Her potential was being slowly buried by New York City rents. "I feel too tired all the time, and not creative. When I look ahead at the next few years I just think, Is this it? Am I going to keep struggling? Is this how it is?"

"No," I decided. "No. You're too good of a writer to get stuck in a dead-end job. There's no way that can be the end of your story."

"Well, it can't be yours either. I think it's clear. You have to leave that place. You just have to figure out how to financially afford it."

"It's hard, though," I prevaricated. "There is so much I love about my work. But honestly, I don't see any way to do this job without working as much as I am."

"We've got to make this the year that we make real changes," Kam decided. "We can't keep living like this. It's too . . . pointless."

"Foin," I reluctantly agreed. Kamala coined the term "foin" when we were in college to mean "fine, I agree, but reluctantly and begrudgingly." "I have no idea how anything can change, but I'll put the intention out there."

"Me too," she declared. "Maybe the universe will kick up some dust and shake things up a bit."

I knew Kamala and I weren't the only ones who felt torn. My friends and I, all working in very different fields and having grown up in families of varying economic status, talked regularly about our similar dreams of having financial flexibility well before the time of official gold-watch-and-golf-course-style retirement to do whatever we want (if such a thing even exists anymore). "Financial freedom" could mean having just enough in the bank to add flexibility to our lives—to stay at a low-paying job we love and be able to easily support loved ones, to work part-time, to have reliable childcare, to quit a salaried job and start a nonprofit, to move to a safer neighborhood, to travel, to simply have a financial cushion in the bank for the apocalypse. To live the life each of us was born to live, whatever that might be. Then there is the ultimate goal: to be truly financially comfortable at the time that we want to fully retire or, even better, to be able to forget the money and just do what we love forever. That's financial freedom.

"Financial freedom" means something different to each of us. To me, financial freedom meant balance in my life: quitting my law firm job, getting healthy, and working with startup companies and entrepreneurs without the pressure of having to work ten hours per day. I wanted flexibility and a financial cushion that was large enough that I wouldn't have to worry about the bills. I wanted to be debt-free.

In my financial life, I realized that I lived with two selves: current self and future self, both of whom wanted to enjoy life and feel secure. Often, though, Present Danielle and Future Danielle were necessarily in conflict. All that New Age-y advice to live in the moment and not worry about the future was great for Present Danielle to abandon it all and tour the wineries of Tuscany, but not so great for Future Danielle to have food or shelter. Putting my nose to the corporate grindstone now was great for Future Danielle, but not for Present Danielle or my family. Living in the antagonistic relationship of my two financial selves felt constantly unstable. Present and Future Danielle needed to have a symbiotic relationship. I had to bring my financial selves into balance.

I had to create that freedom. But I had no idea how.

I started feeling some internal pressure. To figure. This. Out. The jitters started in my stomach. Maybe there was an easy fix? Or maybe there wasn't. The jitters got worse, and I started getting antsy with anxiety. What on earth was I going to do? I needed to physically move. I got up from my big armchair, made some tea, and plomped back into my chair again.

I called my dad. He knows a few things.

"Dad, I'm thinking seriously about my career plan. What can I do to get some financial freedom so I can leave this job if I need to? What I want is to not be depending on this job—or any job, for that matter. I want to be able to do the work I want to do without worrying about financial issues. I want freedom money."

My dad replied, "Honey, that eighty-hour-a-week job at the law firm has clearly run its course for you. I think nature is telling your body that quite loudly. Now you have to figure out how to get some balance in your life and still somehow get the money you'll need for the lifestyle you want, right?"

"Right. I love so many parts of being a startup lawyer, but I want a life too."

"Okay, you love what you do and you're really good at it. So, if you want this career, then the answer is obvious, right?"

It is?

"You have to start investing. Then you'll have the money to have the choice. Right now, you have no choice."

Oh. Of course that's what he was going to say. My mind drifted to all the times he had told me that already.

My father, Phil Town, already has a life of financial freedom: he loves his job and he has the money to do whatever he wants to do. He knows how to create money starting from almost zero because he did it himself.

After dropping out of college and getting dirty for a living as a young lieutenant in the U.S. Army's elite Green Beret unit in Latin America and a platoon leader in Vietnam, while working as a river guide in the Grand Canyon,* my dad had a chance meeting with an investor who ended up teaching him how to use the value-based

---

* 1970–1971: First Lieutenant, U.S. Army Special Forces, S-4, Bravo Company, 8th SFG, Ft. Gulick, Panama; 1971–1972: Security Platoon Leader, 5th Trans Command, Ft. Baxter, RVN; 1972–1980: River guide, Arizona Raft Adventures, Grand Canyon.

strategy of renowned investors Benjamin Graham and Warren Buffett. Value investing is an investment strategy to buy stocks based on financial fundamentals at prices below their value. It was first defined in 1934 by Benjamin Graham and David Dodd in their book, *Security Analysis*.

A NOTE FROM PHIL

The basic ideas of investing are to look at stocks as businesses, use the market's fluctuations to your advantage, and seek a Margin of Safety.

—Warren Buffett

If you want to get rich and stay that way, study Warren Buffett; he is simply the best investing teacher in the world. In 1956, he started the Buffett Partnership in Omaha, Nebraska, to invest his own money and that of family and friends. Over the next fourteen years his partnership returns averaged 31.5 percent per year and his $100 grew to $25 million (about $175 million in today's dollars). A runaway success already, in 1969 he closed the partnership and urged investors to buy the stock of Berkshire Hathaway, a public company that Buffett and his investing partner, Charlie Munger, controlled from Omaha and into which he put his entire fortune. Through Berkshire, which became synonymous with Buffett, he bought shares of dozens of publicly traded companies like American Express and Coca-Cola, as well as entire companies like Geico and Dairy Queen. His original investors saw a $10,000 investment grow to $1.2 billion, which is why people call Buffett the Oracle of Omaha. Today, he is an elder statesman of the value investing world: at eighty-seven, he's worth over $73.4 billion and continues to run Berkshire. Virtually all of the investing knowledge in this book comes from knowledge given to me by Warren Buffett and Charlie Munger.

My dad took to investing like he had a lighted path showing him the way through the fog. After he turned $1,000 into over $1 million in five years, he then developed his own deep value investing strategy based on those methods called Rule #1, a name that pays homage to Buffett's statement that there are only two rules of investing. Rule #1 is Don't Lose Money. Rule #2? Don't Forget Rule #1.

Seems obvious, I know, like "buy low, sell high," but simple isn't the same as easy. My dad's point is deeper than it sounds: buy a wonderful company (my dad calls companies he loves "wonderful") when it is a bargain and only when you are certain that it will be worth more ten years from now than it is today. Then wait, sometimes for years, as the company does what wonderful companies do: becomes more valuable over time. Be so confident that you now own a great company that—even if the stock price goes down—you don't worry and you stay with it until it goes back up and, ideally, you never sell. That's how you "don't lose money." That's Rule #1 investing.

When my dad discovered that other people were interested in his investing strategy, he wrote two books about it—*Rule #1* and *Payback Time*—both of which were *New York Times* number-one bestsellers. I read each of them when they came out and thought they were great, and then promptly forgot everything I read. I only found out recently that my dad correctly predicted the 2008 stock market crash in an appearance on CNBC, and he correctly called the bottom of the market in 2009. Now, he invests, plays polo, and hangs out on his horse farm outside Atlanta. He is incredibly passionate about educating people about how to invest on their own and they travel from all over the world to learn from him.

I had never been one of them.

I grew up in a little town in Iowa, where half the town, including my family, had moved there from other places to be part of a Transcendental Meditation community—with a university, a private school, and group meditation domes. Meditation and yoga were part of my school day. My dad was able to move his family there because his investing work could be done from anywhere.

We had lived in a big house that my parents had designed and built together on a large property with a view of a cornfield and a large lake beyond—very *Field of Dreams* Iowa. My dad and I got into an accident at the house before it was completed, when I was five or six years old. We spent a lot of time together then, and I wandered around the half-built house with him fairly often to check its progress. That day, to shake some fallen cement off some thick drywall slabs that were leaning up against the hallway wall, he pulled the drywall slabs slightly toward us, but they just kept coming, against all his strength. He yelled at me to get out of there while he held the weight for a few extra seconds and backed into the stairwell. Once I scampered clear, the drywall fell over onto him and pinned his legs down, its weight slowly and inexorably crushing both tibias against the sharp, unfinished stair below. I crawled over the drywall slab and sat on the stairs above my dad's head, getting more confused and scared about why he wasn't getting up. "Can you go get help, honey?" he asked. I probably would have been screaming in his situation, but he was calm and no-nonsense. Green Beret training. No cell phones then, and we were out in the middle of nowhere. I started to understand that my dad could not get up, and I could barely breathe. I ran to the car and honked the horn, but we were out on an empty dirt road and no one passed by. There was a neighboring farm some ways away, and I was terrified to go to a big strange house alone, but I had no choice. I ran across the field, summoned the courage to knock on the door as loudly as I could, and whispered to the nice lady who answered that there was something wrong with my dad. I don't remember what happened after that until we were at the hospital and he limped out on crutches with bandages on his legs, making jokes. After a week, he was fine. We had made it out together, as we did many things then, and we resumed our regular walks and bike rides and discussions and house inspections.

Then my parents divorced. I was eleven, and my sister and I primarily lived with our mom, and our parents' relationship could only be described as a war. The war meant that my sister and I suddenly didn't have our dad with us every day, so when we did get to see him, neither of us particularly wanted to spend our dad time talking about long-term savings accounts or financial statements. We were focused on more important matters, like, oh, I don't know, keeping our family together and wondering where we were going to live.

My sister and I always knew that my dad made money and we would be fine financially, but the divorce rocked our world. It was a typical divorce horror show with my sister and me caught in the middle. Haruki Murakami once wrote, "There's only one kind of happiness, but misfortune comes in all shapes and sizes."* Ours was that my dad wasn't around much anymore, and I couldn't see any reason why, except that I wasn't reason enough to stick around.

The war created financial pressure too. Mom got a job teaching at the private school, she sold the house they had built, and we moved with our mom to Maharishi University Utopia Park—a trailer park for university students and faculty. It was a genuinely nice trailer park, but still, it was a big change. The night of our move from our house to the trailer, after a long day of moving and cramming our house of stuff into a trailer that could have fit into our old living room, and after months of being the strong older kid, I broke down and cried.

---

* Haruki Murakami, *Kafka on the Shore*, 2005.

Though neither of our parents wanted it to go that way, we lost access to love and money all at the same time, and that day it became real. I felt horrible about breaking down because my mom was miserable and I didn't want to make her tough day worse, but I was so sad. I was twelve years old, but I crawled into her lap like a four-year-old and cried, and she cuddled me and promised it would be okay.

She was so brave for us; she'd lost her husband, she had to move out of the house she'd designed and built, she was in a brutal money battle, and still, she had the emotional energy to comfort me. I will never forget her courage that night: to keep going, to keep being there. My mom tried to shelter us from the fallout from the divorce while my dad was out in California with his business.

In my hurt and pain, I imagined him without me, out there living the life of a wealthy, single guy. It seemed so unfair, and I was angry about it. Mom made sure we had food and occasionally got to eat out for lunch in our little Iowa town, but suddenly there was no money for much more than necessities.

My dad seemed to parachute in occasionally for the weekend and get a hotel and a Nintendo, and we would have a surface-level great time visiting with him, tinged with underlying horror at the whole situation. It was so stereotypically Disneyland Daddy, it was embarrassing. Mom would struggle to make ends meet and Dad would take us on a vacation to Club Med. It didn't make sense, and yet, my sister and I loved him so much that being aware of how unfair the situation was didn't make us less eager to visit with him.

After two years, Dad came back, got a trailer in Utopia Park five doors down from ours, and my sister and I ran back and forth between their homes while our parents smoothed the waters of our post-divorce world. It was time for a major change for all of us. Mom and Dad moved us all to Jackson Hole, Wyoming, and got two houses within walking distance of each other on a ridge overlooking the valley. We started to put our lives back together as a separated family. It wasn't always smooth or easy but they were both trying to make it better for all of us, and in spite of the wounds from the post-divorce years, it worked out. Money was no longer an issue, and in addition to their divorce settlement, Dad even paid for part of my mom's expenses to go to graduate school. Now we celebrate major holidays with both our parents and they get along well, essentially as acquaintances who have a lot of water under that bridge. It works for us.

In Jackson Hole, once I reached high school age, Dad started talking to me about investing. There was no way I could be convinced that whatever my dad was up to was in any way worthy of my time—to the contrary, it was by definition irreparably blemished by my deep feeling of abandonment. He would harangue my sister and me during a father-daughter meal or on a car ride about how we really needed to start investing, and we half listened and half avoided what he was saying.

To him, investing was the best topic on earth; when he got on the subject, he was like that guy you get stuck with at a cocktail party who doesn't realize that you don't care how his day was—you were just making small talk. He loves running calculations in his head like I love reading celebrity gossip blogs—it's just entertaining enough to be relaxing and neither of us cares if anyone else follows along. He can go on for hours. Eventually I learned to lapse into silence and eat my food until he was done with his math time. Then I'd change the subject and hope to immediately forget everything he had just said, because financial stuff seemed overwhelming and complicated, and the divorce had made things overwhelming and complicated enough already. Anything to do with investing was colored by my memories of my financial anxiety during the divorce years.

Still, when I got into my twenties and discovered that I knew people who were buying stocks or had financial advisers, and that the stock market was something people other than my dad thought was worthwhile, I occasionally thought maybe I was being too prejudiced against what seemed to be a useful skill. My relationship with my dad was pretty good at that point, and I was becoming interested in what my dad did for a living to create wealth. Maybe I could become interested in investing if only I tried, I thought.

So, I tried. I copied some friends and attempted day trading in college, something my dad does not encourage. I didn't know how much I didn't know and lost half my money in about two days, partly because I had so little to invest that the commission ate up potential gains and partly because the stocks just dropped on me despite my surefire combination of gut instinct and getting a hot stock tip from said friends. Quickly, I realized that the stock market was a quagmire I didn't understand.

Then, out of a continued sense that some mysterious "investing thing" would be a useful skill, and probably in hopes of understanding my dad a bit more, I spent one summer doing investment research for him, which really just meant entering numbers into spreadsheets. I was doing it by rote—his way, with his methods, and I didn't try very hard to understand. It was the first time I saw him work up close—seeing how the sausage was made rather than him telling me about it—and I developed a strong respect for how much work he was doing and the investing method he developed. Still, it didn't take.

To a man with a hammer, everything looks like a nail. To my dad, investing on your own was the solution to everything.

I came back to that January morning, and our phone call. "I don't want to do my own investing, Dad," I said to him. "It's too hard and I don't have the time, and it's way too hard." He started chuckling, so I kept going. "I'm busy. I mean, literal geniuses screw up investing in the stock market. It's too hard. I don't have the time to learn it."

Dad guffawed. "Are you trying to say that it's hard and you're busy?"

"I'm glad you could read between the lines, because that's exactly what I'm trying to say."

"Let's run some calculations to see how long it could take you to have the freedom to leave the job and do whatever else you want to do."

"I can't deal with it, Dad. I know what you're going to say, and I'm sure my prospects are dire, but I'd rather just be conservative about this."

"Conservative!" He choked. "What is Rule #1?"

"Don't lose money," I recited dryly.

"What's more conservative than that?"

"I completely agree that not losing money is key, but is the stock market the best way to do that? I don't trust the market. There must be a safer way."

He finally let up and changed the subject, and we hung up soon after. I knew what he would say, but I hoped this time would be different. I'd heard it a thousand times. He would create a spreadsheet and rattle off a thousand numbers too quickly for me to follow and tell me that if I would learn to invest like Warren Buffett, I'd be fine. No details. No real help.

I was too tired to invest like Warren Buffett, whatever that meant. And I'd seen my dad's facility with numbers. I had my talents. Numbers were not one of them. I was certain that I was not someone who should be messing around with my own money.

Surely, there had to be another way that would get me to financial freedom. I put the problem to the back of my mind so I could focus on my legal practice, but as I went about my so-called life over the next few weeks, every time I took my stomach medication I tried to figure it out: What could I do to stop being a wage slave?

The trouble was that the financial services system—which is really such an entrenched behemoth that it should be called the financial-industrial complex—was hardly a friendly face. The master-of-the-universe types yelling at each other on CNBC thoroughly put me off, the books and newspapers used a foreign financial language, and the two major recessions I had lived through taught me that the stock market is an untrustworthy business partner.

I already felt as avoidant of the financial world as I did of learning to invest on my own. Still, I had to figure something out.

The financial-industrial complex tells me that there are only two options to generate more money:

1.   **HOARD**. Stop buying anything fun or extra to save, save, save, and make only the most conservative investments; or

2.   **ABDICATE**. Give my money over to a money manager, to whom I should pay fees for the privilege of handing over my money, regardless of whether or not he loses my money.

I certainly did not want to lose my own money myself, but I didn't want anyone else to lose it either. I had timed my entries into the job market spectacularly badly. I graduated from college during the early-2000s recession and from law school during the late-2000s recession, both times when the financial-industrial complex was in desperate turmoil. These people did not seem to learn from their mistakes. Everyone looked like a genius when the market was going up, but when it dropped, the depth of their ignorance was exposed. Hoarding sounded safe, and safe sounded fantastic. I made an easy decision.

I would become a financial hoarder.

I was thrilled with my decision, and I started madly searching online to learn more. Where were the hoarding success stories of octogenarians throwing dolla-dolla bills in the air?

I didn't find any of those, but I did discover T-bills, which sound like fun but are not. A T-bill, or a treasury bond, is a bond issued by the U.S. Treasury Department and is guaranteed by the federal government, so is therefore considered to be a risk-free investment—at least, as risk-free as any investment can possibly be—because the government has a money-printing press. It's such a worldwide standard for low-risk investing that the ten-year T-bill's interest rate is called "the risk-free rate." Any investment riskier than that would have to provide higher returns than the risk-free rate to make it worthwhile.

Thank goodness the Internet could explain these things to me, because financial language intentionally keeps us "Normals" on the back foot when it comes to financial decisions and needing middlemen to facilitate even simple transactions. The Internet's democratization of information, which let me quickly look up the jargon financiers spout, was the only weapon I had against them.

I hatched my hoarding plan. I was going to, metaphorically speaking, save my money under my mattress. My nice little nest egg would go into a savings account, where I knew it would be safe. It wouldn't grow much, I knew, but it wouldn't get smaller either. I'd save as much as I could without destroying my lifestyle—getting the occasional Americano with a friend from the good coffee booth at the Boulder farmers market gave me life, and I needed those moments. I'd keep at this job as long as I physically could, pay off my student loans, ignore the ups and downs of the market entirely, watch my savings account grow, and maybe buy a T-bill if the interest rate went up. As long as I could hold out a few more years without anything really bad happening to my health, I could then move into a less-stressful position at a company. Done and done.

And that, to me, was a win. In fact, my dad would also consider it a win. I was literally following Rule #1: Don't Lose Money.

Patting myself on the back, I was so excited about my plan to save my money that, when my dad stopped over for a few days in Boulder late in January, I bubbled over. He had business meetings nearby every now and then, and would try to stay over a weekend so we could hang out. We went out for Sunday brunch near my condo downtown, and I triumphantly announced my plan.

"I've decided to save my money under my mattress. I'm going to save and figure out what to do with it later."

Silence. I knew he was thinking that he should have written in his books about savings accounts as a viable option in addition to active investment. C'est la vie, *Dad*. "Why hasn't everyone thought of this genius plan to avoid losing money?" I asked.

"Saving?" he responded. "Just saving?"

"Yeah, I know that savings accounts don't pay any interest. I know it's not a growth strategy. But at least I'm not losing money. I'm following Rule #1 to the letter!"

"What about inflation?" he asked.

Inflation?

"You know what inflation is, right?" he quizzed. I sort of did. I knew inflation existed. Everyone knew about inflation. Inflation means that prices go up and the buying power of money goes down over time. I didn't know why. Something about how the government prints money and that more money floating around means money becomes less . . . less useful . . . less valuable . . . less good . . . just less? Foin, I couldn't exactly define "inflation."

"Inflation means that the purchasing power of your money goes down because, to simplify it, the government wants people to have jobs so they encourage borrowing, and with more money floating around, consumers buy more stuff, and over time, the increased demand makes prices rise. Additionally, because companies try to meet the increased demand, they raise wages or create new jobs, so the economy grows. That also leads to higher consumption, which leads to more demand, higher wages, more jobs, and more consumption. It's called the 'virtuous cycle' of inflation."

He pointed to his Coke—a special Sunday dose of sugar for him. "When I was a kid I could buy a Coke for a dime, and now I can buy a Coke for a dollar fifty. Same Coke. The value of that dime has gone down like a brick. When Ben Franklin said 'A penny saved is a penny earned,' a penny bought almost a dollar's worth of stuff in today's money. Since Ben's time, inflation has reduced the buying power of a penny by more than 98 percent."

"That all makes perfect sense. More consumption, higher wages, more jobs equals 'virtuous cycle.' Why are you asking me about inflation?"

"The only way to simply maintain today's buying power of the money you have is by making more money on your money."

"No, no, no. You're always saying that you prefer to 'sit in cash' instead of investing in overpriced companies and possibly losing money in the market. That's what I'm doing. I'm 'sitting in cash.'"

"Okay, yes, you are technically 'sitting in cash.' But inflation is going to hurt you if you sit in cash for the long term. Inflation reduces the buying power of your dollars over time. So the dollar you save today will literally be worth less in buying power tomorrow. And less the next day, and less the next day, and a whole lot less in ten years, and massively less in thirty years—down to forty cents— without you doing anything at all."

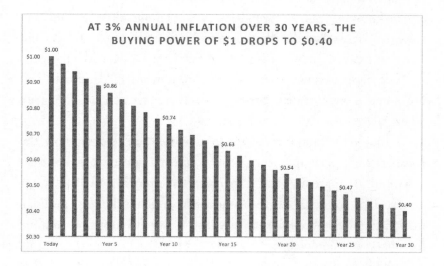

Thirty years from now it could easily cost almost $200,000 a year for today's $80,000-a-year lifestyle.

The deep financial hole created by inflation was beginning to come into focus. The truth was that I had to make 3 percent or better just to keep my money from becoming worth less each year. "Wait . . . you cannot be saying that saving literally makes me lose money without me doing anything wrong. I have to invest just to stay where I am? I have to invest just to tread water?"

"That is exactly what I'm saying." Dad looked a bit flummoxed that I was still surprised. He tried dumbing it down even more. "Inflation has a historical average of 3 percent per year, so you do have to get an average of about 3 percent return per year just to offset inflation."

It wasn't that I didn't understand. I got it, all right. But I had never applied the reality of inflation to my savings. He was speaking as though every adult human knew that they had to invest in order to keep up with the rate of inflation of 3 percent per year. Why hadn't anyone told me before? Why hadn't *he* told me before? Wait, did everyone know except me? I wondered. Was I failing adulting? Did I cut class the day we had the discussion to Make Sure You Get 3 Percent Per Year Because Inflation Is Certain Just Like Death and Taxes?

"I thought of saving as a nice, neutral nonaction." I sighed. "Just put some money aside somewhere each month and let it pile up nicely."

"It doesn't, though." Dad made it worse, and told me how the prices of some very important items go up at a rate even higher than inflation. His parents bought their starter home in Portland, Oregon, in 1951 for $5,000—the same as the annual salary my grandpa made as a novice bookkeeper. Finding a decent home you can buy for one year's bookkeeper salary is hard to do now, and certainly impossible in desirable cities like Portland, where that same house would sell nowadays for $300,000, while even experienced bookkeepers in Portland make about $40,000 per year.

"Inflation grew a bookkeeper's salary by 800 percent in sixty-five years—an average of 3 percent per year compounded. But because of a desirable location, increasing population, government real estate loan guarantees, and tax policies, the price of the same house in Portland grew by 6,000 percent—about 7 percent per year compounded."

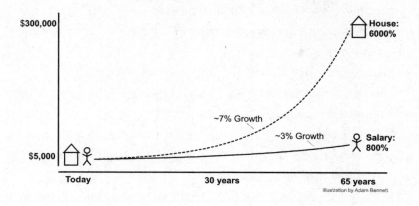

Illustration by Adam Bennett

Dad went on: "If your savings don't grow, even going out to dinner at a good restaurant when you're retired will become difficult, if not impossible. And don't even get me started on health care. So, yes, you have to invest just to tread water, and you might need to make even more than 3 percent to stay above water."

"But everyone says to save! That's the advice! Hoard! Save your money! Keep it safe! Rule #1: Don't Lose Money!"

Now he was openly laughing at me. *Oh Lord, help me not stab this man with my fork.* I'd lose my license to practice law.

"The people who encourage saving mean that you should save instead of spending money. But because of inflation and the fact that what people buy will be more expensive 'tomorrow,' people spend all of their money and whatever they can borrow 'today,' so we need to be encouraged to save instead of spend. Nobody is saying, once you've saved some money, to keep it sitting in a savings account."

Well, crap. I just about jumped out of my chair in frustration. Even the people who had intimated that they thought saving was the way to go meant it only as a prelude to the real work? Saving wasn't enough?

"Saving is not enough," my dad intoned. That he tried not to laugh only made me madder.

"Inflation will actively destroy my savings," I spluttered at him, still trying to process his words. I was slowly wrapping my mind around this crush of crappy information. "How could you not have ever told me this?"

He laughed, maddeningly. "I did! I've told you this!"

Not that I ever remembered. If he did ever say it, he didn't bother to make sure I heard it.

"Good Lord." I talked it out, pretty much to myself: "So, it's inextricable. I'm connected to this economy and this stock market whether I like it or not."

"Yup," Dad confirmed for the fourteenth time. "You look like you want to crawl under the table and hide."

"No, I don't want to hide, I just want to find a solution that isn't me investing my own money! I thought I had found a solution, and now you're telling me it actually loses me money very reliably."

Dad looked at me steadily. "Yeah."

"I am so frustrated," I half screamed.

I needed to move. We walked the few blocks back to my condo, and Dad thought nothing of it when I rolled onto the rug and got into a downward-facing dog yoga pose. My parents had raised me with Transcendental Meditation and yoga as a regular part of my life since I was little, so stretching into a yoga pose had become my own way to keep that frustration from settling in. I inhaled deeply into my lower back to try to put some breath into my solar plexus and flush out that horrid panic of having, for a long time, missed something important. The idea of inflation negatively affecting my savings was sinking in and I was starting to feel my brain turn somersaults, trying to find a way out of this situation. I had felt so safe with my money under my mattress. Now I felt like a rat had made its home under my mattress, and it was nibbling away at my hard-earned and much-treasured dollars one at a time, using them to make a giant rat's nest.

Dad had already plopped onto the couch, so I rolled into my big chair. He had started doing what he always does when he wants to explain financial anything: he opened Excel and made a spreadsheet, then turned it toward me. I half glanced at it. Spreadsheets weren't my thing, and I wasn't interested in deciphering it.

He summarized it: "You can retire after thirty years of saving like Scrooge and living a spartan lifestyle, but your so-called retirement will last four years because the inflated cost of even a spartan lifestyle will wipe out your savings really quickly."

Well, that sounded . . . bad.

"You see why I did what I did and started investing?" He took a breath. "I started thinking about money only after I'd been at an ashram in France meditating twelve hours a day for six months when I was twenty-eight years old. I had to get my Vietnam War experience out of me somehow, and that worked. I needed $4,000 to pay for room and board for the next six months and I didn't have it. It was horrible to know that the only thing that stood between me and total enlightenment was money."

"Six more months of deep meditation would have made you enlightened?" I noted skeptically.

"Well, in hindsight, no." He laughed. "But it was what I wanted to do. It was all about spiritual freedom, at that time. And I didn't get to do it because of money. When I got back to the U.S., I taught meditation and continued guiding river trips, but money was always an issue. I eventually met the guy who offered to teach me investing.* I took him up on it because I was tired of being broke all the time. Once I started learning, I could feel I was doing exactly the right thing—it was as easy as following the river current."

He didn't get it. Investing did *not* make me happy. It made me terrified.

If I did decide to be brave and take the plunge into an investment all by myself, I was certain that I would lose all the money I put in the market. My dad calls this the Emotional Rule of Investing: as soon

---

* My dad's story of how he met his mentor and changed his life is the subject of his first book, *Rule #1*. Did I mention it was a bestseller?

as you buy a stock expecting it to go up, it will go down—entirely because you bought the stock. It's like deciding which line to wait in. I always pick the line that looks the fastest, and as soon as I step in, it immediately slows to a halt. Buying stock seems pretty much the same as line-choosing, only with much higher consequences. But here's the difference: You have to pick a line. You don't have to pick a stock.

When I think about all the factors that can go wrong to cause a company's stock price to go down, I feel like I'm entering a dimly lit parking garage through an enclosed concrete stairwell with heavy doors at both ends, and I didn't pack my pepper spray because it didn't fit in my clutch and also I was afraid I would accidentally set it off in the crowded bar, and *yes* I had a few generously poured aged bourbons and *still* my radar is going off, saying, "Girl, don't go into that concrete stairwell." Tipsy fear is the worst kind, because if you can feel it through the buzz, you know it's real bad. There are two types of people in the world—those who look at the Enclosed Concrete Stairwell and think nothing, and those who look at the Enclosed Concrete Stairwell and think, There's a good possibility that this won't end well for me. The first type is, more often than not, men; the second type is generally women. Men, you know that's true—you have never noticed an enclosed concrete stairwell. Women, you know that's true—you're very aware of the Enclosed Concrete Stairwell on a deeply instinctual level and you also know that most men have never given it a second thought.

Women investors tend to have a lower risk tolerance than men. A recent study showed only 4 percent of women who invested with Fidelity were willing to invest a substantial amount to achieve potentially higher returns, compared to 15 percent of men. At the same time, 90 percent of all women will be the sole financial decision maker for their households at some point in their lives. I certainly was for my own household, but my instinctual reaction to the idea of investing in the stock market was GET THE HELL OUT OF THAT ENCLOSED CONCRETE STAIRWELL AND CALL AN UBER, IT'S WORTH THE SURGE PRICING.

"But you don't seem to react the way I react. I feel like my world is closing in. I have no confidence that I can invest. You seem to have all the confidence in the world."

Dad paused. "I didn't start that way. I had to learn. But being broke can make you brave. That confidence I have now comes from being certain about a company's real value, and then refusing to buy it unless I can buy it at a really low price because things happen that nobody could foresee. We all get it wrong sometimes. That protects me."

"You do like high-risk situations, though. You actually like living on the edge."

"Actually, not at all. Being on the edge only happens when you don't know what you're doing. I like to know exactly what I'm doing."

"I'm a risk-averse lawyer. I don't want to be anywhere near the edge."

"That's a great quality to have as an investor. You shouldn't be gambling with your financial future." Maddeningly, he winked. "You might be more suited to this than you think."

"Eh," I grumbled noncommittally. Avoiding investing on my own had been an extremely logical choice that protected me from the Enclosed Concrete Stairwell feeling, which is very real, and very physical. Not thinking about it, and certainly not doing anything about it, made that horrid feeling of fear disappear. And when it disappears, that's lovely. On the other hand, knowing that my retirement would last four years created its own Enclosed Concrete Stairwell feeling. I started to feel squeezed between that famous rock and a hard place except, in my case, it was this concrete wall or that one.

I pushed our conversation away from anything investment related, and Dad and I both worked at my house for the rest of the day. We stuck to safe topics for the rest of the weekend, until he went back to Atlanta.

That I had missed out on an important piece of information annoyed the crap out of me. To ponder a concept that you've always had some sense of but never actually thought much about is like discovering you have a huge booger just barely hanging on in the inside of your nostril: you knew it existed hidden in the dark hole this whole time, but now you really see it in all its hideous glory. I thought about inflation every day, and every time it came to mind I also wondered, What else had I missed? What else did I not know that I did not know? I couldn't let it go.

Later that week at a work event, I ran into a friend who is a financial adviser. I realized she might need to know what I had learned about inflation from my dad. She would probably want to warn her clients. "Have you heard? About inflation?" I exclaimed.

She waited a beat and said "Yes?" in that voice people use when they're not sure what they're getting into.

"Did you know that it just erodes the value of your money, like utterly and completely, without you doing anything at all?" I was getting loud now. My frustration was coming back in full force.

"Yes?" she answered, and took a sip of her wine. She was not perturbed. Clearly, she didn't understand how terrible inflation is.

"It just takes away your money! So even if I save and save and save, my money just will slowly disappear, dollar by dollar, until I have nothing! *Nothing!*"

"That's sort of true," she pleasantly agreed. "Inflation reduces the buying power of your dollars, generally at an average of 3 percent per year. It's not your actual dollars that disappear, just their buying power."

"So you knew about this."

She shrugged uncomfortably, looking concerned for me personally now. "I didn't know you didn't know."

Maybe there was too much I didn't know. Maybe I needed to investigate.

The booger of inflation is a curious one. It's actually considered by economists to be a positive force on a macro level. Studies done by International Monetary Fund economists and others suggest that as long as inflation stays relatively low and steady, the virtuous cycle of consumption, wages, and jobs creates more jobs or increases wages.* However, if inflation goes up higher than the "good" level, then our money becomes too quickly devalued, and is worth so little that wages and jobs can't keep up. That's when the value of our savings erodes. Of course, inflation also erodes the value of debt, so it encourages borrowing and spending by consumers. But when consumers don't spend, the virtuous cycle stops. Japan has been stuck in a long period of deflation and ultra-low inflation because of too little demand. Their job market has not increased wages and Japanese consumers spend an unusually low amount of their income, preferring to save than spend.† Stock markets, however, typically rise with inflation because company revenue and earnings typically rise commensurately.‡ In sum, inflation hurts savings but helps stocks.

Hmmm. Maybe I really should look into the stock market a bit more seriously.

I rolled that thought over in my mind for about a week, not wanting to make the call, but knowing I really should. It could open an interaction with my dad around money that I wasn't completely sure I wanted. On the other hand, here was this expert, right here in my family and ready to help. I knew what the right decision was for my future.

The next weekend, I took a deep breath and called my dad.

"I could possibly be interested in talking with you about what to do with money," I opened. But he had known I was going to cave. He was ready for me.

"Here's what I think," he ventured.

---

* See M. Sarel, "Non-Linear Effects of Inflation on Economic Growth," *IMF Staff Papers* 43 (March 1996). See also R. Barro, "Inflation and Growth," *Federal Reserve Bank of St. Louis Review* (May/June 1996), and M. Bruno, "Does Inflation Really Lower Growth?" *Finance and Development* 32, no. 3 (September 1995).

† Paul Krugman, "What Is Wrong with Japan?" http://web.mit.edu/krugman/www/nikkei .html; Robin Harding, "Japan Returns to Inflation for First Time Since 2015," *Financial Times*, March 3, 2017.

‡ http://www.investopedia.com/university/inflation/inflation4.asp.

I allowed it. "What do you think?"

"I think that you should spend this year learning Rule #1 investing. In the course of this one year, you will go from the neophyte you are right now to investing your own money with competence and confidence."

Um, what? The Enclosed Concrete Stairwell feeling loomed. I knew that I had to do something to get to financial freedom, yes, but investing on my own still seemed like a last resort. Hoarding was out, obviously, thanks to that jerk inflation, but abdicating to a financial adviser still sounded awfully promising. I couldn't abdicate to my dad because his fund only accepted investors with a high net worth, due to SEC regulations, which my bank account didn't meet, but maybe I could find someone else . . . maybe someone even better.

He could tell that I was unconvinced.

"I know what you're thinking," he said, "and I will show you right off the bat that having someone else manage your money will not get you to financial freedom. I will prove it to you. And once I do that, I will teach you how to invest over the rest of this year."

"You're awfully confident."

"Absolutely. You can do this. No question."

I thought it over. How could I create time to spend on investing? I didn't even have time to go on a date—which, actually, I was perfectly happy with: After ending things with a long-term boyfriend, I had needed some time. I decided not to date anyone until I had the space in my life for someone else. I adored the simplicity of only focusing on myself for once. But even with my life as pared down as possible, I could not continue on as I was. My health and the demands on my family would not allow it. I had to make a better life for them, if not for me. I wanted to do something about my problems, as Kamala and I had promised each other. I couldn't complain about it and then sit by, doing nothing.

I had no choice, really. The universe was offering me a hand, and for my part, I had to reach out and take it.

Which I did, but gingerly. "It could work if I could treat it like a regular practice in my life. If I'm going to spend time on investing, it has to integrate into my life, as my yoga practice does."

Dad agreed. "It will become a seamless part of your life. It's also something that you will get better at over time. I love doing this because I'm constantly learning about new industries or companies or jobs. It's a window into our world."

"Continuing education"—I smiled—"like my legal practice requires. Or a medical practice, or the practice of any other profession."

"I love that. It's your Investing Practice."

Yes. My Investing Practice.

It reminded me of what physician Atul Gawande wrote of practicing as a trainee. He had screwed up putting central lines (a long tube inserted into a large vein to deliver various types of fluids) into patients a number of times, and then, one day, he did it correctly: "I still have no idea what I did differently that day. But from then on, my lines went in. Practice is funny that way. For days and days, you make out only the fragments of what to do. And then one day, you've got the thing whole. Conscious learning becomes unconscious knowledge, and you cannot say precisely how."[*]

If my dad would give me the fragments of investing, I would practice them and hope they would become a whole.

"Tell me how this will actually go," I requested.

"The way that I evaluate a company is by writing their Story. Each month, I will teach you each component of that Story until you can research and write it yourself without even thinking hard. I'll help you create your own Wishlist of companies, and then we'll talk about the timing of buying them and building an antifragile portfolio. You can adjust your practice as you need to for your work schedule. Here's what we'll do."

---

[*] Atul Gawande, *Complication: A Surgeon's Notes on an Imperfect Science* (New York: Picador, 2003), 21.

He described each month:

"This month, January—that's all about becoming brave. It's huge that you're even thinking about this stuff. Most people don't, and I know it's intimidating. I'm so proud of you starting down this path."

I smiled. "Thanks, Dad."

"It's only going to get better. Next month, February, I will convince you not to abdicate by calculating your 'Number'—the number of dollars you will need to be financially free. You'll see that there's no way that handing your money over to a financial adviser will get you there. No question. So that'll be an easy month. In March, let's talk about what the stock market really is and how it works. In April, May, and June, we'll move on to the principles of good investing, how to choose a company, and how to figure out if it's a good business. In July and August, we'll do valuation and how to know what price to pay."

"Ugh." I couldn't help myself.

"I know, you're worried about the math, which is why I'm giving us lots of time to learn it. We'll use two whole months for something that, really, you'll understand in about a day. But you'll have time to practice it and feel really comfortable before moving on."

"Okay, and how about the last few months?"

"September will be right up your alley—we'll cross-examine and invert the argument for companies you like—we'll try to prove investing in those businesses is a bad idea. And then October and November will be about how to put together an antifragile portfolio that benefits from crisis, and we'll wrap it up in December. All of that adds up to the Story of a company. You will know how to successfully invest on your own by the end of this year, and you will have that skill for the rest of your life. You will be well on your way to freedom. Sound good?"

I took a breath and smiled. I promised nothing.

"Only if you convince me not to abdicate first."

JANUARY PRACTICE: The investing process started for me when I realized I wasn't living my life how I wanted because I was so worried about money. Brainstorm and write down what you would do if you had financial freedom, whatever that means to you. Would you stay in your job, work less, volunteer, find a different job, pay off student loans or medical bills, support a family member, travel, donate to charity, or sleep more soundly? Be brave enough to write down how doing that would make you feel.

Knowing Your Number

| February

▶ Primer on the Stock Market
▶ Flavors of Abdication
▶ Calculating My Number
▶ Investment Options Outside of the Stock Market
▶ *Maro*—Thankfulness

DAD HAD GONE BACK TO HIS HOUSE IN ATLANTA A FEW WEEKS EARLIER and, since his visit, I had been mulling over everything we had discussed. I wasn't sold on doing my own investing, so my jitters, added to my normal work stress, were making my stomach worse. Could I really focus on investing for a whole year?

Life has a way of getting really busy, and I was aware that if I had a good structure and accountability, I would have a better chance of focusing all year. I asked my dad if we could have weekly "Investing Practice" phone calls to make sure we stayed on top of it. I thought we would both get busy with other things pretty quickly, and hopefully the calls would help us follow through. I got to thinking it over. The stock market? I was going to trust the stock market?

"Stock market," or "the market," is a generic term for the marketplace represented by the collection of stock exchanges around the world. The New York Stock Exchange (NYSE) is probably the most famous stock exchange, but many countries have their own stock exchanges, and as a whole, they make up the worldwide marketplace of stocks. When my dad talks about the stock market, or "the market," he usually means the collection of stock exchanges specifically in the United States, including the NYSE, the NASDAQ, and other smaller exchanges that, together, trade the stock of roughly six thousand companies. When he talks about "doing better than the market" or "beating the market," he is talking about getting an average return higher than the average return on the U.S. market as a whole.

In the 1600s, the Dutch came up with a history-changing innovation that led to such a marketplace as we now have: they divided a corporation into shares of stock—which just meant owning fractions of a company instead of the whole thing—that were available to be purchased by members of the public. Those shares of stock could then be traded on a stock exchange—the modern name for what was then basically just a bunch of guys sitting around in a bar drinking while speculating on what the corporate shares might be worth if any of the corporation's ships made it to India and back safely.*

This first market of public companies (as opposed to private companies, which do not have their ownership available for sale to the public on an exchange) acted almost exactly like ours do today— sellers yelled out prices, buyers yelled out counteroffers, and eventually a seller and a buyer reached a deal for a certain price. That's how prices in a marketplace move up and down. It's kind of like the local flea market in that no company has any set price; it's entirely down to what a buyer will pay and what a seller will take at any given moment.

Today, the financial-industrial complex is still doing what those Dutch guys in the bar did hundreds of years ago, just on a much bigger scale. The prices on the stock exchange are negotiated like they were in the Dutch bar—people bought and sold in person on a trading floor

---

* One of the most evocative market bubbles in history was also Dutch: the price of tulip bulbs bubbled to the price of a *house* before crashing.

of the stock exchange, a designated area for these sales, except now there's a middleman who facilitates the buying and selling so that prices move up and down smoothly, without so much jumping around. When you buy or sell a share of stock on a stock exchange, you're buying it from a shareholder or selling it to another investor entirely on the stock exchange—the transaction doesn't go through the company—and the guys in brightly colored coats on the trading floor make it happen. I've seen them in the background when my dad was interviewed from the trading floor on CNBC. Since the advent of computers, a lot of the buying and selling is done electronically, which makes it harder to see the process happening, but it is still the same negotiation process, with people involved, happening invisibly in milliseconds instead of taking thirty seconds for a buyer to yell a price at the seller next to him.

And some people figured out that they could make money choosing stocks on behalf of other people, which created the job of money manager and the entire industry of financial advising. As our first call loomed a few days later, the twin walls of the Enclosed Concrete Stairwell felt like they were closing in on me. I decided to get a jump on this Investing Practice idea of mine by checking into using a financial adviser. Maybe I could head off this whole "doing it myself" thing and end the practice right there.

Abdicating by handing money over to a competent money manager was, in the dark recesses of my wanting-to-run-away-from-this-finance-stuff soul, extremely appealing. As wedding planner Martin Short assured Steve Martin in *Father of the Bride*, "Trust me. I do this for a laaahhhving, you know?" I desperately wanted to trust someone to invest for me.

I was cognizant that I was seeking a bad deal. The financial-industrial complex has propagated the value proposition that money managers know what they're doing and I should pay them for the privilege of having them manage my money. By perpetuating the impression that it's so difficult that I should pay them to do it for me, they try to remove my confidence in my ability to do it myself.

And they had done their marketing well. I was aware of their strategy, and still, I almost felt that, even if I paid a professional to lose some of my money, it would feel better than losing it myself. At least I would know it was not 100 percent my fault. All I would have done was choose the wrong pilot. The airplane crash was on him.

To test the waters, I called my financial adviser friend. I didn't really want to mix friendship and business, but I thought it would be entertaining to hear her pitch to me. Instead, she told me she couldn't manage my money because I didn't have enough of it.

I was stunned—hedge funds have SEC regulations keeping them from accepting small investors, but my friend worked for a big typical bank that I had expected to be all about small investors like me. She explained that she doesn't take anyone with less than $250,000 to invest because of her fee structure. I had nowhere near that, so I was out of luck.

Once she brings in a client and charges the client around 2 percent per year for the management, she then might invest in other funds, which also charge fees. She passes those fees along to the client. Clients have to have enough principal to initially invest to afford all those fees and to make it worth the adviser's time. In theory, the financial adviser will get a large enough return to more than offset the fees.

This is, of course, if you are even allowed access to their services. She said many money managers will not take anyone with less than $500,000, and in the case of the more established financial houses, not less than $3,000,000. And they charge that management fee regardless of whether they have made or lost money for you. Money managers charge fees regardless of whether they make money for me or not. I'll say that again: they get paid regardless of their success or failure. We pay for the privilege of being a client. It's not a performance fee. It's a service fee.

I couldn't even pay this bank to let me abdicate responsibility for my money.

I'm certainly not the only one who has wanted to abdicate. There was roughly $70 trillion in stock markets globally in 2017.*

$70,000,000,000,000

That's a lot of zeros. Evidently, most of us are desperate to avoid the stress of actually having to learn about finances and stock markets and commodities and accounting. Frankly, we are too busy living our lives, and we don't believe we can learn it effectively. Still, we seem to want to invest in the stock market, because 85 percent of the money in the stock market is money from little-guy investors like me: money from 401k plans, IRAs, banking accounts, and insurance policies, all of which is given over by ordinary people to professionals to manage.

85 percent of the stock market is OUR money.

We control the market but only by proxy—it is so much easier to pay someone else a fee or a percentage to make decisions for us. Unfortunately, paying someone else means we have to find someone who will do a good job (not easy), pay that someone a good chunk of our hard-earned money (not fun), and often stay in the dark about where our money is going (not a good idea).

Okay, I thought. Abdication comes in a few forms other than through traditional money managers. Maybe a different flavor would work for me. I'd run the options by my dad.

Flavors of Abdication

▶ Mutual funds
▶ Market index funds

---

* https://data.worldbank.org/indicator/CM.MKT.LCAP.CD.

▶ Exchange-traded funds (ETFs)
▶ Robo-advisers

MUTUAL FUNDS: A mutual fund is a collection of stocks and bonds, usually chosen by a financial adviser who charges fees for the service of picking the fund whether the fund makes or loses money. Yup, they make money—even if they lose mine! I didn't believe my dad when he first told me that. And then there are the fees charged by the fund manager, usually 1 to 2 percent plus marketing fees. They call this "actively managed," to indicate that a real person has done something to try to beat the stock market. Until market indexes were created (as described below), mutual funds were the only way for a small investor to easily buy a piece of the market. The reason people still use them is probably because most 401k plans require that you buy their choice of funds from their fund company or fund provider. The total fees charged by a 401k administrator or adviser and the mutual fund manager, whether the fund makes money or not, can easily add up to over 3 percent. Inflation of 3 percent plus fees of 3 percent equals 6 percent gone, again, whether they lose your money or not. Insanity.

MARKET INDEX FUNDS: A market index is a group of stocks that, when averaged, tell us how the stock market is doing overall. These are the ones mentioned every day on the news, but I didn't really realize what they were until I did this research. Standard & Poor's 500 is a classic example of a market index—that's "the S&P" that people on CNBC are always mentioning. Its five hundred stocks are thought to be a good indicator of how the overall six thousand or so stocks in the market are doing. "The Dow" is the Dow Jones Index, which is an index of thirty big industrial companies, also a good indicator of the broad market. A fund company, like Vanguard, buys all the stocks in the index in the right amounts to mimic the index and sells it to us as a fund. Rather than being a collection of "actively managed" stocks and bonds, like a standard mutual fund, market index funds are "passively managed," which is a fancy way to say that no one is actually doing any research to figure out what stocks to buy. You have to buy a market index fund from the fund company or a fund provider. The good news is that fees are lower: anywhere between 0.05 and 0.74 percent, usually with a minimum purchase of $1,000 or more. But if your financial adviser picks the index funds for you, you can add another 1 to 2 percent for their services, for a total of about 3 percent per year.[*]

EXCHANGE-TRADED FUNDS (ETFS): An ETF is a popular option. It is the same index-tracking idea as a market index fund, but you can buy and sell it from a stock brokerage as you would any other stock, and its price goes up and down based on whether there are more buyers or sellers. For that flexibility, they cost a little more than market index funds, with a fee below 1 percent, though some evidence suggests they actually cost 1 to 2 percent, just like a money manager, because of the difference between the ETF's market price and the underlying stock price.[†] Again, bring in a professional to pick these for you and you can watch 3 percent disappear from your account annually.

ROBO-ADVISERS: Robo-advisers are like human advisers who offer a choice of funds, except a computer is doing the advising instead of a person, which makes them less expensive. You find them through an app or website, and increasingly through traditional stock brokerages, which are trying to keep up with these newfangled ideas. Fees range from 0.15 to 0.50 percent. Believe it or not, financial advisers will also advise people which robo-adviser to use, and charge their fees on top, which means the total fees can run up to 2.5 percent.

---

[*] See, e.g., guides.wsj.com/personal-finance/investing/how-to-choose-an-exchange-traded-fund-etf/; https://www.fool.com/investing/general/2015/07/23/vanguard-500-index-fund-low-cost-but-are-there-bet.aspx.

[†] Jason Zweig, "The Expensive Ingredient of Cheap ETFs," *Wall Street Journal*, April 14, 2017.

My Number

Having done my abdication research, I was prepared. Bring on our first weekly Investing Practice phone call! I knew my dad would be pumped to convince me that abdicating would never work, but I had a few things to say first.

"Dad, I researched investing options and I have some ideas."

"Okay, let's hear what you found out."

"There are multiple ways for me to not do this myself, but most of them will cost around 2 to 3 percent or more a year for their service."

"Cool!" he exclaimed, oddly. "Nobody any good is going to take on the responsibility for determining where to allocate your money without being well paid. Now let's figure out your Number and then we'll see if any of the options you found will get you there."

"My Number?" I wanted to talk about abdicating.

"Your Number is how much money you have to save before you can quit your job if you want to."

Are you kidding me? How should I know that? My first thought was "Soon," my second was "Doesn't that depend on multiple factors?" and my third was "Ugh, I hate talking about numbers." My brain stuttered and I said nothing.

Dad ignored my desultory silence and moved on. "And to figure out your Number, first you have to know about the incredible power of compounding."

Ah. I had heard this lecture on the power of compounding before at our father-daughter meals. Imagine one of those charts of breeding rabbits, which start with ten rabbits and then three generations later there's something like 40 million rabbits from only those original ten. Just like those humping bunnies, compounding in investing means if you continue to reinvest the money you make, that money will grow itself, by exponentially compounding the gains on the original amount. For example:

1. I invest $10 and get a 20 percent return at the end of the year. I get $2.
2. Then, I reinvest the $2. Now I have $10 of my money invested, and $2 of "house money."
3. I get a 20 percent return again. This time it's on $12, so I get $2.40.

That extra forty cents is money growing on itself, compounding on the house money, without me putting another dollar of my own money into the pot. It's like magic money, growing and growing and growing without any additional investment. The power of compounding to create wealth is remarkable.

"Every year you don't invest and get a return on your money is a year you lose the power of compounding," my dad said. "The difference starts out small, but it ends up being life changing. One more year of compounding in your account can mean millions of dollars. You won't believe how different the numbers are between people who invest over many years and people who invest for only a few years. Like private-jet-level difference."

"Really?" "Private-jet-level difference" got my attention. I wanted to be on the right side of that one.

"Look, Danielle, you're very lucky. You are young, well educated, and you make good money. You could have a retirement if all you did was save 10 percent of your income, buy the stock market index, and learn to live on what you have left. But people who are older, like me, who did not save and invest and missed out on years of potential compounding, absolutely are in trouble. Only 15 percent of the people my age have saved over $500,000. That means that most of the baby boomers are likely to run out of money in retirement. The good news for you is that people your age have the benefit of many years of compounding. If you learn to invest successfully at your age with your income, there's no way you don't get very, very rich."

Foin. Keep mentioning private jets and being very, very rich, and I'll listen to my Number. No one ever said my dad wasn't a good salesman. "Knock yourself out," I said. "Calculate away."

I could hear him typing over the phone and muttering spreadsheet words like "cell." I was about to be left in the dust of my dad's numbers-running frenzy.

"How much money do you have now?" he asked. Not much, was the answer, but I had one ace in the hole.

"If I sell my condo, I could pay off my student loans and end up with about $40,000."

"Okay. If you really want to change your life, you have to take those kinds of leaps, and save."

He was so blasé about selling my home, like he was recommending pizza toppings: *Well, Danielle, if you really want to taste the best pizza, you've simply got to take a chance on roma tomatoes.* But that's him—Mr. Risk Taker Extraordinaire—and to him it genuinely was no big deal. He went on with his pizza recommendations.

"You have about $40,000 to start with now, and let's say that you will put in about $15,000 per year in a retirement account each year going forward. That's tough but reasonable, right? And again, let's grow what you can save each year by 5 percent from increases in your income."

"Actually, I expected you to say I had to save an additional $50,000 per year or something."

"Nope. If you can earn more and save more than that, great, it will get you to freedom faster, but let's not count on it. Let's start with a really huge return from investing on your own, just to see what happens: Fifteen percent compounded per year. It sounds really high, I know, but it can be done on your own. At 15 percent return per year on your $40,000, save $15,000 a year in a tax-free account increasing the savings by 5 percent each year, retire thirty years from now, then live, in today's dollars, an $80,000-per-year lifestyle during retirement, and you'll still have $615 million when you are ninety-five years old.'"

"Did you say $615 million?"

"I did. That's the difference, thanks to compounding, of making 15 percent per year. Of course, by then, thanks to inflation—your favorite—$615 million will be the equivalent of about $105 million in today's dollars—but who's counting."

"Wait, what? $615 million will actually be worth less than one-fifth of that?"

"Yes. Inflation."

I felt like the Enclosed Concrete Stairwell now had wallpaper with "inflation" printed all over it. Still, at age ninety-five, I could probably get by on $105 million.

"Okay, let's talk about your options to realistically get 15 percent: abdicating to a financial adviser, buying a market index, or investing on your own. You've already heard the numbers if you invest on your own and get 15 percent per year."

Dad pulled up analyst estimates for market growth over the next seven to ten years,† which were 1 to 6 percent. "That's it!" he exclaimed. "Notice that nobody thinks this market is going to go roaring off like in the 1980s and 1990s and from 2009 to now."

Dad did some more typing, and then came back. "Oh. Man. I've also checked two sources that Buffett uses to tell us if this market is high or low overall, and they both indicate that it is crazy high right now. I will show them both to you later this year, but for now, I'd say 1 percent growth for the next few years suddenly looks reasonable, and estimating that the market will average 6 percent growth for the next thirty years is pretty optimistic. But let's get crazy and say that,

---

* We made the following additional assumptions in the calculations set forth in this chapter: 3 percent inflation and 30 percent federal and state tax rate on capital withdrawal from a qualified retirement plan starting at age sixty-five. To play with all of the calculations in this chapter yourself, go to www.danielletown.com.

† Morningstar.

with dividends, the stock market will average what it's averaged for the last one hundred years—about 7 percent."

"Fine," I agreed. I could hear him tapping away at his keyboard and after a few minutes he popped back up.

"Okay, here are some reasonable numbers if you abdicate to a financial adviser who uses ETFs and mutual funds. If the market returns 7 percent per year, but your advisers and managers cost 2 percent per year, you get 5 percent. If you get 5 percent for the next thirty years, and you work and hoard for thirty years, keep adding to your savings like we discussed, and you sell the condo and get $40,000 and save $15,000 per year going forward, you'll run out of money at age seventy-two, after seven years of retirement. And you, my dear, will be working at Walmart until you die."

"Well," I said. "That sucks." What else could I say?

"Now," Dad went on, "let's see what happens if you buy a market index fund with very low fees. And . . . it is still not enough. You will run out of money after twelve years in retirement and you will still die working at Walmart." Basically, he summarized, if the market does its historical average, you can work your butt off for thirty more years, save like Scrooge, and you'll almost certainly run out of money at the ripe young age of seventy-six. And if you are healthy at age seventy-six, you can look forward to living another twenty years or so completely broke. Better hope they fix social security and health care.

We sat there in silence for a minute, processing.

"Well, that sucks," I said again flatly, mostly to myself. "What happened to the $615 million?"

"Thought you'd never ask," he announced. "Let me play with those numbers and show you a different potential outcome."

Dad tapped away at his spreadsheet for a few minutes and then returned, triumphant. "Okay!" Nothing makes him happier than playing with a spreadsheet. "This shows investing returns if you can invest at 20 percent per year."

I coughed. "That's a bit higher than 7 percent—or even 15 percent."

"It's doable, though," he argued. "A study was done that found that if all you did was copy Warren Buffett's trades for thirty years you'd make over 20 percent per year.* If you can learn to achieve a 20-percent-per-year compounded rate of return—and I can show you how very good investors do that—and if you put in the amount we discussed each year, and you work for thirty years, and when you retire you spend the inflation-adjusted $80,000 a year, you will not only *not* run out of money, at age ninety-five you'll leave $7.3 billion for your heirs."

What exactly did I have to do to get those kinds of returns? He was painting pie-in-the-sky numbers, but they were so astronomical that they'd gotten my attention. Now, I was curious.

"And the legendary 26 percent?" I teased him. He had always talked about 26-percent-per-year returns for some reason. "If I managed to really crush it, how many years until I could retire?"

"Warren Buffett said he was certain he could make 50 percent per year if he weren't investing the huge amounts of money he has to move around,† so don't be too pessimistic with your 26 percent. If you'd invested as well as Warren Buffett and other great Rule #1–type investors and made a 26-percent-per-year compounded rate of return, you can stop working after just nine years. Nine years from now! That's life changing. And it won't hurt you at all. You will end up with lots of money at age ninety-five. Almost $15 billion. 'Course you're likely to have a little better lifestyle than $80,000, so it won't be quite that much."

---

* Gerald S. Martin and John Puthenpurackal, "Imitation is the Sincerest Form of Flattery: Warren Buffett and Berkshire Hathaway," SSRN, April 15, 2008, Table VII.
† "Anyone who says that size does not hurt investment performance is selling. The highest rates of return I've ever achieved were in the 1950s. I killed the Dow. You ought to see the numbers. But I was investing peanuts then. It's a huge structural advantage not to have a lot of money. I think I could make you 50 percent a year on $1 million. No, I know I could. I guarantee that" (Warren Buffett as quoted by Amy Stone, "Wisdom from the 'Oracle of Omaha,'" *BusinessWeek,* June 5, 1999).

"Come on."

"I'm serious. Look at the numbers." He e-mailed his spreadsheet to me and I looked. He was right. The chart showed that—starting with $40,000, at 26-percent-per-year returns, sixty years from today I would have $14.9 billion, which was $2.5 billion in buying power after inflation. As long as my spending stayed at $80,000 a year in current-dollar buying power, of course—a not-so-minor point. I would spend more, no doubt. It was surprisingly pretty fun to play around with the spreadsheet and find the tipping point where I could stop working.

The whole thing was incredible. Nine years. Not thirty. The power of compounding was real.

"Twenty-six percent is kind of a strange number to shoot for."

"Twenty-six percent happens to be the exact compounded annual rate of return if you double your money in three years. That's the goal—double your money every three years. There's a great Rule #1–style investor, Mohnish Pabrai, who focuses on 26 percent so much he put it on his license plate. Of course, Mohnish would be the first to tell you that high returns get a lot harder when you're working with hundreds of millions of dollars instead of thousands of dollars."

I heard a voice in the background of the call. "Oh, hold on," my dad said to me, and he said "Thanks" to someone while some loud dings reverberated through the phone like dishware was being knocked around his office. "My housekeeper just delivered my breakfast."

"Oh. My. Lord." I shook my head.

"I know," he agreed, and I could hear him grinning. "Life is good!" He started loudly eating while I was still on the phone and, through his munching, told me about the best investors in the world investing this way and getting those returns, and that they haven't been keeping it a secret. Renowned fund manager Peter Lynch even wrote a book about it. They've been telling people for years that if they invest themselves, they will be better off, and will get higher returns without the fees, than if they give their money over to a money manager and abdicate all responsibility. Warren Buffett does this style of investing, my dad said, and he named other investors who invest Buffett-style. The track record for these kinds of investors, he said, finishing up his breakfast, is often more than 20 percent per year on average over decades, even for investors who are managing billions.*

I slurped my tea directly into the phone to get back at him and digested that information. If those numbers were real, this just became useful. That was a huge "if." "If I can make 15 percent per year, what's my Number?"

"At 15 percent per year, it's $1.7 million, and you can get there in seventeen years," Dad said. "And if you make 26 percent per year and keep working a bit, starting now with $40,000 your Number is $780,000, and you can quit full-time work after nine years."

Nine years. My mind was racing. What could I do to drop it to something like two years? I wanted that.

Dad read my mind. "Start where you are right now and just try to get as much money into your investing as you can."

"I guess a financial adviser who charges fees won't get me to those returns."

"Correct," he agreed. "If you abdicate, you cannot hope for those returns and you won't stay retired long anyway. It's a good bet; a lot of upside if you win, not much downside if you lose."

"And the market index funds and ETFs obviously follow the market, which won't be enough."

"Exactly. Buffett says if you're not going to learn to invest properly, then buying a low-fee index that tracks the market like the S&P 500 is the next best choice—acknowledging that you'll get a market return of maybe 7 percent on average. Basically, you're betting on America going up over time. That's probably a good bet because America has a durable competitive advantage over other nations. We

---

* See "Superinvestors with Audited Track Records" in the appendix for a table of investors and their audited returns.

have a literal moat from two oceans, the world's most powerful military, solid currency, a free press, and trillions of dollars to invest in the future. We also have brilliant minds, hard workers, great ethics, a culture of personal responsibility, fair taxation, and limited government intrusion. Those are the reasons why putting money in the American stock market is investing and it's not a bad decision. Put that same money in the Greek or Argentine stock market and you're gambling. But just investing in an index won't get you the freedom you're looking for, as I showed you, unless you have a lot more money to invest than you have."

"I still wish I could abdicate to some fantastic fund manager," I mused, struggling with coming to terms with the obvious conclusion here—that I should neither hoard nor abdicate, but instead become an investor. It set him off.

"You give them too much credit. The thing is, most of these people barely beat the market, if they beat it at all."*

"Dad, that can't be right. If they didn't beat the market nobody would give them their money."

"It is right. Almost none of them beat the market—but that doesn't seem to matter. Most people are so ignorant about finances they don't care; they just want to abdicate—just like you do. But you would do so at a huge cost."

"Come on, surely there are some good mutual fund managers out there who do good work for their clients and are worth the fees, and that's why their clients stay with them. That's why this job of mutual fund manager still exists."

"Most of the people managing money are so full of baloney they make witch doctors look good. The job of mutual fund manager only still exists because it's a holdover from before the Internet, from

---

* According to a study by S&P Dow Jones, only 5.88 percent of large-cap equity funds beat the market after three years, and by year four, zero of those large-cap equity funds consecutively beat the market. Zero. (S&P Dow Jones Indices, "Fleeting Alpha: Evidence from the SPIVA and Persistence Scorecards.")

before we could feasibly manage our own money, thanks to the information available online. And some fund managers actually just buy funds run by other people. They spend their time bringing in new clients instead of investing because they get paid by bringing in new clients, not by making good investments."

"Wow. Really?"

"Yup," Dad said. "The only incentive they have to do a good job is to be able to bring in more clients by showing as good a track record as their competition and not doing so badly that they lose clients. They feed you this fairy tale that you'll make market-beating returns by paying their fees, and with rare exceptions, while a few people do make good returns for their clients, they only do it for a short time and the rest of the time they're content to just shadow the market. It's not about making high returns, it's about holding on to clients."

"So the real question is how to find the good ones and invest with them," I said wryly. "Like the Rule #1–type investors you just told me about!"

He snorted. "The only way to pick the good ones is to know something about investing so you know enough to evaluate what they're doing. Think of the benefits of learning about investing as much more than being able to invest on your own. You would have a true wealth of knowledge to draw on for any kind of investing—real estate or buying a private business. You can always abdicate. If you do, after learning the Rule #1 principles, you'll know how to evaluate fund managers. You'll know how to tell if they're good or if they're Bernie Madoff. And you'll have enough money to get a good one interested."

"So what you're saying is, even if I want to use a good money manager, that I need to learn about investing in order to find one?"

"Pretty much. Next month, let's get into why they don't beat the market, and why Rule #1 investors regularly do."

"Yeah, let's talk about *that*," I agreed. The weight of what he was saying felt heavy on my shoulders. The only way to evaluate good investors was to learn how to invest. The only way to make enough money to become free was to learn how to invest.

"Okay, those returns would get me to freedom, I see that," I agreed. "But I'm not convinced that the stock market is the only way to get them. I still don't trust it."

"I don't actually think you have to invest in the stock market," my dad explained.

"What?!" I exclaimed. "But you always only talk about investing in the stock market!"

"That's because it's accessible to everyone from their couch. Other kinds of investing, as you've discovered, are less available. But these principles I'm talking about, the Rule #1 principles, can be used for other kinds of investing. They apply to any kind of investment that produces cash flow."

"Like, they apply to real estate?"

"They do. You bought your condo, right? And when you did, we discussed all the different factors that made it a good or bad investment."

"We did. We talked about the space limitations in Boulder, the university providing a somewhat steady source of people, the natural beauty and location, what would happen if the tech scene crashes like it did in 2001, what happened when real estate crashed in 2008."

"And we decided it was a strong investment, not speculation, because of two things: one, Boulder real estate would hold up for the long term, and two, you could rent your condo immediately and get cash flow coming in. That was Rule #1 investing. You did a Rule #1 analysis without realizing it. And you were right about all of it."

I laughed. "Well, that was pretty easy! I understand my neighborhood and my town. I understand the purchase price and what I would have had to pay in rent. I didn't have to read any financial statements or conjecture what an unknown CEO might do."

"It's the same process, though. Maybe a purchase of stock has a few more layers of information, but it's the same process. You want to decide what is speculation and what is an investment. An investment is determined by its certainty."

I thought it over. Focusing on real estate investments to rent out would require a substantial investment right off the bat, and all my money would be tied up in one investment that might be hard or impossible to get out of. Plus, I didn't know how to fix toilets. In the stock market, on the other hand, I could use my money to invest in a few different companies that I could sell any time I wanted from the comfort of my couch. I was still desperately searching for another option. I did not want my dad to be right. I did not want to trust the stock market.

"I've got an alternate idea for you," he piped up. "A friend of mine made enough money to play a lot of polo by building Domino's Pizza franchises. They're a great business for him. It's all about location and the brand and maintaining the brand. If you can do that, you rake in money. I think he has over forty locations now."

"Yeah, and I'd have to run a business in which I have zero experience."

"You'd have to do what he did—work there, manage one, then buy your own. But you're right, that probably wouldn't be your strength."

"Um, no. Not that I couldn't learn it if I had to, but is that going to be my natural oeuvre, to leave my legal career and open a pizza joint? No."

"Yeah, just the fact that you use the word 'oeuvre' indicates that. Elitist," he teased. "It's also really hard to get franchises, actually. There's pretty much already a fast-food restaurant in every good location, so you have to either put one in a suboptimal location or get a franchise from an up-and-coming company, which of course is less of a guaranteed investment."

"I could found a tech startup," I suggested.

"Oh really?" he said slowly, but not unapprovingly.

"This, I actually have some experience in. Okay, not directly, but

I've worked with dozens of them. I actually have a lot of experience in the problems startups typically run into. I know what the pitfalls are, I know what's important, I know what most of the first-time founders don't think of."

"That's true," he said slowly. "It's a hard life, though." Dad had funded and run a few startups. "No matter how many books are written about failure being good, failing is usually a personal disaster. You see the successful entrepreneurs, the serial entrepreneurs, the successful venture capitalists. You don't see the people who have done seven different failures and have no career or savings to show for it. The people who are fifty years old and haven't had a success. It can be a very tough life if you're not really good at it and really lucky. And you have to be both."

I remembered why I went into law instead, and loved that I got to work with startups without actually risking my own neck.

Well, that was that. I had no more arguments. I was stuck. I saw no way out other than investing my own money in the stock market, and the thought made my stomach hurt. I really did not want to lose my own money.

"Honey," he said, "take a step back and notice the problem that is stressing you out right now. You're getting all worried about failing at the opportunity to prepare for a better life, but you're missing that you have the opportunity to prepare for a better life!"

A dose of perspective. He couldn't have been more right.

"Staying in your current situation is worse than taking the chance. Come on! You're worried about losing out on the very few years of retirement that you can hope to achieve without learning to invest. Don't get too wrapped up in how terrifying it is. The alternative is pretty damned scary too. So just be grateful you aren't stuck with it like most people. Remember Wahei Takeda?"

Mmm. The name barely rang a bell.

"Wahei Takeda is the Warren Buffett of Japan."

"As in, he made billions from investing, or as in, he's a famous value investor?"

"As in, both. I met with him at his home when I was in Japan a few years ago, remember? He invests like Buffett, of course, but I wanted to know if he did anything else that he thought was significant to his success. Do you know what he said?"

"Don't lose money?"

Dad grinned. "I'm sure he was thinking that."

"He didn't want to steal Warren's line."

"He actually answered, for real. He called his secret *Maro*. 'Thankfulness.' One of the most wealthy, successful investors in the world, and his secret was gratitude."*

I laughed. "That's probably just something he trotted out to answer annoying questions like 'What's your secret?'"

Dad stopped laughing. "Except that he's famous for it in Japan. It's the centerpiece of his investing. He has institutionalized regular thankfulness in all of the companies he invested in."

Whoa. That's putting your money where your mouth is.

"When he invests in a company, he asks that company's CEO to implement a policy of thankfulness among the whole company. Employees get reminders to be thankful; thankfulness to each other is part of their meetings, and becomes part of the culture of that company. If the CEO does not do it, Takeda will sell his stake. He told me he has developed the habit of being thankful one thousand times per day and it is the key to his success."

"One thousand? You wouldn't think about anything else. Even ten times a day is an awful lot to focus on."

"Yeah, so fine, let's assume we don't do it a thousand times per day, but could you think about it twice a day? Once a day?"

"Of course." It was actually a really nice idea. Thankfulness is generally good. But I've tried to consciously feel thankful more of-

---

* There has even been a book written about Takeda's thankfulness practice: Janet Bray Attwood and Ken Honda, *Maro Up: The Secret of Success Begins with Arigato: Wisdom from the "Warren Buffett of Japan"* (Amazon Digital Services, 2015).

ten, and it has felt forced, and then I feel fake, and then I feel guilty for feeling fake about thankfulness. "I don't think forced thankfulness really works for me."

"Yeah, I get that." He thought it over. "Can you take things you're not happy about and find a silver lining? Say a thank-you for your problems? You don't have to force yourself to feel anything, just say thank you for some part of the experience."

I thought it over. I liked it. Finding pointed problems and looking for the good turned their energy around. It moved them away from the dark side and into the light.

In that moment, I was thankful for the stress in my body revealing how urgently I needed to change my life. I was thankful that my dad had the knowledge, experience, and time to help me. I was thankful that I had found the courage to face my financial reality that month, and doing so made the knot in my stomach loosen ever so slightly. My thankfulness was very real.

My dad said, softly, "I'm thankful that you're being so brave about this and for letting me help you. It's not easy."

I did not know what to say to that. He had never admitted before that leaping into investing was anything but utterly, obviously, ridiculously easy. I did not know what to do with a dad who acknowledged that investing could be intimidating. Or, even more surprising, that he really wanted to help me in an extended, invested way. It made me feel like I didn't have to protest quite so much to him. Maybe he empathized with me, just a little bit. I stopped wanting him to not be right quite so much, and unclenched a bit internally.

Dad cleared his throat and moved on to summarizing: "Basically, there are four pretty straightforward mathematical components to achieving financial freedom:

1. Minimum annual spending
2. Years remaining to invest

3. Money to invest

4. Required rate of return on the investments

"The first one, spending, is up to you. I lived on less than $4,000 a year for thirteen years and I didn't notice I was poor. I think my top pay in the Vietnam-era army was $441 a month and that included extra pay for jumping out of planes and being in a combat zone. You're going to need more than I had or you will definitely notice you're poor. The second one, years, is fixed: you only have so many years in your life starting right now to compound successfully. So you have to begin now. The third one, money, is also fixed—unless you can do something magical to suddenly start making a lot more money. Most of us can't, and the weird thing about making more money is that somehow our expenses rise to match the increase in income and we still don't save enough."

He had a point, I thought ruefully.

"You've gotta fight that and get as much money into your investments as possible, especially at the beginning, when you have the most time to compound those dollars."

"I wish you had started me early," I ventured.

"I tried! You didn't listen to me."

"That's true."

"That's why you've got to do it now. And listen—the fourth component of reaching financial freedom, the required rate of return, is also fixed for most people. There is no point whatsoever in attempting to achieve a higher rate of return than the market unless—and this is a life-changing unless—unless you are willing to learn to invest like Buffett and Munger."

"But that's a full-time job," I protested. "I would be doing it part-time, so I can't put in the research that you can. And I don't even have any time to put toward it at all! I'm barely treading water as it is."

"I know shooting for a 26 percent compounded rate of return per year is an incredibly high goal, but what if you could take the shot with less risk than putting money in an index? If you put a bit of time into it now, the rewards will be huge in the future. If you don't, you'll be—"

"I know," I interrupted. "Working at Walmart till I die." Present Danielle and Future Danielle were fighting in my head. I didn't have the time, but I couldn't afford not to make the time, not with the potential to get to a whole new life in just a few years.

"I don't want that for you, obviously. This is the single most useful and protective thing I can teach you. What's stopping you?"

He had opened the door away from a yes-or-no answer. His first mistake. All my fears came flooding back and I jumped all over it.

"How about the fact that the macroeconomic world affects the stock market in ways I can't possibly predict or imagine? How about the fact that in 2008, I had no comprehension or clue that there were real estate securities that were going to bring down our economy? How about a world war? How about companies that lie to the regulators? How about not knowing enough about an industry to know if a certain company in that industry is a good investment or if the whole industry is going down?" He had knocked down my practical objections, and now my deeper worries were coming out in full force. "There are *so* many things to know, and I know you have some certainty about your investments, but I don't know how you get there. I mean, really, the question is, how do I know when I know enough?"

Dad knew I was worrying about getting good information. "Okay, now *that* is a good question. You will know, because I will teach you."

I wasn't sure I would know. Companies are made up of people. People make mistakes. People act emotionally, and they have things happening in their lives other than their jobs, and they have incentives to lie and pass the buck to the next guy, and they want to do the right thing but don't. Sometimes people steal and cover it up. The view of a company as a monolithic entity that cannot be shaken is dead wrong. I had to be able to tell from my research if a monolith was quavering.

"I first want to show you how choosing wonderful companies works on a broad level," Dad interrupted. "Then, we'll dive into the details of choosing particular companies and how to get good information. The secret to good investing is to wait. I won't let you do anything before you're ready and the market is ready."

"That makes me think of the Four Levels of Mastery you talk about."

"Yes, exactly!" Dad exclaimed.

My dad often mentions an old saying about the Four Levels of Mastery of a skill, and it has stuck with me. The first level is Unconscious Incompetence, when you're completely incompetent at that skill and don't even worry about it because you don't know anything about it. I'm Unconsciously Incompetent at yacht racing, now that I think about it.

The second level is Conscious Incompetence, when you know what you need to know but you can't do it very well. I'm Consciously Incompetent at singing karaoke and I'm not trying to get better at it. I'd rather curl up in the corner of the booth, drink old-fashioneds, cheer my friends on, and dance when a Britney song comes on. That's what I call Not a Bad Night. For a skill I do want to be competent at, though, being Consciously Incompetent feels excruciatingly painful.

The third level of mastery is Conscious Competence. That's when you know what you need to know, and if you stay focused and conscious about what you're doing, you can do it well. The good news about Conscious Competence is when you get there, you become even better quickly; the brutal days of Conscious Incompetence are gone and better days are ahead.

The fourth level of mastery, Unconscious Competence, is the experience of doing something well without thinking about it. Athletes often call the extreme experience of Unconscious Competence "the zone," a state of activity that is experienced as a kind of mindless witnessing of, say, the ball effortlessly going through the hoop. Warren Buffett says he can decide in minutes if he wants to buy an entire company. I imagine he is in that state of Unconscious Competence. Me, I'd happily settle for Conscious Competence.

"You are going to become Consciously Competent faster than you can imagine," Dad promised me.

My dad was so nice to offer to spend his time teaching me. He's a busy guy, and I didn't take his offer lightly. I wasn't completely confident that he would see it through the whole year, but he seemed to want to show up, and there was nothing I could do but see what happened. Future Danielle needed this, that I knew. Maybe, I thought, Present Danielle would get something out of it too. I spent my days taking care of projects and tasks and questions for other people. This Investing Practice was something I could do for me, and me alone. And maybe I'd get to know my dad a bit better—or differently, anyway.

One concern remained, though. There's a reason I went to law school instead of business school. Numbers swim around in my brain until they float out of my ears, never to be seen again. To me, accounting statements look like impenetrable columns of tiny black numbers. I can feel them physically hurting my mind as each minute ticks by, like electrolysis on my brain. I know I'm not the only one to whom accounting is intimidating, and for good reason. The Enron accounting scandal proved that financial accounting can be a mysterious art even to those who are certified professional accountants.

"You know I'm terrible at math, right? Financial statements are not something I enjoy."

Sheepishly, he said, "I gauge whether my investing students will be able to follow something by trying it out on you. I know that if you can understand it, they can."

I laughed. "Good, so we're on the same page, then. Am I teachable?"

"Of course you are. I will teach you how to value a company.

We're not trying to jump over six-foot hurdles, as Buffett says. We're only taking on six-inch hurdles. You'll be fine. Don't worry."

"Am I going to have to buy stock soon? I don't really want to."

"No! You're not even allowed to buy stock, how about that? You're probably going to get impatient and want to buy stock before you're ready."

I gave him a major side-eye on that one, which he couldn't see, but he seemed to feel it anyway. "You should not expect to buy a single company until this year is over," he went on. "You've gotta get centered in the knowledge first. 'Established in Being, perform action,'" he quoted from the Bhagavad Gita.

I knew what he meant. Along with Transcendental Meditation and yoga, I had grown up reading Vedic texts in both English and the original Sanskrit—exchanging a quote in a five-thousand-year-old dead language from the Bhagavad Gita was perfectly normal for us. My parents were weirdos who somehow became successful, what can I say? Dad meant that my investing knowledge had to be established within me so that my instincts would be true. Which was perfect, because I dreaded putting real money in the market.

"Don't worry, Dad. I don't think I'm going to want to jump the gun on buying anything. I'll probably want to wait longer than you want me to!"

"I think you'll get into this more than you think you will."

Nothing I could do but take his word for it and plan to focus on each step of this practice. If I'm going to learn to invest, I'm going to do it right, I decided. I didn't have years to mess around and the potential to get to a life of freedom quicker than I ever believed possible was like a magnet drawing me in.

We said our goodbyes and hung up. He had convinced me that abdication was not an option. I was going to do this myself. I felt an oddly layered mix of curious, anxious, and empowered. I was going to do this myself.

I was going to do this myself.

FEBRUARY PRACTICE: I didn't want to know my Number, but finding it out did make me feel that reaching it might be possible. Make your own choice to know your Number, and to have more control over it, play around with the different returns and other inputs to see all the different paths to financial freedom. To make finding your Number easier, I put a "Your Number" calculator on my website: www.danielletown.com. Most important, practice consciously and regularly acknowledging and being aware of your problems, and find a reason, however tiny, to be genuinely thankful for each of them.

Voting for a Mission with My Money

| March

MY OBJECTIONS HAD BEEN SWATTED AWAY, AND I HAD COMMITTED TO this Investing Practice with my dad. All my excuses were still true—I was still busy, still bad at math, still overwhelmed by how much information there was to take in. How could I integrate learning to invest into my life so well that I would stick with it? I had to think practically now.

When I feel overwhelmed, organizing has always been my saving grace. Organize my stuff, and my mind feels equally less cluttered.

The next cold Saturday morning at home, as my picture-window sunrise view was being filled up by blue sky, I sat in my big chair and started to think about logistics. Where and when would I practice investing? In my yoga practice, I had my yoga mat to ground me—as long as I got on my yoga mat, even if only for five minutes, I considered my practice for that day done. Recently, I had gotten so desperate for time that my only yoga practice was when I would lock myself in the handicapped bathroom at work and try to imagine I was somewhere else while I breathed and touched my toes a few times. I avoided touching the floor like the plague, but in my mind I was on my yoga mat, and at least it was something. At least I was trying. For runners, lacing up running shoes and leaving the house is often enough to get going. What was the equivalent of my yoga mat or my running shoes for investing?

Investing was something I was doing on time borrowed from other items on my to-do list. If I didn't have an inviting environment that would spark the desire to spend time on my Investing Practice, I would probably let it peter out as the other items on my to-do list inevitably became more pressing.

Indeed, I had no investing environment whatsoever. I didn't have a home office, nor did I even have room for one in my tiny apartment.

Marie Kondo, the expert on tidying up, says to visualize in concrete terms the ideal space.* I snuggled into my big chair and stared out the window at the stately university campus across town, as I often did, and thought about what would spark the fire of my practice. It would have some reminders of why I was investing, it would have some useful investing props, and it would have space for me to pile up papers and other investing debris. I set about creating my investing space.

The Magic of Creating Investing Space

Buffett acolyte Guy Spier wrote in his book, *The Education of a Value Investor,* that he has a treasured photo of himself and Warren Buffett in his office to remind him who his hero is, uses a standing desk to stay alert, and stays away from analyses about companies as much as possible to keep his own counsel unsullied. My dad, on the other hand, mostly sits at his desk computer and regularly reads analyses as a counterpoint to his own viewpoint. He has some photos around him, but they're all positioned behind his back, so he doesn't actually look at them often. To each our own.

---

* Marie Kondo, *The Life-Changing Magic of Tidying Up* (Berkeley, CA: Ten Speed Press, 2014).

Every corner in my tiny box of an apartment was spoken for. Marie Kondo was right, though: visualizing did put what was most important to me into my mind. I always gravitate toward working in the dining room or kitchen—where there's some energy, and some room to spread out, and some snacks. Snacks are very important to completing good work.

I decided my actual Investing Practice was going to have to be done at my dining room table. However, that meant my investing stuff would have to be cleared off and tucked away, often, so I would fill a box with investing paraphernalia to serve as a kind of mobile office. Where my investing box was, my investing office was.

I put a few talismans in a box to remind me which way to point my intentions and my brain, along with a few practical items any office needs. First, my talisman to remind me to be thankful for my problems—*Maro*. I had heart problems years ago that were difficult to diagnose, and my doctor gave me a heart-shaped stone after it was all over to remind me that things do get better.

Second, something to remind me why I was doing this when I got tired and didn't feel like focusing on investing anymore. My North Stars, so to speak, to remind me of the tradition of value investors from whom I was learning. My dad's presence was already every-where when I sat down to do Investing Practice—on the phone, in my e-mail, in my head. Plus, on the bookshelf next to my dining table, I already displayed in the place of honor first editions of his two books with his handwritten inscriptions to me. Dad was there.

Books were a good idea, though. I piled up other books to serve as a laptop stand: additional copies of *Rule #1, Payback Time,* and *The Education of a Value Investor;* Yvon Chouinard's *Let My People Go Surfing;* Gretchen Rubin's *The Happiness Project;* and Atul Ga-wande's *Complications.* I put *The Life-Changing Magic of Tidying Up* on the stack of books to remind me to be tidy and efficiently ruthless in the organization of my finances, and *The Big Short,* to remind me that I had to look deeper than surface level and think about macroeconomic forces in the market, and that things can go very wrong when they look like they're going very right.

Spier keeps photos of his father, one of his first investors, in his office to remind him who he's working for. Not that they necessarily need me, but being able to take care of my mom and my sister is a big part of how I envision financial freedom, so I picked a photo of us off the shelf and put it next to my computer. It was okay, but not quite right. I already had photos of my family all over my tiny house. I propped up a photo of myself, Kamala, and two other close friends from a night out in New York, and being inspired by them felt right. I also grabbed a photo that a friend took of me hiking in some amazing mountain scenery and gave to me as a gift, because it made me feel expansive and reminded me that my idea of financial freedom meant having days available to go to the mountains . . . or to the ocean . . . or to a city . . . or to do whatever I chose. I loved these photos and wanted to see them, and the only way I would see them was to pull them out of the box and set up my investing office. A small incentive, but a nice one.

What else . . . I thought of something to entice me to open that box and create an inviting atmosphere. I put a scented travel candle in the box for some good smells when I sat down to practice. And a lighter so I wouldn't have to search for one each time.

I considered putting headphones in the box so they would be easily available, but I only had one pair of quality headphones and I wanted to use them for non-investing time too. I decided I could easily grab them from their usual spot in the entryway key bowl and left them out of the box.

Finally, and I wasn't sure why, but I grabbed a small prayer wheel that I bought at some touristy stall in Kathmandu a few years before. It was slightly off-kilter and nothing fancy, but I felt things about this prayer wheel. In Tibetan Buddhism, turning a prayer wheel while praying sends the energy of your prayer into the universe. I put it on the shelf next to my dad's signed books and turned the wheel. It sent my wishes, my prayers, my hopes for my Investing Practice into the universe. It also reminded me, by its presence, that wishing for something won't make it happen on its own. I have to turn the wheel. I have to practice investing.

So that was my office, contained in an ugly plastic storage bin stowed on my bookshelf, all classy-like. A pile of books, a candle, talismans, photos, and a computer on my dining table. Not exactly Guy Spier's perfectly curated library. Oh well. I reminded myself not to let the perfect be the enemy of the good.

Doing something to set up my space, even these small things, made me feel more in control. I felt like I was running headlong into that dense fog swirling around, but for goodness' sake, at least my stuff would be organized.

Then I prepared my computer. I made a folder titled "Investing Practice" and placed it prominently on my desktop. I already used a note-taking app* to keep and organize news clippings, so I made a new notebook also titled "Investing Practice." I wasn't sure what would go in each of these folders, but at least I was prepared. I wanted to set it up so that two or eight or ten years from now, when I wanted to know everything I had found on a company, I would be able to easily find it and I wouldn't have to duplicate my work.

Now that I was set up, I could think about what I was actually going to invest in. The corporate form, I knew. It was the basis of all stocks and public markets, and understanding where it came from was key to understanding how it worked today. Executives get paid millions of dollars for screwing up their companies because of the evolution of corporations and liability, and I wanted to make sure I knew the underpinnings of the system to which I was going to subject my money.

Corporations: A Short History of a Legal Fiction

Corporations provide our products, transportation, food, shelter. Of course they do; corporations and stock markets are just people, and

---

* As of this writing, I use the app Evernote, but there are many great note-taking and file-organization apps and websites out there.

we the people have invented these constructs (we lawyers like to call them "legal fictions") so that we can invest in them without being personally on the hook for what they do. Their history led to me standing in my apartment that day, reviewing my investing office, thinking about how I would protect myself from subjecting my money to an unscrupulous corporate management team.

Corporations have existed for thousands of years, but several hundred years after the Dutch invented the stock exchange, the British added their own history-changing innovation: limited liability for the owners of corporations, which is exactly what it sounds like—liability of company owners was limited to the assets of the company, and their personal assets could not be reached by company creditors. It spurred entrepreneurship like nothing else, because once limited liability was enacted, no one worried about their families being ruined forever by the failure of a company. Limited liability, while fantastic for entrepreneurship, would turn out to be a double-edged sword for corporations and investors. The British economist Adam Smith's fundamental premise, that people will always act rationally in their own best interest, is modified substantially when the penalty for unconscionable behavior is muted by a corporate shield.

The United States gradually adopted the view that even with the occasional corporate excesses, the benefits of corporations outweighed their drawbacks. The evolution of the corporate entity permits both angels and monsters: one corporation brings the comforts of kings to the middle class while another destroys communities; another corporation makes poor people rich and another makes rich people poor. I knew that if I was going to be an investor, I wanted to be a values-driven, Mission-oriented investor who could distinguish between the angel companies and the monster companies. Which businesses are behaving honorably, following the values I believe are important? I wanted to know. Which are not?

Addressing the Asymmetry

From my corporate legal work, I was constantly aware of the inherent asymmetry of information between public companies and their shareholders. If I were going to invest in my field of professional expertise, an early-stage startup, I would first get to know the founders personally to decide if they were worth betting on. Similarly, large investors in companies traded on the stock market do the same: they often meet with the executives, visit the company's offices and manufacturing facilities, and have experts who review the financials. Little-guy investors like me don't get to do any of that. One thing that scared me about investing in public companies was that shareholders have less information than company management and, as such, are at an inherent disadvantage. The information the company has and the information the shareholder has is never going to be exactly the same.

Shareholders are the owners of a company, but shareholders do not run a company—a fact about corporate structure that, as a lawyer, I find fascinating, but as a potential investor, I find daunting. Limited liability has given me, as a potential owner, the option to invest, but also to essentially check out of governance. There's that double-edged sword again. Instead, shareholders vote to elect the people who sit on the company's board of directors, which makes major decisions for the company. The board of directors then hires and appoints the company's executive officers, who run the operations of the company. The board of directors has a fiduciary duty, a legal and ethical responsibility, to make decisions for the company for the benefit of the shareholders but with great latitude in how it accomplishes that purpose. In this way, in theory, shareholders indirectly control the company, and if a director is doing a poor job, shareholders can elect someone else to that director seat (or use other methods of recourse if there are egregious violations of that director's fiduciary duty). In practice, and depending on the company, many board members are eager to get something like $250,000 per year for a few hours of meetings, so they avoid rocking the boat and often rubber-stamp the CEO's decisions. Consider executive pay, for example:

The board is incentivized to hire executive officers who will grow the company and make the stock price rise, and the officers are incentivized to make the board happy with their performance and to, usually, make the stock price rise. Shareholders like a higher stock price, but this incentive structure sometimes perversely encourages short-term corporate decisions instead of longer-term growth. Is it any wonder that executive officer compensation at some companies has become higher and higher . . . and higher? The incredibly high compensation has created mercenary CEOs who, even if the long-term results of their decisions harm the business, still get their millions in annual compensation and a golden parachute at the end.

In 2015, the CEO of the oil-drilling company Schlumberger was paid total compensation of $18.3 million, including a 12 percent raise in the cash he took home. The same year, the company cut 25,000 jobs, or 20 percent of its workforce, because it lost 27 percent of its revenue and 41 percent of its profit from the year before. Enron, WorldCom, Tyco, and HealthSouth top the list of companies that have been run by CEOs to make themselves rich or even just to make themselves look good. Unfortunately, there are many examples of this kind of morally corrupt disparity between CEO pay and company performance, as well as employees' pay, and it has only gotten worse over the years. Fifty years ago, CEO pay at major corporations averaged twenty times that of their employees; today, CEO pay averages three hundred times that of their employees.*

It's a stock market driven up by the short-term thinking of mercenary CEOs. Many companies participate in it, but some don't.

As an investor, I wanted to support the ones that don't.

---

* Robert Reich, *Saving Capitalism* (New York: Knopf, 2015), 94.

Voting for a Mission with My Money

As I thought more about corporate practices, I decided to look for the few companies I could find that I really love, corporations that are wonderful in the sense that they share my values and they walk my talk. I wanted to support the Andrew Carnegies, Steve Jobses, and Oprah Winfreys of the world. They were not driven only by greed. They weren't perfect; they were driven by the personal desire to be the best, to create the best product, to invest their lives in making the best thing they could. It's not idealistic to say so.

How was I going to figure out who the good guys were? I used to think the alluringly underachieving Lloyd Dobler in *Say Anything* was exactly right, when I was wary enough to avoid investing in any business: "I don't want to sell anything, buy anything, or process anything as a career. I don't want to sell anything bought or processed, or buy anything sold or processed, or process anything sold, bought, or processed, or repair anything sold, bought, or processed. You know, as a career, I don't want to do that." Fair enough, Lloyd, you boom box–playing, tall, cool drink of water. But that wasn't me anymore. A few months ago, yes, but not now. What I wanted to do now was invest in people who were into everything Lloyd was not: people who were selling quality goods, who were buying things they'd carefully chosen, who were behaving with integrity. Some of my friends think we live in a dystopian world of corporate fascism driven by the greed of faceless men. That might be true if we do nothing. But I could cast a vote for which corporations and CEOs would occupy my world in the future.

I suddenly realized I could vote with my dollars in a larger way. Every day we, you and I, act on our morals with our money. We choose to buy organic food, sweatshop-free clothing, or American-made cars. But we have the opportunity to vote with our dollars in a much bigger, more impactful way than just buying dolphin-free tuna at the grocery store; we can support the Mission of a right-acting company by buying its stock. By voting with all of our dollars, we could fix this stock market mess.

As a consumer, I had voted with my dollars every single day for what I wanted to see more of in the market. I wouldn't buy conventional produce grown with herbicide expecting that my choice would increase the amount of organic produce next year. If I bought organic, it encouraged more organic—and indeed, the organic grocery market has gone from nonexistent to changing the face of the grocery industry in the last thirty years, thanks largely to consumers voting with their dollars at Whole Foods, which forced conventional grocery stores to offer more natural and organic foods in order to compete.

In exactly the same way, I now could expand voting with my dollars to the stock market. Rather than being limited by my physical proximity and my immediate consumer needs, my dollars could support companies that consider all of their stakeholders when they make major decisions run by leaders with integrity. If I had to invest, I wanted to invest in companies that understood that the bottom line, net profit, is required for their existence, but that it is not the only reason for existing. I wanted to vote for companies that had a Mission to change the world for the better just as much as the founders of the startups I loved did. The more I thought about it, the more I felt that these companies, with a strong Mission I supported, would be better custodians of my money than anyone else.

I did not want to support a company that took advantage of good people looking for honest work by paying its employees the bare minimum and treating them poorly, like Walmart does. A company can do extremely well financially without treating its employees well, as Walmart has, but I don't think it has great long-term prospects. There is a slow decaying process to a company with a lot of employees who are unhappy. Aside from the ethics of how they are treated, those employees are definitely not going to give the extra hour needed to make something perfect, they're not going to provide excellent service to customers, and they probably won't stay at that company if they can find a viable alternative job. Similarly, I didn't want to own a company that buys chickens raised crammed into tiny cages and filled with antibiotics, like McDonald's. It matters to me to not shop in those stores and not buy that food, when I can help it.

In the same way that I wouldn't shop at companies that I didn't agree with, I wouldn't invest in them either.

Investing might actually be useful in this world, I realized. Good companies need me, and others like me, to vote for them with our dollars for ethical animal farming, organic strawberries, and well-paid workers. I can buy Whole Foods stock regardless of how close the nearest Whole Foods is. I can buy lululemon* stock whether or not I buy any clothes from them this year (ha!). I can buy the public company that owns Jack Daniel's, Brown-Forman, to support my bourbon obsession even when I'm trying to be a good teetotaler. I get to vote with my money. The vote exists whether I'm conscious of it or not, and it definitely exists whether I want it to or not. I could ignore that fact, as most investors do. Or I could embrace it.

I'm not the only one who could vote with my money. Of the $70 trillion in the world stock markets, 85 percent of it is our money, remember? Most of the Wall Street professionals and robo-advisers out there don't consider investing to be a vote, and they don't consider Mission at all. Their focus is solely on the bottom line. Those that do try to invest in right-acting companies almost always do so at the expense of making a good return.

If we combine Mission with a growing, well-managed, income-generating company, the impact would be incredible. I would do well for Future Danielle by generating income to bring me to financial freedom, and I would join the rest of us 85 percent to support and invest in companies that deserve my hard-earned money—companies that are consciously capitalist, in which doing good actively supports and enhances the bottom line. It has happened already: Investors took their money out of companies and organizations that supported

---

* Yup, they don't capitalize the name of their company.

or benefited from apartheid, and apartheid died. Investors took their money out of cigarette companies, and they have been severely weakened. Investors put their money into organic and natural foods companies, and now even conventional grocery stores not only offer natural and organic products, they position them right up front where they're easy to find.

Money talks. The largest investors in America aren't Warren Buffett and Bill Gates; they are retirement funds like CalSTRS, the California State Teachers' Retirement System pension fund with over $110 billion invested in the stock market.* That $110 billion is all schoolteacher retirement money. Little-guy money. If all of us small investors took our money away from the control of Wall Street pension funds like CalSTRS and invested it individually in what we want to support in the world, those companies without good Missions would either change or die. The long-awaited ethics revolution in corporate America would happen quickly because the stock price follows the money. Take the money out of that stock, the stock price goes down, the CEO gets fired, and the board gets replaced. We're talking months, not years. That thought gave me a little shiver.

It could be the end of overpaid CEOs and crony boards, the end of exploited workers, the end of polluters. It could be the growth of companies that use American workers and pay them well, that make products in America, that make sound environmental choices, that consider their stakeholders when making major decisions. It could be a market takeover of well-run, ethically managed, Mission-oriented companies that make excellent returns for their investors. If we all acted like we are adults who take responsibility for our financial decisions, we would have massive power. It would also make this investing thing a lot more fun.

We don't have a way of controlling institutional fund managers. All we can do is take our money away from them and do it ourselves.

---

* https://www.calstrs.com/portfolio-holdings-asset-category.

I started to feel a bit like an entrepreneur of my own investing portfolio—where would I pivot next? What would I do to change the world next?

Massively impressed with my own do-gooderness and surprised by how excited I was to vote for a Mission with my money in the stock market, I noticed that I didn't feel quite as afraid of investing anymore.

I jotted down the threads between all the companies I liked and called it my List of Missions.

My List of Missions

▶ Treat employees decently and pay a living wage: a company that isn't ethical is not putting good vibes out into the world; it's creating employees who don't like it. It'll eventually go down.

▶ Treat products decently: if animals, humanely; if products, be environmentally friendly; if food, use sustainable farming practices.

▶ Prefer local and small: support the community and use local information about the company's environment, local reputation, and employees.

I also noticed what was not on my List of Missions. There was nothing on there about specific industries or products. Some people who are against firearms, for example, might never buy Smith & Wesson as a matter of principle. I didn't have any hard-and-fast positions like that, but others certainly do and they should be voting their values with the same enthusiasm I was going to vote mine.

Some might say that my investing dollars were so minimal that they would not have the slightest impact on any company I bought. It's the same argument as "I don't vote because one vote doesn't make any difference," or "I just buy the cheapest/closest/easiest thing because it doesn't matter anyway." But one vote or purchase, multiplied by thousands of similar votes or purchases, could have a huge impact. More important, I knew I would be doing everything I could to put my own conscience at rest. I believe karma exists, and I wanted mine to be good.

I stood there in my newly minted investing office, and I felt truly eager about this endeavor for the first time. Consciously capitalist companies, I realized, matter to me. I thought about buying a share of a company with a great Mission, like Whole Foods. When I had thought of buying stock at lunch with my dad two months ago, I felt the Enclosed Concrete Stairwell closing in. Strangely, now I felt like a warrior. I now saw myself as a Mission-oriented impact investor, asking which businesses are behaving honorably, following the values I believe are important, and which are not.

I thought Dad would like my idea of voting for companies with Missions, but I wasn't sure how he would react to my adding my own ideas to his methods. I knew he wanted to teach me exactly how he invested and would push me toward his answers. When I was a kid, he used to quiz me on long car rides about matters of philosophy and religion using the Socratic method. Socrates, like my dad, infuriatingly asked leading questions to guide his subject toward the answer he wanted. No wonder the Athenians killed him.

Dad and I had another Investing Practice call toward the end of the month. We weren't exactly hitting our weekly call plan even a few weeks in, but we were both trying hard to make time for them, which was good enough for me.

I blurted it out: "Dad, I have to invest in companies with values that I want to support with my money. Otherwise, I'm going to feel bad about what I'm supporting, and that's going to eventually make me lose interest and not want to do it anymore."

"Good! Vote for your values. I love it. The Mission of the business and their values are part of what I call the Story of a company."

I had no idea what he was talking about. Like, its history?

The Story of a Company

"As I do my research into a company," he went on, "I naturally concoct in my head a tale of how that company came to be, who runs it, and why it does what it does. I call this tale a Story. I follow a kind of simple outline to create a Story about a business: meaning, management, Moat, Margin of Safety. I know we haven't gone into them yet, but we will, in depth. Another very important part of the Story about a business should be that its values are what you want to see more of in the world: Mission." Research into a company, he explained, can quickly broaden in scope: you start with Apple and end up studying superconductors in Chinese plants. Keeping the Story in mind, Dad said, keeps him focused on the most important issues for determining if this was a good investment.

"Do you write the Story down or say it out loud?"

Dad thought about it.

"I guess I've been doing it so long, I don't take the time for a formal statement. I kind of do it in my head, and then I usually talk it out to a few people I trust."

Well, I knew right then I would do things a little differently, though I didn't tell him that. I had a method of making an argument honed by years of law school and practicing, and I knew I needed to see an argument written in black and white. I write it. Writing it down forces me to be precise. The choice of words matters. It's not casual.

He laid out his Story system for me. It starts with how he found the business and if other investors are buying it. Then comes understanding the business—in particular, what protects it against competition, who runs it, and what is its value. He then describes the industry, its competition, and why this business has a durable competitive advantage backed up with compelling historical consistency of performance and a solid management team. The Story goes on to state the value of the business, the price at which he would buy the business—the buy price—and what Event put this business on sale, along with how long it might take the business to recover. Finally, he summarizes with three great reasons to buy the company.

"You're going to explain all this stuff to me, right?"

He laughed. "Of course, that's the rest of the year."

I thought about how I would evaluate a startup company as an investor: What is this company all about right now and what is their plan for the future? That's pretty much what I wanted to make sure I knew. As a lawyer for emerging companies, I had quite a lot of experience in looking for issues that could derail an investment—attorneys invert stories for a living. "I like that you call it a Story. It reminds me that it's my perspective on that company. My Story of Apple might be different from your Story of Apple."

"Absolutely—especially when you add your values—what you're calling the company's Mission. Describe its Mission and values and why you really love it and want to see it prosper in the world. I love that you do that. Your Missions are different from mine, so our perspectives on a certain company's value in the world is probably going to be different."

That was so sweet. I felt gratified that my dad appreciated my contribution to my own Investing Practice, but also to his Investing Practice. It felt a bit like we were walking this path of learning together, instead of him always leading me. He seemed to be listening to me and taking in what I had to say. He had done that before when he asked me questions of law, for example, but now we were on his turf, and he seemed okay with a few changes to the landscaping. It made me trust him a little more in this practice.

"Really? You don't mind my adding something to your investing method?"

"Not at all," he assured me. "In fact, it tells me you're a natural at this. You'll only invest in a few companies over your entire life anyway, so they should be companies you absolutely love. Buffett only invests in companies he loves—but the companies he loves are probably different from the companies you love. At a recent annual meeting, Buffett was asked why he still invests in Coca-Cola; doesn't he see that all that sugar is bad? Buffett said that he drinks six Cokes a day and it makes him happy. Then he added that he's been to Whole Foods and that nobody's smiling at Whole Foods."

"What?" I choked in mock shock.

"He was joking, but not about his values. He puts his money where his mouth is."

Of course the master had already thought of voting for a Mission with his money. So much for my stroke of genius. And his Missions were different from mine, because of course they were. We're different, and that's the point: I'd vote for my values, he'd vote for his, and we'd see what happened—but at least we didn't pretend our money was voting for nothing.

I remembered the fourth level of mastery, the level we all aspire to: Unconscious Competence. I imagine it as the birds singing, the fog lifting, and a spotlight from heaven shining upon me. That was my goal. I wanted to learn from someone on that level. It sounded like that was where Buffett was.

We had long planned a family trip back home to Jackson Hole, Wyoming, and I showed up inundated with work, remotely plugged into the office the whole time. Still, it was too good of an opportunity for Dad and me to be together and talk investing, and do a different sort of work.

First, I wanted to know the underpinnings of this "value investing" shenanigan that Warren Buffett and my dad liked so much.

And I knew others would want to learn too. As we sat in the living room together, I mentioned, "I think we should start a podcast about this. I'm not the only one in my situation, needing freedom. I know lots of people who would benefit from learning this Investing Practice along with me."

"Oh yeah?" Dad said. "What's a podcast?"

"Something you couldn't get for a nickel when you were a boy." *Old people.* I showed him on my phone.

He immediately understood that it would be a great way to reach people who, like me, avoid the financial-industrial complex. *InvestED: The Rule #1 Podcast* was born. I hoped having to talk regularly with my dad about investing would keep me on track in my practice, and I knew it would help others do the same.

Much like the law, investing has a language unto itself, and it's not taught in school. We Normals needed this help.

When I started my first year of law school, I felt like I was trying to drink from a firehose. Decisions were written using words I had never read before, so I spent a lot of time with *Black's Law Dictionary* next to me and four colored highlighter pens to color the different parts of the case. Our criminal-law professor told our class that law is a language, and you have to learn the language before you can function smoothly in it. It took me about six months of law school before I had a moment when I realized I had just read a case without consciously struggling with the format or the vocabulary. I had learned the language.

I was having a strange sense of déjà vu to those first days in law school, as I thought about understanding a company in which I might potentially invest. All these words my dad used effortlessly—"compounding," "returns" . . . "inflation," for God's sake—were part of a foreign language, and they implied that other words would have to be used, and then more new vocabulary learned on top of that. I knew it was only going to get worse. But, like any foreign language, all I had to do was put some effort into learning the language. Or so I told myself.

"Buffett is the best, right?" I asked my dad.

"He's the best. We're not starting with him, though."

We're not?

"We're going to start with his business partner, Charlie Munger. If any investor is as smart as Warren Buffett, it's Charlie. Munger laid out the basics of their investing strategy in four simple principles in an interview he gave to the BBC. Everything I do in investing, and everything Munger and Buffett do, is derived from these four principles."

MARCH PRACTICE: Spend ten minutes creating your investing office. What will create your own atmosphere of financial freedom? What will support you to keep going when your practice is difficult? Then, in your investing office, brainstorm how you already vote with your money. What are the values you're supporting? Do you want to keep supporting them? From that, make a list of the Missions you choose to vote for with your investing money.

The First Principle of Value Investing

| April

"FIRST," DAD STARTED, "WE'VE GOT TO BACK UP SO THAT YOU HAVE THE context in which to understand a given company. Let's talk about the market and why it works the way it does."

Efficient Market Hypothesis (EMH)

"Let's assume people are rational," Dad began. "A reasonably rational fund manager wouldn't sell a stock worth $100 for $50 and wouldn't buy a stock worth $50 for $100. I wouldn't, you wouldn't, and none of the thousands of smart fund managers would either."

"Well, I agree with that." I nodded.

There was even a theory that explained it: Efficient Market Hypothesis (EMH). EMH says that if people are rational actors who buy and sell based on what a stock is worth, then a stock's price is completely rational and—here's the key—fully reflects all available information at any given moment in time. All of the possibilities of a stock going up or down are immediately factored into the price by thousands of smart people who have all the information and are bidding on the stock, all at the same time. The theory says that the pricing of stock based on information available at every given moment makes the market *efficient*. Therefore, the *price* of the stock at any given moment is exactly the same as its underlying *value*.

"If, in an efficient market, information is priced into the stock almost instantaneously, that explains why hardly any professionals can beat the market," Dad summarized EMH. "The moment that there is new information, the bidders will adjust based on that information, and the stock will immediately reset to a price that reflects its new value."

I remembered discovering that almost no mutual funds beat the market more than a few years in a row. My dad told me that EMH perfectly explains why: any attempt to outsmart the market by picking "good" companies would be futile because every good and every bad company is already priced to where it's a 50 percent probability that the stock price will go up and a 50 percent probability that the stock price will go down.

Well. Hmmm.

But there is a counterexample to EMH: $10,000 put into the first Buffett Partnership in 1956 would have grown to $2.5 million by 1973, while the same money in the stock market index would have only grown to $50,000. If EMH is true and nobody can beat the market, then how do you explain Buffett's success?

One academic said Buffett was, like a lottery or slot machine winner or a monkey flipping coins, just lucky.* If the odds are fifty-

---

* In 1973 Burton Malkiel, a professor at Princeton University, published *A Random Walk Down Wall Street* to explain EMH to the general public, and in the book, he raised the

fifty on each coin toss, and a monkey tosses a billion coins, the monkey will get very close to exactly 50 percent heads and 50 percent tails. But, if the monkey only tosses one hundred coins, is it so hard to imagine that one very lucky monkey could get one hundred heads in a row? There are always a few results way out on the tail of the bell curve. In other words, in a random stock market we should be surprised if there wasn't at least one Warren Buffett.

This all made so much good solid sense that several Nobel Prizes in Economics were awarded for the EMH work being done to show how rational and efficient the market is, and thus that the only way to beat the market was to get lucky over and over again for a long time—as Warren Buffett was thought to have done.

Lucky Monkeys

Warren Buffett, having essentially been called a lucky monkey, responded by saying . . . nothing.

For nine more years, he let his investing returns do the talking. If Malkiel had invested only $1,000 with Buffett when his book came out in 1973, he would have had $2,378,280 by 2015.*

In 1984, Buffett let everyone know that, yeah, he was well aware that he caused the conversation and, boy, did he have that paper. He published an article in the Columbia Business School magazine titled "The Superinvestors of Graham-and-Doddsville," in which he argued against being a lucky monkey. He made the point that if you found lucky monkeys that all "came from a particular zoo in Omaha, you would be pretty sure you were on to something . . . That is, if you found any really extraordinary concentrations of success, you might want to see if you could identify concentrations of unusual characteristics that might be causal factors."

---

elephant in the EMH room: Buffett. Warren Buffett had been crushing the stock market for nearly twenty years at that point and Malkiel dismissed it.
* http://uk.businessinsider.com/warren-buffett-berkshire-hathaway-historical-returns-2015-3?r=US&IR=T.

Buffett's "zoo" was founded by his teacher and mentor, Benjamin Graham, who pioneered what would become the basis for Buffett and Munger's investing strategy. The Benjamin Graham "zoo" of value investing strategy had produced quite a few "monkeys" who had gone out on their own, and Buffett cited the records of several other of these "monkeys" who all used Benjamin Graham's investing strategy of "mentally, always buying the business, not buying the stock" at a lower price than its value. He pointed out that their stock picks were all entirely independent—they had not discussed them with each other and their overlap was extremely low. "These records do not reflect one guy calling the flip and fifty people yelling out the same thing after him," he noted. Their results? The worst track record of the group crushed the stock market index. The best record, Rick Guerin's, even crushed Buffett's.

Buffett concluded that there has to be inefficiency in the market for all these investors, all independently investing with the same method, to be able to exploit gaps between price and value. "When the price of a stock," he declared, "can be influenced by a 'herd' on Wall Street with prices set at the margin by the most emotional person, or the greediest person, or the most depressed person, it is hard to argue that the market always prices rationally. In fact, market prices are frequently nonsensical."* Remember those Dutch guys in the bar who created the first stock exchange? Buffett was talking about guys like those influencing each other, and the ensuing herd mentality that starts when they worry they're going to be left behind. Buffett's point is that fund managers commonly buy and sell based on fear or greed, not on ruthlessly rational, fully informed decisions.

Warren Buffett and Charlie Munger saw that emotion often drives decisions, and they exploited it. They bought when the herd

* Warren E. Buffett, "The Superinvestors of Graham-and-Doddsville," 1984, reprinted from *Hermes,* the Columbia Business School magazine.

was selling out of fear, and sold when the herd was buying out of greed. Clearly, by their track record of high annual returns, it worked.

So, did economics professors take Buffett's point that emotions and inefficiency affected the stock market, and that the market was not as ruthlessly efficient as EMH claimed, and immediately stop teaching EMH? Nope. They just ignored Buffett or declared him an exception and stuck with EMH. Then, in 1999, Robert Shiller, an economics professor from Yale, published his book *Irrational Exuberance*. The title is from a quote by then-chairman of the Federal Reserve, Alan Greenspan, who in 1997 said, "The stock market has become irrationally exuberant." He said that the supposedly rational and efficient market was manic; that the market was acting on emotional whims, not reason. Shiller proved that Greenspan was right and the market regularly behaved irrationally. This was the first major shot fired into the EMH paradigm by a well-respected academic, and it was not the last. In 2013, Shiller received the Nobel Prize in Economics.

Suddenly people remembered that Buffett and Munger had been saying for years that the market moved nonsensically, and their formula was to buy when the market was full of fear and sell when it was full of greed.

The next shot into the hull of EMH was *The Black Swan* by Nassim Nicholas Taleb, a former options trader turned academic who tore into the 1997 Nobel Prize–winning EMH theories of Robert Merton and argued that the market is not random, nor a bell curve, nor is it unbeatable. "Black swan" is a Taleb term that means events that were thought not to exist, like black swans were thought not to exist—until they were found in the wild. Taleb found that these supposedly rare events actually happen with regularity.

Recent examples of black swan movements of the stock market are the rise of the Internet (that was greed to get in on a high-growth industry—a bubble), the 2001 dot-com crash (that was fear of wildly overvalued tech stocks—a crash), and the 2008 real estate crash (that was major fear in response to the discovery of fraudulent financial instruments, almost Depression-era fear), and now that the market has been in a nonstop upward trend for ten straight years, greed is kicking in again.

Two Israeli behavioral economists/psychologists, Daniel Kahneman and Amos Tversky, added to the EMH attack by proving over the course of their thirty-year academic careers that, contrary to Adam Smith's and EMH's hypothesis about human behavior, humans do not act rationally all the time. In fact, they showed that in conditions of high stress, uncertainty, and rapidly changing data, humans can usually be counted on to act on what they called "fast thinking"—thinking based on biases and emotion. Instantly running away when you think a lion is about to attack is fast thinking that can save your life. But this predisposition humans have in situations of high stress and uncertainty to leap to an action that worked in the past can result in wrong action in the present.

In the stock market, it isn't always right to run from uncertainty. Considering that the stock market can be a high-stress, rapidly changing environment, their work suggests it is more likely than not that the market can be driven in an irrational direction by the mass of traders operating on unthinking biases, particularly when there is an unexpected event that creates fear. Kahneman got the Nobel Prize for his work in 2002.

The torpedoes into the EMH boat are increasing. Richard Thaler, a behavioral economist from the University of Chicago, was awarded the 2017 Nobel Prize for proving that the underlying assumption of EMH—that we all make totally rational choices in pursuit of our own self-interests—is wrong. But the old guard isn't going down without a fight. Eugene Fama, also at the University of Chicago and a Nobel Prize winner for his work proving EMH back in the 1960s, once said of Thaler, "His work is interesting, but there's nothing there."* Despite the recent Nobel Prizes, EMH is still being taught in every business school in the United States. And Buffett is still making 20 percent per year on the follies perpetuated by the EMH paradigm.

What all this means is that value investing works. It really does. Find a business you really like. Wait for the inevitable economic recession to reduce earnings of public companies to start a cycle of fear in the market and the mass selling—also known as a stock market crash—that will bring prices below their values. As most fund managers sell when other fund managers sell, there will be fewer and fewer buyers and the prices go down. Wait for your favorite business to go on sale. Buy. Now sit back and wait for the economic cycle to increase earnings and for the inevitable greed to kick in as earnings recover, and market prices tick back up as more and more buyers show up. Sell. There you go. Now what will we do for the rest of our weekend?

"Well," I said, sitting across from my dad, "if it's so obvious and so simple, why doesn't everyone do value investing?"

Events, or Sh!t Happens

Dad answered with a real-life example. "In 2011, the Arab Spring made it look like it might be hard for Egypt to ship its cotton. A public company called Gildan is the number-one T-shirt-manufacturing company in the world. It makes T-shirts for Walmart and it buys a lot of cotton from Egypt to make those shirts. The potential shortage in cotton made the cotton price get so high that Gildan's CEO publicly said there was no way his company could be profitable for the next year. That's what I call an Event."

An Event is the linchpin of the Rule #1 strategy. As distinguished from a terminal problem in a bad company, a Rule #1 Event

---

* Frank Armstrong III, "Richard Thaler, a Giant in Economics, Awarded the Nobel Prize," *Forbes*, October 13, 2017.

is an unexpected, yet temporary and rectifiable, disaster that creates short-to-medium-term uncertainty about the cash flow of a company. It could be an Event that affects only that company, only that industry, or it could be market-wide. The key is that it is temporary and we know, by doing research into the company and industry and understanding how it works, how long it will take before the Event is resolved and things go back to normal.

"But here's the thing," Dad went on. "The CEO also told us the cotton shortage was temporary. They'd seen it all before and knew it was a one- to two-year issue. With the cotton price that high, farmers in Georgia would plant cotton from one end of the state to the other, and when that bumper crop came in a year later, prices would fall back to normal."

"Which is too long of a time horizon for the big investors," I realized. The practical realities of a fund manager's job proscribe riding it out. Fund managers' clients—mostly pension funds—do not like to pay fund managers to do nothing, particularly when the market is going up. By waiting to find discrepancies between price and value, a fund manager risks being beaten by the market month after month. If his performance does not keep up with his peers' quarter by quarter, within a year or two his clients will move their money to a different fund manager and he will get fired. Fund managers live in a world of competition that makes the NFL look like kindergarten.

"I guess so," Dad agreed. "I always thought they just didn't know how to do anything but follow the herd. Because you're right, they sold off Gildan stock like it was poison. It's irrational."

But I wasn't sure I saw it like that. "I see what you're saying but I don't think fund managers are acting irrationally," I thought out loud. "They are acting rationally within the rules of their world that you just described. If an Event happens that raises uncertainty, fund managers are forced by the nature of the industry to sell. Long-term to them is ninety days. And the recovery for this Event was much longer than that. If a fund manager owns Gildan and he knows everyone else is going to bail, he can't just sit there and watch that part of his portfolio crash down 70 percent when his peer group is outta there. He has to exit too even if he would rather not."

"I can see that," Dad acquiesced.

Well, that was a revelation. Dad agreed with me. He concluded, "You see that EMH can't be true—the price does not equal the value."

"Yes," I concurred, "and I can also see that we should expect funds to exit if a long-term Event happens. I should not get freaked out by that."

"Exactly. You should be pleased because them selling will make the price go down, and that gives you the opportunity to buy."

That's incredibly good news for me because that means I don't have to be smarter than the pros on Wall Street; I just have to play by a different set of rules. Buffett's rules.

Market-Wide Events

Crashes and bubbles in the market were really what I was worried about. Bubbles start because buyers think there is someone else out there who will pay even more than they did, not necessarily because of value.

One of the first stock market bubbles in history was created when the British trading company the South Sea Company, was granted a monopoly by the Crown to colonize South America. The near impossibility of actually conducting business in Spanish-controlled South America was not exactly public information, but everyone had heard stories of the fabulous wealth to be had there, so without South Sea having any revenue, speculators piled into the stock and drove it in a single year from £110 per share to almost £1,000 per share in 1720. This is a classic example of the potentially devastating information asymmetry between a company and its investors. There was suddenly so much demand that the facts were not at all taken into consideration when setting the price, and it didn't end any better for the poorly informed then than those of today. The bubble burst before the year was out and the stock dropped back to £100. Now, did this prove that all the information was correctly priced into the stock price at any given moment? No, of course not—quite the opposite.

A bubble or crash was nothing more than that happening on a much larger scale, with multiple companies being priced inefficiently and incorrectly. They seemed to happen out of nowhere.

"Ah." Dad smiled. "It does seem like that if you're not paying attention, of course. I will tell you how to find out when it's priced wrong. I've got two sources for market-pricing information; one was recommended by Buffett and the other by Robert Shiller. When the market is rocketing to the moon and I'm being left behind, I keep my eye on the Shiller P/E and the Buffett Indicator."

Shiller P/E

The Shiller P/E is an indicator created by Robert Shiller, author of *Irrational Exuberance,* mentioned earlier. To determine how over- or underpriced the market is, Shiller calculates the cyclically and inflation-adjusted earnings of the S&P 500 over the past ten years and divides that number into the total market price of the S&P 500—a cyclically adjusted price-to-earnings (P/E) ratio. Which sounds like a food-processed mess of words, but I discovered that a chart helps a lot to understand. On the opposite page is a chart of those points going back to 1870.

The average Shiller P/E over 140 years is 16.4. Since 1870, the Shiller P/E has risen above 25 only three times. In 1929 it rose to 32, and then the market crashed down 90 percent. In 2000, it rose to 44, and then the market crashed down 50 percent. The third time is now. The Shiller P/E went above 28 in 2016, and as of October 2017, it had risen to 31.

Dad added, "Shiller got the Nobel Prize for this analysis, and the discovery that the market can behave quite irrationally and does so regularly. The Shiller P/E doesn't indicate an imminent crash; it's

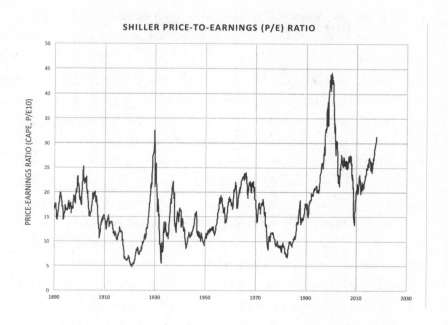

Data courtesy of Robert Shiller from his book *Irrational Exuberance* and updated on his website as of November 17, 2017.

just an indicator to know when the whole market is badly mispriced. The market might tumble next week, or it might go straight up for another two years, or it might not go anywhere for three years."

Buffett Indicator

Buffett called the ratio between the market as a whole and national revenue "probably the single best measure of where valuations stand at any given moment." One measure of this is called the ratio of Wilshire 5000 Total Market Full Cap Index/Gross Domestic Product, colloquially called the "Wilshire GDP." The Wilshire GDP ratio is tracked by the Federal Reserve Bank of St. Louis (the FRED) and can be found at fred.stlouisfed.org.

To find the Wilshire GDP, the FRED takes the stock market index that covers the most stocks, the Wilshire 5000, and calculates its capitalization (how much the entire index is worth) and divides it by the gross domestic product (the total revenue created by U.S. businesses).

Dad explained, "If the Wilshire GDP ratio is around 60 percent, then, overall, the market is priced under its real value. If the ratio is over 100 percent, as it was in 1999, 2007, and now, it's an indication that the market is overpriced." In other words, if the market is disproportionately high compared to the country's production of real products and services, then we should be prepared for a big market downturn.

The Wilshire GDP went over 100 percent in 2000 and the market crashed. And it went over 100 percent in 2008 and the market crashed again. That time, however, an extreme intervention in 2009 by the Federal Reserve Bank with a $4 trillion infusion and interest rates at zero percent kept the Wilshire GDP from crashing further, and the resulting lack of alternatives for yield to investing in the stock market had the intended consequence of driving the market and real estate back up higher than before the 2008 crash.

Now the Wilshire GDP has blown through 100 percent to the historically unprecedented 155 percent it hit in the third quarter of 2017. At this level, the market price has disconnected itself entirely from the historical relationship between the actual revenues being produced by companies in the United States and the prices of the companies producing those revenues. This is not likely to be a permanent change.

"If you watch the Shiller P/E and the Buffett Indicator, you'll have a good sense of where we are in the economic cycle. And where we are now is at the top."

"What if we don't see a crash? What do I do, wait for ten years without investing?" This was sounding kind of terrible, actually. All this work, and I was going to end up hoarding anyway?

"Where the market is priced right now, relative to GDP and earnings, there has never been a time in our history when it stayed there for longer than a couple of years. Something is going to send it tumbling. But if it stays overpriced like this, there will still be opportunities to invest in specific companies in specific industries. You just keep researching, keep reading, keep looking. That way, you'll be ready when an industry-wide or market-wide Event happens. Have a little faith in the strategy; Buffett isn't keeping $100 billion in cash for no reason."

"Wait, what? Buffett has $100 billion that he's just keeping and not investing? That's crazy."

"Yup. So just remember that he's waiting for an Event also."

Charlie Munger's First Principle of Investing: Being Capable of Understanding the Business

With that as our context, we sat across from each other with a microphone between us to record our first podcast. Dad started fiddling with his phone. He pulled up a video on YouTube of an old white guy in a suit who clearly didn't care what anyone else thought. He looked like someone who would think voting for a Mission with my money was liberal-young-person nonsense destined to land me in the poorhouse. He looked like someone who would use the term "poorhouse." "This," Dad said, "is Charlie Munger."

A NOTE FROM PHIL
In 1959, Charlie Munger, magna cum laude graduate from Harvard Law School, met Warren Buffett, the only person to ever get an A+ from Ben Graham at Columbia Business School, and two of the smartest men in the world became lifelong friends and investing partners. Buffett had been trained by Graham in the art of buying $10 of value for $5, but Munger added to Buffett's strategy that "it's better to buy a wonderful business at a fair price than a fair busi-

ness at a wonderful price." Working from that revelation for the past fifty years, Buffett and Munger bought businesses they would never sell—relying on the power of a great company to compound the investment over time and provide the highest rate of return. To Munger, the key ingredients of great investing are to be aware of what you don't know, stay rational, and wait for a great company you understand to go on sale. Munger was so good at waiting and turned down so many potential buys, Buffett now calls him the "abominable no-man." Munger counters that it was only fifteen patiently awaited deals that put them in the top ranks of all investors. Munger's wisdom about life, integrity, rationality, patience, focus, inversion, divergence, antifragility, the power of sloth, mispriced gambles, the dangers of overconfidence, and other human foibles is legendary in the investing community.

This was the guy who is as smart as Warren Buffett?

"Charlie Munger is Warren Buffett's partner. They've invested together for most of their lives. And in this interview I'm going to show you, he breaks down Rule #1 strategy into four principles. These four things are all you have to know to do well with investing."[*]

The relevant section is one minute long. In that one minute of talking, Charlie Munger succinctly summarizes eighty-five years of investing experience that started with his and Buffett's mentor, Benjamin Graham, in 1930. For Charlie Munger to put money into a company:

---

[*] The video Dad pulled up is an interview Charlie Munger did with the BBC in 2012. You can find it on YouTube under "Charlie Munger Reveals Secrets to Getting Rich."

1. it must be a business he is capable of understanding
2. it must be a business with some intrinsic characteristics that give it a durable competitive advantage
3. he would like it to be a business that has management with integrity and talent and
4. it must be a business that he can buy for a price that makes sense and gives a Margin of Safety.

The Margin of Safety, Charlie explains, gives us comfort, considering the natural vicissitudes of life (though I had no idea what he meant by Margin of Safety). Then he says, matter-of-factly, that these ideas are so obvious and so simple that there is nothing left to talk about. That's it. How to invest exactly like the best investors in the world (and presumably make the same billions they do), in one minute or less.

I thought, Great, there is nothing left to talk about.

Those principles did seem simple. In summary: be able to comfortably predict the long-term prospects of a company and buy it at a price lower than its value, given—my favorite phrase, asserting that ups and downs are completely natural and inevitable—"the natural vicissitudes of life." Charlie had explained it just fine. (By the way, though I should probably call him Mr. Munger because of his well-deserved status as a senior statesman of the value investing world, I'm going to call him Charlie because I feel such fondness for him, like he has become my crotchety great-uncle who serves up wisdom while complaining about "kidz today," and "kidz" means anyone under the age of fifty, and I note that he does not remove himself from such annoying kidz but rather chooses to make himself available to kidz like me with this BBC interview, which I take as an indication that he secretly enjoys either us or the attention or both. And thus, to me, he is Charlie.)

"Oh no," Dad warned. "There's plenty to talk about." I internally rolled my eyes at this guy who just disagreed with Buffett's investing partner.

"We are going to go through his principles one by one," Dad said, "and it's going to take a few months."

"Really?" I side-eyed him. "Months? They seem pretty simple and straightforward."

He laughed. He laughed at Charlie!

Oh, no, wait, I realized. He was laughing at me for thinking Charlie's principles were so easy. *Hmph*.

"They do seem simple," he chuckled, "but they're deep. There is a lot there, as you'll see once we start to talk about them. The principles are in a specific order of importance. I'm going to go through them one by one. This month we'll work on what he means by being 'capable of understanding.'"

I have never been so dead wrong. Charlie may have distilled his investing methodology into four easily soundbited principles, but there is a Hoover Dam–size depth underneath them. They have framed our entire discussion about investing. They frame my investing decisions now. I doubt we will ever stop discussing them. And that is why Uncle Charlie is the master.

His first principle is a doozy. Being capable of understanding sounds simple, right? Should I put my mind to it, I'm capable of understanding pretty much anything.

But how could I ever consider myself capable of truly, madly, deeply understanding a publicly traded company? There are vast amounts of information about these companies that I can never know. The distribution of information between a company and its investors is wildly misaligned. Plus, truly understanding a company requires understanding its competition and its industry, which is a whole other endeavor. And understanding an industry requires understanding its relationship to other industries, which requires understanding those industries individually as well, and obviously I'd need to understand the market as a whole to understand how this industry and company fit in to it, and how can I expect myself to understand the market as a whole when I'm just beginning at all this and ENCLOSEDCONCRETESTAIR-WELLFEELING.

The stairwell is deep. And I was burrowing my way into the damp darkness, right there across from my dad. I started to see what he meant when he said there's a lot to these principles.

I took a step back, noticed that I was mentally spiraling down, and took a breath. "Dad," I ventured, "on one level I'd say I'm capable of understanding right now, and on the broader macroeconomic level I'd say there's no way I'm going to be capable of understanding until I've been working at this for years. What is he talking about?"

Dad nodded. "Notice that Charlie did not say that he has to currently understand the company. He used the future tense, not present. No, he has to consider himself 'capable' of understanding in the future, rather than currently understanding it from the get-go."

Ah. That was a big difference. It was being able to project that, should I put the work in, I would be able to understand that company. *Not* that I had to understand it at the beginning.

Even Charlie doesn't understand companies straightaway. That made me feel better.

"Okay," I pondered, "so how do I know in advance that if I put the work in, I can understand a given business and industry? I don't have time to waste on chasing dead ends."

"Think of this business like buying your condo," my dad suggested. "Just like with buying a condo, you've got to know the neighborhood and the long-term implications of that location. For public companies, the neighborhood is the industry. That's all. Understand it the way you would understand a neighborhood. What has it been through, what are its cycles, what are its good spots and bad spots, and where do you think it's going over the next ten to twenty years? Are the schools getting better or worse, stores opening or closing, incomes going up or down, prices going up or down?"

I got it. Two seemingly opposite ideas can be true at the same time: I am completely capable of understanding some companies, and there is such a vast amount of information that knowing all of it is impossible. Both things are true. And they are true for every single company, from a kid's lemonade stand to a rental house to Enron. As investors, we live in the tension between those two truths, and when we find between them the sweet spot of understanding how this company is expected to behave in response to unknowable events, we invest. Thinking of my condo purchase helped a lot. I could handle a condo analysis. I could do condo.

"Here's the key," my dad concluded. "Here's the key to the whole thing that will keep you safe. If it's not condo-in-Boulder obvious, don't do it. If it's not that obvious, it's not a good investment for you. We want to jump over six-inch bars, not six-foot bars. You're just starting out with this. Keep it obvious."

"Keep it simple, stupid." I laughed.

Dad didn't laugh. "Exactly."

He called it his Rule of Obviousness, and it made me feel better. I didn't have to push myself into anything I wasn't 100 percent sure of, or anything I wasn't ready for. I thought about the condo. Durable competitive advantage. Location on Pearl Street Mall. In a great building. In Boulder. Beautiful, backed by the University of Colorado, and forty minutes to Denver. Basically, if the price was right, a no-brainer. That was a six-inch bar to jump over. I could jump that. I had jumped that.

"Buffett"—my dad grinned—"has a box on his desk. A 'Too Hard' box. He wants to put companies in the 'Too Hard' box. He's dying for an excuse to throw things in the 'Too Hard' box. And you should be too. Don't be afraid of saying something is too hard. Find the low bars to jump over, not the high bars. Charlie is saying that to look into a company, you should use your own innate knowledge and experience to determine if this company is potentially in your sweet spot, or if it's just, right now, today, too hard."

"The thing is, though, everything seems too hard."

"That's an excellent observation about where you are in the process. Right now, you have no idea if it's even possible to understand a business because you haven't studied or researched even a single company. But once you start reading and getting a sense of what's out there, you'll quickly get enough perspective to start to know when you're capable or not. And just to put this process in perspective, experienced Rule #1 investors expect at least 90 percent of what we look at to be Too Hard or an outright no."

"Ninety percent! That's nuts. Almost nothing gets through."

"That's exactly right. Remember that. And for beginners like you, it'll be even fewer."

"Okay, so I only need to find a few companies at first, and then build up."

"And you need to understand the industry. Which you can totally do. Just choose one that's an easy one for you. You don't get any extra points for studying industries that you know nothing about. You live in the world; you know lots of industries, actually. Choose one you know something about."

To determine if I was capable of understanding an industry or a company, I needed to do some preliminary research to see if I was familiar with its basic concepts. If I wasn't, it was Too Hard. I needed to review the market-wide indicators to see if the overall climate was one that supported companies being on sale or overpriced. And I should look for Events.

Events were a way to use my fear as a lever to get incredible investing results. I knew that if I was initially fearful, others were too. However, they would act on their fear by selling, while I would act on mine by waiting.

To be ready to act aggressively when fear is everywhere seems to be one of the great paradoxes of Rule #1 investing. Our practice demands extreme patience and extreme courage to invest when smart people are running for the hills. Dad said Warren Buffett called it "laziness bordering on sloth," but, really, it's the patience of a hunter to do nothing when companies are overpriced, and to strike aggressively and buy when companies are priced far below their value.

I noticed that all the information I had learned so far was actually attacking my fear of the unknown. Instead of trying to eradicate my fear, which was probably futile, being aware of the fear might help me to avoid dumb investments. If I was feeling afraid, other investors probably were too. That feeling gave me valuable information about the market.

The hard part was going to be discerning when the fear was irrational and when it was warning me of real danger. I wasn't going to figure that out on my own. I needed my teacher.

I was getting a bit of a sense of the vastness of information that real investors like Charlie have, and that I could learn not only from my dad, but also from Charlie and other great investors. It was a quick reminder that, just as in yoga, I'll always be a student in this practice. Warren Buffett, Charlie, other major value investors, and my dad were all my teachers. I wouldn't be alone in this, nor would I be reinventing the wheel they had already designed and crash-tested. The tradition of masters my dad was talking about was real. These master investors had been making millions and even billions of dollars since the 1930s. This was definitely not something new and untried. I felt more confident. It was the unknown that scared me, but the information that this investment tradition had been working so well for so long was alleviating my fear. And I now had some tools that gave me perspective on the market overall, which was rather extraordinary. Knowing nothing about what was happening in the market overall had been one of my huge fears a few months ago.

Then we dialed it down, from the vastness of the market as a whole to specific companies. Research time.

Circle of Competence

"Right now, I'm going to teach you about your Circle of Competence. We're going to talk about how to research companies, and how to create your own focus on one or two industries. Buffett calls this focus your Circle of Competence.* You already have one, without even knowing it. Think of all the companies you have opinions about."

I tried to think of a company I had an opinion on. He explained, "Having an opinion is a good clue that there's an industry you might know pretty well already because you already have some perspective on it. I spent years in the army becoming something of a weapons expert, so it was easy for me to have an opinion when it came to putting my money in a firearms company. I already had an opinion about those companies. I already knew what I thought about those companies' products. I just had to look into their company structure and management to see if the companies themselves were good investments, because I didn't know about that stuff without researching it."

I remembered the Four Levels of Mastery. You'll know you're Consciously Competent when you know what you don't know. That's the edge.

"Okay," I thought out loud. "I need to choose where to start my initial Circle of Competence. How do I choose where to spend my time? I suppose there are some industries I know about, just from life. I like yoga. I like cooking and entertaining. I like startup tech companies. But I don't know exactly what 'industry' the financial world divides those into."

"Let's do this," my dad suggested. "There's an exercise that Jim Collins uses in his book *Good to Great* to determine what companies I should be focusing on that I use for investing. We'll make three circles, and the convergence of the three is where you start creating your Circle of Competence."

"A Venn diagram of competence?"

"Exactly."

I grabbed a legal pad from my shelf of legal pads. A legal pad and

---

* http://finance.yahoo.com/news/buffett-munger-circle-competence-221834144.html.

a good pen go a long way toward my happiness—just one more example of money supporting my happiness—so I keep a joyful stack of them for times exactly like this one. I drew three circles overlapping in the middle, and he told me to label them: "Let's make the three circles what you're passionate about, what you vote for with your money, and where you make your money."

We took a fifteen-minute break so I could fill in the circles.

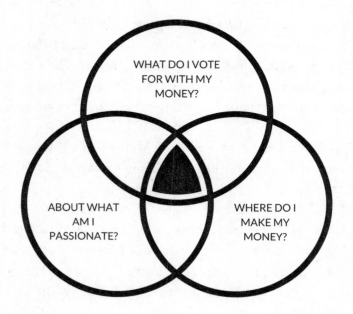

The first circle was fairly easy— *about what am I passionate*: yoga, cars, startups and legal stuff, eating healthy foods, cooking, throwing dinner parties and entertaining, sleeping as much as I can, snowboarding.

For the second circle, I had to think for a while about where my money was going, and therefore, what I had already been voting for in the world without thinking too much about it.

▶ Grocery stores like Whole Foods and Safeway
▶ My mortgage—with Chase

- ▶ Furniture and home-goods stores like Restoration Hardware, Crate and Barrel, T.J.Maxx, Williams Sonoma
- ▶ My car—a Nissan
- ▶ Clothing stores like Zappos
- ▶ Air travel on United, Delta, Southwest
- ▶ Restaurants like Chipotle, Subway

I checked my Amazon account to see what I'd been voting for with my money recently. I had even ordered toilet paper on Amazon. Charmin. I searched online for "who owns charmin toilet paper." Procter & Gamble bought it in 1957. Charmin developed the SitOr-Squat public-restroom finder. *Parenting* magazine called SitOrSquat "one of the best apps for simplifying a parent's life." Roto-Rooter said Charmin was used by more plumbers than any other brand. *Better Homes and Gardens* named Charmin Ultra Strong to its "Best New Products of 2013" list.

I am not making this up. Charmin sounded fantastic and I had never viewed my toilet paper with such interest.

I added Procter & Gamble and Amazon to my list.

Second circle—*what do I vote for with my money*: groceries, household goods, startups, yoga, cool cars, healthy food, travel, snowboarding, clothes.

The third circle was the easiest—*where do I make my money*: legal work, startups, and—I didn't, but I was pretty sure I could make money on this—dinner parties and entertaining.

My overlapping circles were: startups, yoga, cars, healthy food, and entertaining. It was actually pretty helpful to see it drawn out in black and white so I could refer to it going forward as I searched for companies. I showed it to my dad, and he nodded in approval.

"Now what? Is that my Circle of Competence?"

"Almost," he said, "because the three circles don't quite make your investing Circle of Competence. Doing the three-circles ex-

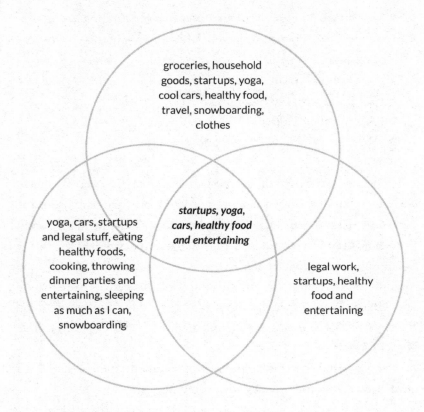

groceries, household
goods, startups, yoga,
cool cars, healthy food,
travel, snowboarding,
clothes

yoga, cars, startups
and legal stuff, eating
healthy foods,
cooking, throwing
dinner parties and
entertaining, sleeping
as much as I can,
snowboarding

*startups, yoga,
cars, healthy food
and entertaining*

legal work,
startups, healthy
food and
entertaining

ercise narrows down the industries you should start with. We start
with businesses and industries we already are involved with in some
way. Then we narrow down, again, to create the Circle of Competence for investing."

"Should I only end up with one industry to start with?"

"Yes. Focus and start with one. Do the work on that one. What
companies are in it that you already know? In a high-priced market, mostly you're just putting companies that are wonderful on a
Wishlist to be bought later when the market makes its inevitable
downturn. Don't worry about actually buying anything at this point.
You're just going to build a shopping list."

"I need to find out what industries startups, yoga, cars, and healthy food fall into. It's not toilet paper." I mentioned how much fun I had investigating Charmin. He replied that he had encouraged his guests on his Grand Canyon river trips, for their visits to the "bathroom," to try out using smooth river rocks that had been warmed by the sun. Helpful.

"But see," he pointed out, "you have an opinion about toilet paper, and you didn't even realize it. That's going to be true for many companies and industries as you get more into this. You'll find that you know a lot more than you think, once you put your attention on it. For now, though, to start out and practice, stay focused on your Circle of Competence. Find out what other companies there are in the industry and learn how they relate to each other. What are the economic cycles of that industry? Is the company you're interested in going with the overall trend of the industry or against it? Are there regular ebbs and flows or does the company's profit usually go up with the economy and down with a recession—or is it counter-cyclical?"

All righty, then.

I went through my results. Startups can go public, but that's a whole other game of speculation. That left cars, healthy food, and yoga.

I thought about my Nissan Xterra, which I loved as an off-roading beast, but not particularly because of its Nissan-ness. But the auto industry could be very interesting. Then I thought of Whole Foods. Now, that was a store that I had feelings about. I really loved that company for helping change the world in so many ways, from making natural and organic food a normal and expected offering at the store to its consciously capitalist attitude toward business.

I could extrapolate from specific companies like Whole Foods to the industry: grocery stores. Or from Nissan to the automobile industry. But yoga was harder. There isn't an industry called "yoga." There aren't many publicly traded companies that have to do with yoga or its accessories, like mats and yoga videos, specifically, but I thought of lululemon, and their efforts to reinvent their image and expand their brand. If you go to a yoga class, I promise that at least half of the women will be wearing lululemon. Their clothing is expensive, but it lasts, and I wear their gear more than most of my other clothes so the per-wear dollar amount ends up being quite low. lululemon, though, had a problematic founder who had made comments that lululemon's yoga pants weren't meant for larger women—and indeed, their pants weren't made in sizes larger than 12. From an athletic-wear company, that's a particularly poor message. A month after his comments, he was forced out and the stock price dropped a third and kept going. They have since gotten a new CEO and have been recovering.

So how did I find the industries of things I like if the industry isn't obvious? My dad offered some help.

"You can use my website, Rule One Investing, or another one like Yahoo Finance to find out. Here's a free website, InvestSnips, that has an 'Industries' tab. Click it and scroll down to 'Category Links' and you'll see about 450 categories, from Advertising to Zinc. This site reclassifies companies according to category of interest. The yoga category, for example, has two companies—lululemon and Gaiam. We know lululemon makes yoga clothing. How would you find out what Gaiam does?"

"I'd start with the annual reports." I sighed.

The U.S. agency that regulates companies, the Securities and Exchange Commission (SEC), has tried to solve the information deficit and protect investors by requiring a comprehensive annual report from each company on the stock exchange (among other filings). That's me, the potential investor who needs to be protected.

The annual report is a written document that tends to be very long, and is submitted to the SEC on its Form 10-K, so it is interchangeably called "the annual report" or "the 10-K." It describes, in great detail, the work of a company, its plans, its financials, and all the ways the company could potentially fail. I have to determine from my research if a monolithic company is quavering, and the annual report is the first place to look.

I have read many annual reports in my practice as an attorney but, thankfully, have never had to write one. They are notoriously boring. Still, they're like the celebrity gossip blogs. Once you read a few, you learn where to sniff out the really juicy stuff and just skim over the rest.

Public companies also file reports every quarter, called the 10-Q, and hold calls with analysts every quarter that are recorded and transcribed. These can all be found on the company's website for investor relations, or, if they don't have a good website, on the SEC's website. My dad thinks the SEC's website, called EDGAR, is tough to use, but I don't find it that difficult, and I like getting things from the official source.

"Reading annual reports is a major project," I complained. "You want me to randomly read them?" I started to think that maybe I could wander around in these weeds forever. Was there an easier way to do this?

"Yes, there is. Another way to narrow down is to start looking to other investors," my dad announced. "I call them my Gurus. I look at what they're buying and check it out."

Gurus

I thought about it. Everyone running a fund of $100 million or more must report quarterly to the SEC the equity positions they have bought and sold in the previous quarter.

"That's a great idea. They have to file publicly anyway, and the information is a little old, but that's not a big deal for a value investor." I thought about it some more. "Wait, why aren't I just copying what they're buying?"

He laughed.

"No, I'm serious. Why do I even need to do all this work on my own when they can do it for me? Why couldn't you have told me this months ago?"

Dad stopped laughing. "Actually," he agreed, "you're right. It's my favorite way to find great investments. There were two professors who wanted to see what would have happened if all you did was copy Warren Buffett from when he started to be quite famous until recently. They got the data from his quarterly 13F filings with the SEC from 1976 to 2006; to model it as conservatively as possible, they 'bought' the stock he was buying on the last day of the month that it was public knowledge that Buffett was buying and they 'sold' it on the last day of the month it became public that he was selling."

I vaguely remembered Dad mentioning this study back when he was convincing me that I could successfully invest on my own. "And?"

"And it worked. Their model made a ton of money just by copying Buffett."

I wanted to see details. We looked up the study by Professors Martin and Puthenpurackal. They found that an investor who did nothing but copy Berkshire Hathaway's public company investments for those thirty-one years would have gotten a 20.43 percent compounded annual gain,[*] while the market index would have returned half that amount.[†] The two researchers concluded that Buffett's returns were not due to luck. Furthermore, while Buffett's rate of return was approximately twice that of the market, his actual cash return was five times larger. This is a feature of compounded returns: a small change in the compounded rate of return can, over time, result in a very large change in actual dollars.

"For professors to admit that it's not luck is pretty unusual," my dad said. "They don't like to admit that choosing individual companies can beat the market."

I thought about the study. I wouldn't have even had to buy stocks at all, except Berkshire. *Huh.*

---

[*] Gerald S. Martin and John Puthenpurackal, "Imitation Is the Sincerest Form of Flattery: Warren Buffett and Berkshire Hathaway," SSRN, April 15, 2008, Table VII.
[†] According to Moneychimp, the compounded annual growth rate of the S&P 500 index from 1976 to 2006, including dividends, was 12.86 percent.

"Dad, forget doing all this work. Why don't we just buy Berkshire and be done with it?"

"If we buy Berkshire when it's really cheap, then yes, that's a great plan. You'll get no argument from me. But how will you know it's cheap? It's the same as when you wanted to abdicate. Fine, but you have to know how to evaluate them, and that takes investing expertise. Same thing here: Buying Berkshire might be a good call, but how will you know if it's a good price without learning investing?"

Silence from me. *Stop telling me I have to know something about investing in order to copy other people!*

Foin.

"I won't know when it's a good price," I admitted. "I have no clue."

"Right," Dad affirmed. "Plus, Berkshire isn't cheap often, and that means we're probably better off copying what they're buying. Also, Buffett isn't going to run Berkshire forever. He has great people in place, and has assured us they will do a good job, but who knows? Still, if I can buy Berkshire cheap enough, I'm going to buy it."

"Keep my own counsel," I said, half to myself. "And I can always buy the companies Berkshire buys if they fit my Mission."

There is a short list of other investors who invest in the Rule #1 style and get high returns year over year—sometimes even in markets that are strangely inflated, like this one. Dad looks to Buffett and Munger, obviously, but also Mohnish Pabrai, Guy Spier, David Einhorn, Bruce Berkowitz, and a bunch of others. Dad has a list of Gurus he follows for ideas on his own website. I can find their 13F filings on the SEC's EDGAR website.[*]

I could copy them, but I was already seeing a few problems with my idea. It's the lawyer in me: I poke holes even in my own argu-

---

[*] As of this writing, other websites that collect data from 13F SEC filings include my dad's website, www.ruleoneinvesting.com, as well as www.dataroma.com and www.gurufocus.com.

ments. "Dad, the obvious problem is that, because they are reporting one quarter after they purchase or sell, the information is always old. I should take it with a mountain of salt?"

"Well," Dad said slowly, "imagine you could get forty-six of the world's best investors to call you up personally about what they've been buying or selling over the last ninety-day period. That would be pretty valuable, right? Even information a year old would be valuable, if only for ideas and examples. Many times, I've found that the price of a company has actually gone down since great investors bought it more than a hundred twenty days ago. For example, Warren Buffett bought a bunch of IBM stock repeatedly from 2011 to 2016 at prices that averaged about $170. You could have bought IBM in 2016 for $120. That happens all the time. But you do have to know what you're looking at. You still have to do the homework."

"And even more importantly, make sure their Mission matches my Missions," I added. "A Guru might buy a company that is antithetical to my values, and I refuse to blindly copy them."

"Exactly." Dad nodded vigorously. "Copying someone else blindly is a lot like abdicating. You've got to do your own homework to know if what they're doing is a good thing or not. The other thing to remember is, keep a Guru's purchases in perspective against their overall fund. Buffett has about $100 billion in cash right now, and none of that shows up in his 13F filings. If you didn't know about how much cash he's keeping, you'd think he was fully invested, when in fact, he's sitting on the largest pile of cash in his whole life just waiting for the inevitable economic storm to put everything on sale that he wants to buy."

Additionally, it is extremely important to know that 13F filings do not report "short" positions. Some investors hedge stocks by selling weaker companies "short" (betting they will go down instead of up) while buying stronger companies with the expectation that if the market goes up, the strong ones will go up more than the weak ones and they'll make money on the difference; same thing if the market goes down, but in reverse—the weak companies will drop faster and farther than the strong companies. Watching the 13F filings can be misleading if you aren't aware of the whole picture, but even so, following the 13F filings of the right people can be quite an advantage. Every quarter, the list of new buys comes out—around five hundred to six hundred companies to look at each quarter, and that's just from the Gurus my dad follows. Get an idea of if what they do is in your Circle of Competence and then, if it is, go deep in your research. But always remember that while it's a really cool shortcut to finding something you might want to buy, the 13F filings paint an incomplete picture of any Guru's holdings.

My skeptical legal training kicked in, and as I reviewed the companies Gurus had chosen, I noticed that either I could not guess why they bought a company or I did not support the Mission of a company they bought.

I refused to blindly depend on my father or any other Guru. Professional investors are smart people, but investing is not about being smart; it is about knowing that what you're buying will be worth more in ten years and being patient. Many professional investors get scared and do stupid things. Charlie Munger says that he and Warren Buffett wouldn't be so rich if smart people didn't do so many stupid things. My job in this practice was to avoid being one of those people. This, my dad believes, is the key to successful personal investing: learning how to use predictably irrational and emotional short-term decisions of others to my advantage.

I felt like I was getting comfortable with knowing if I was capable of understanding a company, but I hadn't really tested it out. I needed to work on my Investing Practice. I needed some perspective on my own skills, quickly. How could I create a good baseline of investing research?

My Investing Intensive

"Read Warren Buffett's letters," Dad advised for a second time. "He's written letters to his shareholders for about forty years. They are an unbelievable education in value investing, and they're a pretty good read." I searched online for "warren buffett letters to shareholders" and got a link to Berkshire Hathaway's shareholder letters, available for PDF download. All of them since 1977 were there. I hadn't known the provenance of Berkshire Hathaway, but Warren Buffett, I discovered, used the vehicle of a textile company called Berkshire Hathaway to form an investing company. Berkshire is not a fund. He simply uses this company, which is public, to purchase other companies—public and private ones.

And he writes a letter every year to his Berkshire Hathaway shareholders. These letters are held up as the pinnacle of shareholder letters because it is incredibly rare for a public company executive to write to shareholders the way Buffett does: openly, straightforwardly, and honestly about what the company is doing, about its failures as much as its successes, about its plans for the future, and about its intentions regarding its values and where it is going. Value investors talk about these letters like they're the Bible.

I figured Dad was on to something—I'd better read the letters. Reading the Buffett Bible would lay the groundwork for my research to come. So, read the Buffett Bible I would. Reading three letters per day would take me about two weeks to finish all of them since 1977. When I went home to Boulder, I got started.

In yoga, a multiday focused practice is called an intensive. I planned my two-week Investing Intensive to ground the information I had learned over the last few months into skills. *Water the root to enjoy the fruit.* It was an old maxim from my Transcendental Meditation upbringing, and it was a good one that I remembered often. In the meditation context, it means that meditation is the food or water needed by the consciousness so that out of meditation, one can enjoy the fruits of that time spent turned inward. In my Investing Practice, it reminded me to learn. The water was the knowledge about how to do Rule #1 investing, the root was my practice, and the fruit was financial freedom.

I wanted to read Buffett's letters, since my dad spoke so highly of them. And I wanted to start developing more perspective on the market.

In my legal practice, I often found myself advising clients simply on what was normal—normal deal terms, normal issues a startup often runs into, normal conflicts between founders, normal documents they should have at the ready. It was vital information to a startup or venture capitalist that we could provide because we handled so many deals. I noticed that I had no clue about what was normal in the stock market, and I knew I had better find out before I put my own money into it.

The letters to shareholders are fundamental. What else? I decided to back up. Instead of checking celebrity gossip in the morning as I drank coffee and woke up, I'd start every morning by reading a business newspaper. Losing my moment of gossip Zen would be a major sacrifice, but it was probably good for me.

Well, maybe I would make myself wait to skim the gossip until after I read the *Wall Street Journal*. Yeah, that sounded a lot better already.

I looked up the *Wall Street Journal* and discovered it was quite expensive to subscribe. Then I went to the *Financial Times* website. Similarly expensive. I checked the *New York Times*. Also expensive. Good Lord, I quickly realized that if I subscribed to four or five news sources at their full prices, I'd be at $100 per month. Twelve hundred dollars per year of investing news was a serious annual expenditure for me, and one that would cut into my investing budget.

This practice apparently required not only a time investment, but some financial investment, and, really, what better place to put my money than to support strong business journalism? The fourth estate protects me, the small investor, better than the SEC or any regulatory agency could. It finds scandal and publicizes it, bringing light to the dark corners of back rooms and trading desks.

I decided to pay for the *Wall Street Journal* and see how much I really read it. If I decided paying for the other newspapers would be worthwhile, I could add them to my reading list later. I made a folder in my Web browser bookmarks called "Investing" and added the free websites my dad had mentioned.

Every day for two weeks, I read "one plus three" as my Investing Intensive: one *Wall Street Journal* business section in the morning and three shareholder letters by Warren Buffett by bedtime.

The Buffett Bible was exactly as good as my dad had described. Buffett has an incredible ability to explain financial concepts to Normals like me, and that is rare. Too rare. Maybe it is a clue to why he is so good at commonsense investing.

APRIL PRACTICE: Starting research is hard, but this is the month to do it. It took me a few tries and some boredom before I started to find the good stuff, so be prepared with snacks and a sense of humor. Run through your own three-circles exercise so you know where to focus your investing research, and then just . . . start. Choose a newspaper for business news and read it regularly. Maybe do your own Investing Intensive and read the Buffett Bible. Look at some 13F filings. Think about what would work best for you and your schedule, and then go for it.

Charlie's Moat and Management

| May

IT WAS THE STRANGEST THING. ALL THIS THINKING ABOUT FINANCIAL freedom and working toward it seemed to create . . . freedom. In ways I didn't expect. For years, I had been promising my grad school flatmate to come visit her in Zurich, Switzerland. I switched law firms to a boutique firm focused on startups, and in between jobs, I had the opportunity to go. I wandered around the city alone while she was at the office, and after work hours we sunned ourselves by the lake and drank good wine, and I felt purely myself, more so than in a long time. I felt free.

On the last night I was in Zurich, she invited a friend over for a game of Risk, and by the end of the game I liked that man sitting next to me more than anyone I had ever met. Nuno was Portuguese, gallant, and devastatingly smart. He was a strategy consultant to banks, which was why he lived in Zurich, and he seemed fascinated by my efforts to improve my life, which I appreciated because I still felt a bit hesitant to tell other people about my Investing Practice. They seemed to immediately assume I knew all about investing, and I certainly did not.

I was scheduled to stop at Oxford for an entrepreneurship conference for a few days on the way home, and Nuno asked if he could come hang out before I went back across the Atlantic. I was in vacation mode and said "Sure!" and only realized the next day that a virtual stranger might follow me to another country. Our mutual friend assured me he was trustworthy, and I remembered his dark gray-green dreamy eyes and the way he looked at me with a certain unwavering intention, and I remembered that I was on vacation and this didn't matter. I let him know where I would be. After he flew to London, rented a car and a hotel room, and showed up to meet me at the King's Arms pub in the center of Oxford, I was impressed. Three days later, I was very much in danger of falling in love with a guy who lived in Europe. When I went home, Nuno asked to come visit me in Boulder, and I decided to let him.

Before Nuno came to visit, Dad stopped in to Boulder again for business, and we made sure he could stay over the weekend so we could talk about Charlie's Principles in person. I was becoming accustomed to this constant contact with my dad. We used to talk every two or three weeks; now we talked or texted at least once a week and e-mailed each other articles we found about value investing or companies we ran across that we thought were cool. It was, actually, really nice. He was sticking with me.

We sat down in my living room. It was time for Charlie's second and third principles: ensuring the competitive advantage of a company, and then evaluating the people running the company. We got down to business.

Charlie Munger's Second Principle of Investing: Intrinsic and Durable Competitive Advantage

This second principle is mega. To me, it's the crux of Charlie's Principles of Investing. Charlie says that once we have decided we're capable of understanding the business, the next thing to determine is whether the business has an intrinsic competitive advantage that is durable. In Buffett's investing strategy, this concept is referred to as a Moat.

A Moat is exactly what we all think of—the body of water surrounding a castle to prevent attacks. In investing, the castle is the business and the Moat is the competitive advantage the business intrinsically has that makes it near-untouchable by competitors for long-term cash flow. If a business has a good Moat, it's going to be hard for competitors to breach the Moat and take the castle. Not impossible, but difficult. So difficult that they won't try. So difficult that if they had all the money it would cost to buy the whole company, they still couldn't compete with it.

"Think of the life cycle of a company," said Dad. "The company is founded to meet a need and solve a problem; they solve that problem and meet that need, and probably over some number of years the problem or the need becomes obsolete. There are very few companies that last one hundred years. Notice where a company is in that life cycle and what gives it a long-lasting, durable, intrinsic competitive advantage to stick around as long as possible."

"Is this Moat you and Charlie are talking about different from a company doing a good job when it comes to meeting a need or solving a problem?"

"Totally! Totally different. What makes a Moat different from pure competitive advantage is that it is a competitive advantage that is, first, intrinsic to the business, and second, durable. 'Intrinsic to the business' means that their advantage cannot be separated from their business. It's inherently there. 'Durable' means that it is so difficult or expensive, or both, to overcome that intrinsic characteristic that no competitor is going to try, so we can expect that it's going to continue for a long time to come."

"Sounds like a typical competitive advantage to me."

"It's not at all. This is competitive advantage that can't easily disappear. Ask yourself whether it's possible to start a company that would compete and take over that company."

"The answer is that it's always possible."

"Maybe. So, the next question is how much would it cost for a new competitor to get started and grow to the level of being able to compete with and beat our company? If the cost is so huge that no one would do it, it's impracticable; then you know our Moat is pretty strong."

Hmm. Okay.

"Think of durability from the opposite perspective," Dad suggested. "Is a company you're researching just trying to compete with a 'me too' product that is priced lower than competitive products? Are some of these companies making typewriters at the beginning of the personal computer? Are these going to be going strong in ten years, or maybe not?"

So if nothing was going to threaten it, I considered, its competitive advantage was incredibly strong. "And the intrinsic quality? Like, they're the first ones into an industry or something like that? That would be intrinsic to the business."

"Exactly like that," Dad replied. "Being the first mover into an industry is even part of one of the kinds of Moats I'm going to teach you."

"There are kinds of Moats?"

He had so much energy now he couldn't even keep it in. He started bouncing in his chair. "Oh, there are many kinds of Moats. Five kinds, maybe six."

The Five (and a Half) Moats

1. **BRAND.** When a company has a brand that is so strong that it would be very difficult for another company to cre-

ate an equally strong brand to compete with them. Sometimes created by being the first mover into an industry and thereby having that industry identified with them. Example: Coca-Cola and Pepsi. Pepsi has spent millions to improve its brand and compete with Coca-Cola, and has created a strong brand. Still, Coca-Cola is stronger, especially worldwide. In some regions, people even say they want a "coke" instead of saying they want a "soda," no matter what type of soda they are actually asking for. With a great Brand Moat, customers think in terms of the brand name rather than the generic name of the product: Coke, not cola; Harley, not motorcycle; iPhone, not smartphone; Kleenex, not facial tissue.

2.   **SWITCHING.** When it is very difficult, expensive, or painful for a customer to switch away from using a company's products or services. Example: Apple computer products are an integrated environment using one operating system. As a user of an Apple iPhone, laptop, and iPad, I can confirm that it would be difficult, painful, and expensive to switch to an Android or Microsoft system. That doesn't mean I can't or I won't switch, but the pain of switching deters me—even if my current products are not as good as their competition.

2.5   **NETWORK EFFECTS.** A subset of the Switching Moat, when a company provides an exclusive network to which the user wants access. The act of switching itself is not difficult, but switching away from the network would mean losing that access. Example: Facebook. That said, those of us who used Friendster know very well that all that has to happen for this Network Effects Moat to be breached is for people in your personal network to switch to a different host. Still, there is a certain quantity of users before this Moat gets established or broken.

3.   **TOLL BRIDGE**. When a company has a monopoly or near
      monopoly in their industry. That is, a Toll Bridge is the
      only product in a big niche. This is usually created by gov-
      ernment regulations or intervention, which of course can
      change. Other kinds of Toll Bridge Moats are geographic
      or driven by the unbelievable cost to enter a market. Or
      all of the above. Example: The intercontinental railroad
      is my dad's favorite example of a Toll Bridge Moat. Burl-
      ington Northern Railroad controls the railroad tracks. It's
      not that another company can't build a railroad, but the
      government regulations, the expense, and the right-of-way
      it would have to procure make doing so, for all practical
      purposes, impossible.

4.   **SECRETS**. When a company has proprietary secrets that
      protect it from other companies copying it. These might
      take the form of patents, or trade secrets, or other forms
      of intellectual property. Examples: A pharmaceutical com-
      pany like Pfizer or Merck with a patent on drugs has a
      strong Secrets Moat, until that patent runs its term and
      generics can be made. A company like 3M might choose
      not to patent an invention to avoid announcing how to cre-
      ate it (a requirement of patent filing) and instead protect it
      as a trade secret, to keep it well hidden from reverse engi-
      neering.

5.   **PRICE**. When a company is the low-cost provider because
      it can make its product, or provide its service, more cheaply
      than anyone else, and it is intrinsically able to sustain that
      advantage. Example: Costco can sell their products cheaper
      than anyone else because they use their huge buying power
      and low display costs to have the most profit, at any price
      point, of any competitor. If they get in a price war with an-
      other company, they can drop their prices lower than any-
      one else can and still make money. Any company trying

to compete with a nearby Costco on price would quickly become a cautionary tale of economic Darwinism.

It was early May, and Dad and I got lucky with a clear and crisp Rocky Mountain weekend, so I suggested we go for a hike. I could think through these Moats better in the foothills around Boulder.

To me, the hard part of the Moat wasn't determining if a company had a competitive advantage. I could make an argument that most decent companies had a competitive advantage. No, the hard part of Moats was determining how intrinsic and durable a company's competitive advantage was. The key question was: Is it really a full Moat that is intrinsic and durable to the company?

As we hiked up First Flatiron, I tested out analyzing two well-known companies mostly to myself, both of which I've already mentioned: Coca-Cola and Apple. They seem easy, right? Dad stayed relatively silent and let me work through my thoughts on my own while he focused on breathing steadily at a mile-high elevation.

Both Coca-Cola and Apple are consumer-facing companies, which gave me the advantage of direct knowledge about and experience with them. I could understand them because I use their products and because they're just about everywhere. I can go to a grocery store and see that Coca-Cola's display power is as strong as ever. And I can drop into an Apple store and see that it is the busiest store in the mall. Coca-Cola's Moat is Brand; Apple's Moats are Brand and Switching. But it was easy for me to go down the rabbit hole, even with these companies.

Coca-Cola

Coca-Cola has a Brand Moat, obviously. Does it also have a Secrets Moat? Their secret recipe for Classic Coke, from 1886, is one of the most famous company secrets. It has been reverse-engineered by competitors, and recipes published in newspapers and online are said to be the original recipe, but the company still famously perpetuates the story that its recipe is a secret. The truth is that whether the recipes out there publicly are real or not, Coca-Cola uses its origin story to its advantage. It probably is not that hard to reverse-engineer a beverage with the taste of Coke. But it is impossible to re-create the taste of Coke and package it in a Coke bottle or can, which adds that certain je ne sais quoi to its brand.

Coke doesn't have a Secrets Moat at all. What it does have is an incredibly strong Brand Moat, in which the appearance of secrets is an important part of its brand mythology. Coca-Cola's secret formula has contributed to its mystery and therefore its Brand Moat.

It's incredibly easy to choose a non–Coca-Cola product in the store, so they do not have a Switching Moat, nor do they have any Toll Bridge Moat protection. But cans of Coke are awfully cheap. Do they also have a Price Moat? Nope, because they are not the low-cost provider of cola. A major part of their business model is to be inexpensive—often cheaper than bottled water—but not as cheap as generic store brands. The Coke brand still carries a price premium, which, again, contributes to its strong Brand Moat. Do you really want to serve up generic cola at your party? I mean, c'mon.

But I can argue the other way too. Yes, Coca-Cola has an obvious Brand, but how durable is it? Sugary sodas are becoming very unpopular in the United States and Europe the more they are linked to obesity, and there are even additional taxes on soda in some cities, such as New York, meant to deter buyers. Coca-Cola has already acted in response to that trend by buying beverage brands that stand for energy or health and nutrition, which it does not brand with the Coca-Cola name: Monster, Honest Tea, smartwater, and Odwalla are all Coca-Cola owned.

I really like Honest Tea. It was created to provide yummy healthy drinks without additives and with organic ingredients, including fair trade–certified tea. In short, these guys have a great healthy-food Mission I love and a great-tasting product that I buy. And it is now owned by Coca-Cola, but you would never know that without some digging. For a socially conscious product that is aiming for the health-food market, Coca-Cola's brand would probably harm Honest Tea rather than help it. Coca-Cola has used its display power in grocery stores to get Honest Tea a lot of shelf space it couldn't have gotten without the Coca-Cola brand power, but has hidden their connection.

As a potential investor, I look at Coca-Cola's investment in new products for a very different market than their core market, and I see vision and preparation for the future. Coca-Cola's sodas are still massively popular worldwide and probably will continue to be for longer than ten years from now, but they are focusing on new brands anyway. Buffett himself has been excoriated for owning Coca-Cola shares because of the cola's sugar content, but I was starting to see why the master stayed with that company. Coke's Brand Moat looked good.

Apple

Apple has a Brand Moat, obviously. It is also bloody difficult and painful to switch from an Apple platform to a PC, or from an iPhone to an Android phone, so it has a Switching Moat.

But, just as with Coca-Cola's Moat, I can argue the other way. It's not impossible to switch away from Apple, and if it becomes unwieldy to use Apple products, the relative pain of switching becomes lessened and lessened. Apple has changed since Steve Jobs passed away, and I'm not impressed. I can easily buy a roughly Apple-equivalent personal computer or smartphone from any of its competitors, and Apple is only getting more expensive. However, Apple does own thousands of patents, has an incredible operating system, and has a strong culture of product secrecy, so I would say it has a Secrets Moat. With its Brand and Secrets Moats, it is going strong, but its Switching Moat is weakening with poor decisions on user interfaces like iTunes and by driving the prices up on its products.

I'm not impressed by Apple's competitive advantages because I'm not sure they rise to the level of Moats.

I gave my dad a run-down of my argument for each one.

"Competitors attack a Moat in basically two ways," he said. "First, by saying, I'm going to do what you do, but cheaper or better; or two, I'm going to do something that eliminates the need for you."

I nodded. "The second is being a typewriter company when the computer came around."

"Exactly. If you're facing that kind of obsolescence, there's nothing you can do about it except foresee it and sell your company—or join the new wave, as IBM did. IBM is a selling machine that has a Switching Moat, and they have held their Switching Moat by buying new technology as it comes out and providing it to their customers quickly enough that it's not worthwhile for them to switch."

"And the first? Cheaper or better? I mean, every single company is attacked on price constantly."

"Right. What keeps customers from leaving is the Moat. It could be that the company has a brand as a high-quality product, or it could be easier not to switch, or the company could lower its prices to match its competition's. You should be able to anticipate how a company you choose will handle those Moat attacks by looking at how they have handled them in the past. Apple has been repeatedly attacked for forty years and they're still here. But you don't only have to depend on your subjective research to know how strong they are."

I stared at him blankly. "I don't?"

"Nope." He grinned. "There are numbers."

Oh no.

"Don't panic," said Dad. "There are only a few numbers you need, and I'm going to tell you exactly where to find them on the financial statements when we get back to your house later. That will give us much better information about how strong the Moats are."

Oh Lord. It couldn't be time for the financial statements already. I thought I would be able to avoid dealing with numbers until our discussion rolled around to Charlie's fourth principle about price. I took a deep breath and remembered that I had tackled financial statements in law school and had handled that just fine. But I felt so unaccountably nervous about it now. Sure, Dad could tell me which lines on the statements to read, but I needed to understand what those numbers meant to be capable of understanding a company. This was where the whole investing thing might break down for me. At least I'd find out sooner rather than later.

A NOTE FROM PHIL

The SEC requires public companies to file their financial statements according to a standard set of accounting principles, determined by a board of accountants, called the Generally Accepted Accounting Principles (GAAP). In financial statements, a public company will provide standard GAAP-compliant accounting. Additionally, it will often provide non-GAAP accounting for a different picture of how the company is doing financially. Check the explanations and footnotes in the financial statements to know how the company calculates these non-GAAP numbers, because they are often designed to mislead an investor into thinking the company is doing better than it is actually doing. Any time they use "adjusted earnings" or "EBITDA" ("earnings before interest, tax, depreciation, and amortization"), be suspicious and skeptical.

Financial Statements

INCOME STATEMENT: How much money are you making (revenue)? How many expenses do you have? Subtract expenses from revenue and get your profit. Profit is how much you have left over. You make a salary of $80,000, your expenses this year were $75,000, and you have $5,000 left over as profit.

BALANCE SHEET: What do you own (assets), what do you owe (liabilities), and what's left? You own your house and a car and an inheritance from your grandma, and it adds up to $500,000. And you owe $400,000 on the house and $10,000 on the car, so your liabilities are $410,000. What's left is the $90,000 that you could actually get if you sell everything and pay off everybody.

CASH FLOW STATEMENT: How much actual cash you have in the bank tells you:

▶ the actual cash you spent and got from the business operations (operating cash);

▶ cash that went to investing in equipment or buying a business or came in from selling part of the business (investing cash); and

▶ cash from loans or stock sales (financing cash).

This statement is necessary for public companies because they use accrual accounting, which lets companies count as income payments that haven't actually come in yet, and expenses as they are owed rather than when they are paid.

The cash flow statement lets us know what's actually in the bank account. You know the money arrives from selling your house, but the money won't land in your bank account until escrow closes in three weeks. It will not show up on your cash flow statement until the cash comes in.

As we continued on our hike, I tried to feel my feet being heavy and grounded into the dirt and rocks below me with each step. The concentration helped with the shaky feeling of panic that had hit me behind my eyes.

"Okay," I said. "Let's do this. How can numbers tell me anything about something as intangible as a Moat?"

Dad smiled. "They're hugely important clues. Remember that the real point of a Moat—this intrinsic characteristic that helps a company remain durable—is the ability to roughly predict the future. That's the whole point of it. So we want to see that four major numbers are consistent over time because that might mean these numbers are predictable in the future. A big, durable Moat should let the future look a lot like the past. If the Moat is good enough to be consistent in the past and predictable for the future, then we know something about what we're getting. If there's no reason to suspect it's going to change, it's so much easier for us to understand the business, roughly predict the future cash flow, and find the value."

We finished our hike, and once we got home, Dad ordered in dinner. He wasn't taking any chances of me getting out of this one. It was our first discussion of financial numbers. Big moment.

He listed the Moat numbers found on the financial statements that he would want to see grow each year. Dad calls them the Big Four Numbers:

Big Four Numbers

Number	Which Financial Statement?	Definition
1. Net Income (also called Net Profit or Net Earnings)	Income Statement	Profit after all costs of making that profit have been deducted
2. Book Value (also called Equity) + Dividends (if any)	Book Value: Balance Sheet Dividends: Cash Flow Statement	Value of the business if it were closed down and all its assets were sold (assets minus liabilities), before any dividends were paid out
3. Sales	Income Statement	Amount earned from selling (revenue)
4. Operating Cash	Cash Flow Statement	Actual cash received from business operations

Note: Some of the accounting numbers are called by various names depending on which section of the financial statements they are in. I'm sure there are very good reasons for this, but it's confusing and frustrating to an accounting novice like me. However, there's an easy work-around: if I run into a term that I don't know, I search for it online to turn up its synonyms.

"I'd like to see each of the Big Four Numbers growing at 10 percent or better each year," Dad said. Those are called the Big Four Growth Rates.

"Remember," Dad declared, "these numbers are out the back window of the car. You're looking into the past, and the past doesn't promise anything about the future. That's why we do all this other research as well, to decide if the company will reliably continue these trends."

But wait a second. "You said the Big Four have to grow each year. This company can never have a down year?"

"No, no, no, it can. The most important thing is not actually the 10 percent growth. The most important thing is that it's consistent and predictable, looking over the occasional valleys and mountains. For example, one of Buffett's companies, See's Candies, is growing at about 4 percent per year for the last forty years; it hasn't been linear but, looking at the long view, it's been very consistent."

"Well below your 10 percent goal."

"True. We would *like to have* 10 percent per year, but in a case like See's Candies, its growth is steady and predictable and it generates great profits, so we know it has a durable Brand Moat. Other candy companies might also have a Brand Moat—it's not exclusive within an industry. If there's a down year on any of the Big Four Numbers, find out why. If it makes sense to you, and the company recovered fairly easily, then don't worry too much about it."

That made sense. Look for a reliable pattern and look for how the company responded to breaks in that pattern. "Now," Dad explained, "take the Big Four Growth Rates and choose one overall growth rate to use for the company."

"You mean, use the average growth rate?" I asked.

"No," he said emphatically. "Definitely not the average. This is a judgment call you're going to have to make based on your research. You have to choose what you think is the most likely growth rate going into the future. Remember, all the numbers you have are in the past and there's no guarantee they will continue. Only your understanding of the company will let you make an educated guess about how much this company will grow. So you've got to just choose the growth rate you're going to use. It's like taking the 'windage' into account when you're shooting a gun. The wind could push the bullet either way and you've got to estimate the aim based on your experience."

"What!" I cracked up laughing. "The *windage*? Like, the wind pushes the bullet and that's called 'windage'?"

"Yup!" Dad laughed.

I loved it.

I named the growth rate that I was supposed to choose the Windage Growth Rate. The Windage Growth Rate was based on research into past growth rates and into what analysts thought the growth rate would be going forward. It was up to me to be conservative with a lower estimate of growth or aggressive with a higher estimate of growth.

Having relayed this knowledge, Dad decided it was enough. We had dinner and the next day, he flew off to Florida to play polo.

Later that week, I laid out my investing office and tested it out. I was proud of myself: I actually sat down and pulled up the financial statements for a few real companies, and organized the Big Four Numbers for each company on a spreadsheet.

I'm not going to lie: it was painful. Accountants. They seemed to call everything by a different name: "operating cash" might be called "cash from operations" by another company. Or, they put the financial statements in a strange order that made it hard for me to find what I wanted. The "Search" tool became my friend, along with the Internet in general, which told me what terms to search for. I discovered that most financial statements have three to five years of data on them, so a shortcut to getting ten years of data was to pull the most recent 10-K (annual company financial report available on the company website) and the one from five years ago. I calculated each growth rate for each year; ran the most recent 10-, 7-, 5-, and 3-year average growth rates; and, based on my limited understanding of the company, made an educated guess at the Windage Growth Rate.*

Coca-Cola's Windage Growth Rate was the most difficult, because the company's numbers were a bit of a mess and recently had negative growth. I went conservative and chose zero percent overall.

Apple, on the other hand, had been growing slowly and steadily across all four growth numbers. Easy. Except that its growth was slowing and included a few negative numbers in recent years. Overall, I chose 8 percent. That's Windage for you.

That was enough for now. I was a bit excited to move on to researching the people running these companies. That, it seemed to me, was where the rubber met the road for my Mission. Could I trust them to do a great job?

Charlie Munger's Third Principle of Investing: Management with Integrity and Talent

I felt like I could research management myself, so I tried it out. It felt nice to take the initiative for the first time in this practice.

A venture capitalist I know describes the process of finding a good startup investment like dating. You've got to hang out with the founder to see if you see the world the same way and if the chemistry is there. Is this someone you trust and want to spend a lot of time with? Because, as a venture capitalist, you've got to have both in a founder. VCs do all that founder dating in person. As everyone who's ever been on a blind date knows, people are often very different in person than they are on paper.

Researching public company management is the same dating process, but most investors rarely get the chance to meet a CEO in

---

* Besides the annual 10-K document, this data is easily found on many stock research websites, including Yahoo Finance, Google Finance, Morningstar, GuruFocus, and my dad's toolbox, www.ruleoneinvesting.com. For more information about how I worked out these growth rates, go to my website, www.danielletown.com.

person, so I had to learn to depend on secondary sources. I found a few CEOs I wanted to look into, created a folder in which to save the articles I found, and started searching online.

I looked at:

▶ **BIOGRAPHY**: A lot of my biography questions are related to how easy or difficult it has been for this person to come up in the business world. Running a public company is no easy job. How did this person get there? Did they pay their dues, or was the path smoothly paved for them? Neither is better than the other—in fact, a well-connected and well-integrated CEO can be far better for a company than a hardscrabble, pulled-himself-up-by-the-bootstraps type who knows no one but has mad skills—but I like to get a sense of their background.

▶ **MANAGEMENT STYLE**: Are they a skydiving-on-the-weekends entrepreneurial type like Richard Branson, or a stay-the-course, keep-growth-steady-and-low type whom you've never heard of? The Branson types make good copy for business writers who have to make stories interesting to make a living, and some subjects are easier than others to write five thousand words about. But the other types often make more reliable managers.

▶ **FOUNDER**: If the current management team does not include the founder, they might be reacting to the founder's departure. Steve Jobs left Apple the first time because the board thought someone else could run the company better than he could and forced him out. While the board might have been right at the time, what they missed was that no one could make Apple products better than Jobs could, so the company went into decline until he came back. When he returned, older and wiser, he not only saved the company, he led the creation of iconic products that changed entire industries. Knowing that story is pretty important to understanding the current managers of Apple and the length of Jobs's shadow on them.

- ▶ **BOARD OF DIRECTORS**: The board of directors hire and fire the management team. I tried to see if I could determine how they have handled doing both of those things.
- ▶ **OWNERSHIP**: Sometimes CEOs leave knowing they're out before the problems hit, so I look for founders or executives with a large shareholding stake, so they are literally invested in the long-term success of the company.

As I read the press about a given CEO, gradually, article after article, I got a feel for what they were like. Were they warm, authoritarian, family oriented, community oriented, Mission oriented? Were they an industry specialist, a CEO for hire, a serial entrepreneur? Did they manage time well, have business loyalty, or move around a lot?

I looked for clues and developed a bio in my notes. And I acknowledged to myself, constantly, that this bio was only based on impressions I'd gathered from incomplete information. Except for a very few famous CEOs, not all the information I wanted was out there. For many CEOs of non-famous companies, almost no information was out there about them. The absence of information told me that this was not someone who had been under the press's microscope.

The conclusions I could draw then and now from researching CEOs are dependent on what an online search turns up, on how much press attention the management and the company have gotten, and how much scrutiny that attention has given the officers. This is where we hope the fourth estate protects us potential investors. We can't have access the way the press can, so we are stuck depending on their choices and on what's called for editorially that week or that month. There's a lot we don't control or can't know about.

Dad, taking time out from his polo practice schedule in Florida to talk to me on the phone, sounded a bit pained when I mentioned I had been looking into management. "Management is one of the hardest parts of this whole thing. Did you notice that Charlie said he would *like* to have a management team with integrity?"

"That was kind of weird."

"Well, it's because it's so hard to know if people are trustworthy or not until things go bad. Charlie and Warren are masters at judging people, but they haven't been able to describe how they do it and they definitely have made some mistakes over the years. As a counter to making a mistake about management, Buffett once said that you should only invest in a business an idiot could run, because one day an idiot will."

Another way to gather information about executives is to read their letters to shareholders, though they hardly ever reveal anything important—which is, in itself, a notable piece of information. Rule #1–style hedge-fund manager Matthew Peterson advised, "When management is talking in terms of per share growth and free cash flow and internal rates of return, it is a signal that they share a value investing mindset and consider things through a capital allocation lens. Watching the vocabulary in public statements can be very informative."[*] Warren Buffett's shareholder letters are famous for being the apotheosis of "straightforward," to the point of bluntness. How open is the CEO in the letter? Does the CEO announce bad news will come, and does he or she do so in a way that is intellectually honest? I had the massive advantage of 20/20 hindsight. Did what the CEO predict come to pass? How closely to the time frame and the description the CEO gave did the prediction happen? What's the scuttlebutt around the Internet about what the company's employees think about their management team?

I saved all my research so I would never have to search for it again and wrote, for myself, an overall pronouncement on each CEO I researched, however vague. For example: "Seems decent enough. Can't get much of a read. College and business school, then straight

---

[*] "15 Questions with Matthew Peterson," Gurufocus.com, September 21, 2016.

into management program, seems to have been moving up the ladder since then."

While reading business news and news about CEOs, I noticed that I regularly came across executives whom I had not intentionally researched. I created a list of "executives to watch." Executives move around to different companies sometimes. That person may not be at a company I want to focus on right now, but maybe in ten years they would be, and I would have already done the legwork to get a feel for them. Plus, then I'd have ten years of evidence to see if my feel was right on.

This reading contained great gossip. Who had worked with whom? Who left which company for another company after an embarrassing personal scandal? Who got paid way too much? I love the inanity of celebrity gossip, and looking into management is basically the same thing. There are scandals and divorces, and bad guys and good guys, and undisputed kings and queens of the financial world. It's even a glamorous world, though in a different way from Hollywood.

Still, I did find it difficult to get all the information I wanted. Business journalists can be quite good, but they can't cover everyone, and they can't see into opaque companies. Someone hiding that they are embezzling from their company isn't going to be caught by a reporter doing a puff piece, nor even by an investigative reporter, necessarily. How many fawning articles about the Enron officers were there, probably in which they posed with leather-bound books in rooms that smelled of rich mahogany, before Enron went down? While the most well known public company officers are certainly scrutinized—a takedown of them would be front-page news—for smaller companies, no one in the press has the time to care as much.

I called my dad back the next day to tell him how much I was enjoying researching management.

"Studying management is the best part of this whole thing," I exclaimed. He laughed, incredulous.

"I thought you'd hate how you wouldn't be able to get much information."

"No, it's totally like celebrity gossip, but I do feel a bit like I'm looking through the lens of the news, and it's all a little fuzzy."

"I have a part of the solution, actually," Dad replied.

"Really?" I said, excited.

"Yup. Numbers."

I balked. "Management can't have numbers."

"Oh yes, management can," he retorted gleefully, loving how much I wanted to avoid this, "and they will help you determine who is a good manager with an insight that is different and more objective than reading the gossip about them will."

I sighed. *Foin. I was just starting to love my management gossip, and he throws it back to the numbers. Bloody f-ing numbers.*

"All right, give them to me."

Management Numbers: (1) Return on Equity, (2) Return on Invested Capital, and (3) Debt

"Remember book value, one of the Big Four Numbers?"

"No," I admitted.

"Book value is the same as equity, which typically means ownership in corporate law. It's on the balance sheet. What we want to know is what return the company is making on that equity. That's what matters! And 'your money,' in financial speak, is 'equity.' It's a number called—get this—return on equity. This is major."

I couldn't help it. I laughed at him. "It's *so* major."

"It is!" he insisted. "And, you're going to love this: return on equity is an easy number to find. Multiple sites online will tell you what it is. It's a standard number that any finance source will have calculated."

"Wait. It's not on the financial statements?"

"Well, not as such. It's a calculation from numbers that are on the financial statements."

Return on equity is: net income (found on the income statement) divided by equity (found on the balance sheet).

RETURN ON EQUITY (ROE) = NET INCOME / EQUITY

"Return on equity, or ROE, tells us the return the company is getting on our shareholder investment. It calculates how many dollars of profit a company generates with each dollar of shareholder equity, which tells us if the management is doing a good job with our money. Now, a high ROE can be financially engineered just by the company borrowing a lot of money."

I groaned.

"Return on invested capital is the other number we're going to use to look at management. Return on invested capital tells us the same thing as return on equity, but in addition to the money put in, it also includes the company's debt."

RETURN ON INVESTED CAPITAL (ROIC) = NET INCOME / (EQUITY + DEBT)

"What is a good and what is a bad ROE and ROIC number?"

"Look for a company with an ROE and ROIC at 15 percent or better, each year, for the last ten years or so. Ten years probably means they've been through a down economic cycle, or they've outgrown their startup phase, or they've been through a change of executive team. If they still have a strong ROE, this is a company to look at. Charlie wants us to look at durability, and shorter than ten years is not enough to prove that a company is durable."

Just as it is with people, consistency is important in a company. Consistency doesn't necessarily mean I can predict what it will do in the future, just as inconsistency doesn't necessarily mean that the company will continue to be inconsistent, but consistency does lend some confidence to the idea that a company will do what it says and says what it will do.

"One last number to check the management," Dad noted. "Debt. Debt can be corrosive, and if they have a lot, it might give management an excuse to go into a prepackaged bankruptcy where they can dump the shareholders and emerge owning a big part of the company. If there is any long-term debt held by the company, we require the company to be able to pay it off with one to two years of earnings."

I want the debt to be zero, preferably. Debt scares me. Debt is a great way for management to be able to manipulate the financials, and I know enough about myself to know that I'm not good enough with financial statements to suss out manipulation.

Let's review the management numbers on a company my dad and I made up: a lemonade stand. We use this example because it's straightforward, plus, I had a few real lemonade stands when I was a kid in Iowa, and there was an early Macintosh computer game in which you manage a lemonade stand that I was obsessed with and played for hours after school. Lemonade stands have all the same components as a more complex business. We brilliantly named our example business the Lemonade Stand.

The Lemonade Stand has:

$1,000 of equity
$1,000 of debt
$2,000 total

The company made $100 on that money.

The ROE is 100 / 1,000 = 10%
The ROIC is 100 / (1,000 + 1,000) = 100 / 2,000 = 5%

> On the equity alone, the company made 10 percent. On return on invested capital (equity plus debt) the company only made 5 percent.

I discovered a cool shortcut to checking the debt when looking at the management numbers: by looking at the difference between ROE and ROIC, I quickly know if and how much debt is involved in this business. With zero debt, the ROIC will be the same number as the ROE.

"Guess what," my dad teased. "You're already reading financial statements without even realizing it. All those numbers you just used for Moat and management? From the financial statements."

"Oh yeah." I smiled. He was right. I didn't love pulling them, but it wasn't hard, and I knew why I was doing it and how to use those numbers to develop my argument for or against a company. In the service of my own knowledge, the financial numbers became useful to me, and that made all the difference.

I still didn't want to move on to valuation. It had been a heavy-duty Investing Practice weekend. When I reflected, I felt uncertain about my company evaluation and financial skills. I felt like I had started learning a new language. Sometimes I recognized the words or lines of numbers, but most of the time I didn't. I didn't want to get ahead of myself and push too much new information into my brain too quickly. I needed to practice what I had learned for a while before adding to it.

"Go play polo," I told him. "Don't forget rule number one: don't fall off the horse."

"I'll try not to!" he promised. We hung up the phone.

Formal Investing Practice time was over, but I was thinking about how to organize all this information I had gotten that month. I needed to add something to my own development of my practice.

Checklists

I use checklists for repetitive tasks in my legal work to great effect, and it was time to get one going for my Investing Practice. I found I had great support from the value investing tradition of masters: investors Mohnish Pabrai and Guy Spier have both written at length about how useful checklists are to their Investing Practices. It sounds like a Pippa Tip from Pippa Middleton: checklists are terribly useful for many endeavors in which you need to remember certain items, such as grocery shopping, lawyering, and investing. It's like that feature in *Us Weekly* of paparazzi photos of famous people getting coffee, grocery shopping, wiping at a stain on their shirt called "Stars, they're just like us!" This is "Super Successful Investors: They're just like us!"

But, uh, yeah, they are. And checklists work.

The beautiful thing about checklists is that they are not emotional. In his seminal book, *Complications,* about training as a surgeon, Atul Gawande explained that doctors are human and they screw up, and that checklists have been a huge component of cutting down on doctor error. Doctors are intelligent people who still make mistakes because they are 100 percent sure they can remember everything—but they don't always. That arrogance can have dire consequences. And it is so easily remedied with a simple solution: Write it down. Then follow what you wrote down.

A checklist has to have a reasonable number of items. Too many, and it's overwhelming and you spend more time checking off the checklist than using it. Too few, and you'll skip things. It becomes useless. Checklists that are too detailed, for instance, have actually contributed to airplane crashes. There's a strangely addicting Canadian TV show called *Mayday* about investigations into plane crashes, and while it's not my favorite thing to watch reenactment after reenactment of terrible airplane crashes, I've learned a lot about what to do in an air emergency. In one crash, the engine literally fell off the airplane. It turns out—I swear this is true—there is a "Your Engine Has Fallen Off" emergency-procedure checklist, which was too long for the pilots to complete before the plane crashed. And a checklist's entire reason for existence in this world is to be useful for its purpose. Otherwise, tear it up, burn it, feed it to the dog; it ain't no good.

MY CHECKLIST

Charlie's Four Principles

1. **Be capable of understanding**
   - ❏ Is this company inside my Circle of Competence?
   - ❏ Are any of my Gurus buying or selling this company?
   - ❏ What is my overall level of confidence with my research into this company?
   - ❏ Describe the business and industry in one paragraph.
   - ❏ Describe the challenges and economic cycles of this industry.
   - ❏ What are the company's plans for growth?
   - ❏ Will growth peak within ten years?

2. **Moat**
   - ❏ What is the Moat?
   - ❏ How hard is it to compete with this company?
   - ❏ Compare this company to its competition.
   - ❏ What are the Big Four Growth Rates? Are they speeding up or slowing down?

- ❏ What is the Windage Growth Rate? Is it speeding up or slowing down?
- ❏ Does the company have enough cash to last several years if it loses money?
- ❏ How were sales and earnings during the last recession?

3. **Management**
    - ❏ Does the CEO have integrity?
    - ❏ How candid is the CEO's letter to shareholders?
    - ❏ Does management talk freely to investors when things are going well but clam up or disclaim responsibility when trouble occurs?
    - ❏ How happy are its employees?
    - ❏ Does the company have any debt? If yes, could it be paid with one year of free cash flow?
    - ❏ Has the company indicated that it plans to take on debt any time in the future?
    - ❏ Is the management team buying or selling its company's stock?

4. **Reasonable Price with Margin of Safety**
    - ❏ *NADA*

My checklist got a little thin at number four. I was begrudgingly reminded that I hadn't focused the slightest time or attention on determining what a good price for a company was. How would one value a company, exactly?

In the meantime, I was a little distracted. Nuno flew across the ocean, came to my house, and stayed for three weeks.

MAY PRACTICE: It's crazy that it's only the fifth month of
practice, but we already know Charlie's first three principles.
Choose three companies you've gotten interested in from your
reading and calculate the Moat and management numbers of
each one, as well as the Windage Growth Rate—and notice
how you're using financial statements and financial terms like
a boss.

Circling Competence

| June

IT HAD BEEN SIX MONTHS OF INVESTING PRACTICE, I REALIZED WITH A start, as I laid out my investing office on the dining table and started preparing for my investing call happening soon that day. Nuno's visit had gone really, amazingly, shockingly, surprisingly, happily well.

I barely knew the guy when he showed up, and I was nervous that my vacation brain had made a mistake I would pay for over the next two weeks. I'm an inveterate introvert and I needed my space, plus my condo was a small studio apartment, plus I was back at work again, with all the stress that entailed. Was he dangerous? Or worse, boring?

I made sure my sister knew his last name and employer so she could track him down in case I turned up dead, and I went to pick him up at Denver International vibrating with anxiety. But when the opaque double doors at the arrivals gate finally opened up and he bounced out, jumpy and eager and feeling to me exactly like the guy

I remembered, and somehow, magically, smelling wonderful after nine hours on an airplane, I was pretty sure we were going to be okay. (I asked him later if he had been nervous when he arrived, and he said, "No, I was *excited*.")

I still liked him more than anyone I had ever met. I noticed that he pulled less energy from me than any person I had ever been around; he, also utterly introverted, noticed the same about me. I wonder if that's what we recognized in each other the night we met—a rare equilibrium. Ease. *I'm in trouble*, I thought to myself one morning in my office toward the end of his visit. I was at the point of no return. I either had to pull back, tell him to leave, and keep my life straightforwardly simple, or jump irrevocably into the unknown with this man from another culture and continent.

Love is like enlightenment. To move into that new state of being, there is necessarily a death of the previous version of you, an abandonment of what was before. It is for such a good cause that it usually happens unconsciously and gladly, but I viscerally felt my decision and what it meant for my future. I knew that it might not work out, that I might get hurt beyond hurt, that it might be beautiful, great, enlightening, and that it would change everything.

I chose to jump.

I had kept up my Investing Practice reading while Nuno was visiting and discovered that, to my surprise, it was a bit of fun to share the public companies I liked with someone else. I got to share the gossip. I told him about Whole Foods, obviously, which he fell in love with from our very first visit to the flagship Pearl Street store. He started going there without me while I was at the office and bringing home new products I hadn't discovered. I'm not saying it was a relationship litmus test, but if it had been, he had just passed it.

I had still been searching around for other companies to follow.

"Did you know lululemon is public?" I offered. Everyone knows about lulu.

"Lala what?"

Oh right, he didn't do yoga. Suddenly I felt like I was conveying a hot stock tip.

"My yoga pants."

He was suddenly interested. "Ohhhhh."

I tended to think everyone knew about the same consumer companies, but—um, obviously, I realized at that moment—we don't. Nuno, a car aficionado, told me why he liked certain car companies that I hadn't known much about. My world of investing possibilities was expanding, and I had only been doing research for a few months.

I was already more attentive to the companies in my world than I was before starting my Investing Practice. It happened, without my even trying, in prosaic activities like doing the grocery shopping. I thought that I had been an engaged consumer, aware of what I bought and where I put my money, but this was a new level of conscious consumerism. I had always tried to buy products made by Boulder companies, and I pointed them out to Nuno proudly—until he asked if everything available in Boulder had been made by a Boulder company, and then I toned it down. But I started looking at everything as a possible investment.

I'd walk down the grocery store aisle and the brands popped out at me like superimposed thought bubbles. Toothpaste companies! Nut-free-protein-bar companies! Frozen-burrito companies! Who owned which? Where would the eventual down-the-rabbit-hole parent-company search lead? Some of the products on the shelf were biologically related to each other, having been born of the same parent, but gave us no indication. Others were related by marriage, from mergers or purchases of companies. And it was all a big treasure hunt. Some companies were public, and I could actually buy them. Which was a crazy thought. It made this whole investing thing seem a bit more real, and it made a regular mundane chore like the weekly grocery run a lot more meaningful.

So it was odd, in that moment after Nuno left, when I put out my photos and lit my scented candle, that I didn't feel so excited about my investing call that day.

We were halfway done with our year together, Dad and I. The thought brought on a deep breath.

It felt a bit heavy, this Investing Practice of mine.

My trepidation had subsided considerably since beginning my practice. After six months, the financial world was no longer a total black hole of mystery, and I was getting ever more sure that I could do this investing thing myself just as well as one of Those Finance People without paying their fees, thankyouverymuch.

Still, in my less guarded moments, my reservations persisted. If I was honest with myself, I felt uncomfortable truly committing to my Investing Practice. I had come a long way in the last six months, I acknowledged, trying to give myself a little pat on the back for all the work I had done. I'd been giving my practice the good old college try by following what my teacher said to do: practicing, reading, and even experimenting with my own versions of Investing Practice. But I continued to feel like an outsider looking in on value investors as a whole.

It was like being at a great party of investors where I knew only the host, and I was awkwardly wallflowering around on the outskirts, trying to find anyone else I knew so I could join in. I could see everyone having fun, I was there, but I wasn't really a member of the nucleus.

This sense of detachment made little rational sense. After all, I actually was starting to like this stuff. I wanted to learn it. I spent time on it. I had found ways to make it my own, as with my investing office, but doing so also emphasized to me how different I was from Those Finance People. Why wasn't I truly passionate about it yet? Why hadn't I found my friends at the party?

Despite my growing comfort with it, when I thought of the financial world, what came up were those same old feelings and images: stress, uncertainty, the unknown, it being too complicated to ever know, fear, lying liars who lie, numbers, financial statements, calculations, computer models, fees, the Great Recession and depressions. It felt nasty. It felt like the opposite of the freedom I was starting to feel in my Investing Practice.

In my mind, I tried something—I skipped to imagining I had achieved the end goal: feeling free. Immediately, I saw the words "abundance" and "happiness," and imagined getting to do the stuff I wanted to do, relaxed, stress-free. I saw myself looking happy. Even the stress in my stomach felt a bit lighter when I imagined financial freedom.

I reminded myself that my bridge to that freedom was my value Investing Practice, so I tried to picture myself being a successful value investor. I surveyed my investing office, closed my eyes, and tried to visualize it.

I tried. But I couldn't.

It was the strangest thing: I literally could not picture myself as a successful investor. In my mind's eye, I was there, but there was dark fog obscuring that image of me—the same fog that my dad seemed to have a lighted path through.

It occurred to me—wouldn't it make sense that my image of myself as a successful value investor be modeled on my dad? Didn't I have a real-life role model for it? Shouldn't this be the easiest visualization exercise ever? But no, my image of a successful investor didn't look or feel at all like my dad. And I noticed that I felt a bit panicky in my chest after having that thought.

Did I not want to be like my dad?

I felt nauseated. I needed to sit down. I pulled out a dining chair and tucked myself into the table with my head in one hand, messing with my prayer wheel with the other. I was tapping into something hard, something tough, and something very old, and I didn't like it one bit.

I had gone into my corporate, big-law legal career to save myself from the fear of the financial world by not having to deal with it. I'd make my money another way, and feel the financial freedom without ever having to touch that side of money. But it hadn't worked—at all. My career hadn't created any of the feelings I associated with financial freedom—on the contrary, it had seemed to make everything worse.

I got some water. Took a breath. I was tired of dealing with these mysterious feelings of stress and avoidance. In my mind, the joy of financial freedom had not fully entwined itself with the idea of investing. They were actually separate and opposed—which made no sense. I had tried a few times to get closer to what my dad did in investing, and eventually had avoided it each time. I wanted to know what was up with me and handle it, so that I could move into being a successful investor. I had started on this path of my Investing Practice, I was in it, and I wasn't going to turn back now. If facing the fog and understanding whatever it was that was making my tummy hurt was part of it, then better now than later. I had years of compounding returns ahead of me and I wasn't going to let some old, mysterious emotional hangover derail this train.

I thought about it being June a second time. We were halfway done already? My dad had stuck with me so far, but I only had about six months more before he might fade away into other busyness. I didn't even really know how to research a company yet. All I had done were bits and pieces in the service of Charlie's Principles, and I had no clue how to make a final decision on a company, from the vast universe of companies out there.

Sitting there, confused and lost, I realized it was time to call my dad. Just like we all do when we have to go to work, as I had done a million times at my job, I tried to shake off my confusion and set about my task. There was nothing I wanted to do less at that moment than talk to him.

I reached for the one positive thing I had thought of. "Dad," I said haltingly, "we're halfway through our year. We've actually done a lot."

"Wow," he said, "that happened fast. We've got a lot to cover. We need to talk more about your Circle of Competence. Now that you've got Charlie's first three principles down, you can start doing serious research into Moat and management."

"Yeah," I agreed, "I don't have the time to waste on companies that aren't going to be real options. I need to know how to research so I can really do this on my own."

Dad said, "Of course, and you shouldn't randomly choose what to research. You don't have all the time in the world. You've got to be strategic about this. Choose an industry you like, one you know something about the companies in and want to learn more about, and go deeply into it."

"I like the circle metaphor in the Circle of Competence. The circle widens only when my competence grows."

"Exactly. I learned the hard way what happens when I stepped outside my Circle of Competence."

Yikes. That sounded juicy.

"Back in my early investing days, I invested in a bioengineered organic fertilizer company. Dr. Jonas Salk—the inventor of the polio vaccine—lent his credibility to the company as chairman of the board and I thought I understood the product and industry well enough."

"You didn't."

"Well, I thought I did, and I was right in that the bioengineered products actually worked well and the company succeeded, but maybe I could have avoided becoming its CEO if I had known more. I had a lot of money invested in it, from me and one of my funds. One day I showed up at a board of directors meeting and the rest of the board were already there, coffee cups half empty. Peter Salk said that the board had met a bit early and decided to let the CEO go and then voted on the next CEO. Me. I asked why me. He said because I was the only board member that didn't have a real job."

"What?" I had never heard this story before. All I had known is that he had run a bioengineering company.

"Doctor Salk got me into Harvard Business School's Small Corporation Management Program and then I ran the company for a couple of years and then, finally, the board brought in more-experienced management and eventually the company went public. It all worked out."

"Dad, that's amazing. I've never heard about this. Really?"

"Yeah. But the point is, I probably shouldn't have made the investment in the first place. I really didn't know enough about it. It is so crucial that you know what you don't know. I made the mistake of thinking I knew when I didn't."

I couldn't relate to having the confidence to invest in something I didn't understand. I was even worried about investing in things I did understand. I asked him how you know if you know enough.

He paused and thought about it. "Charlie says that is one of their great secrets—he and Warren know what they know and what they don't know better than most people. I think the answer is to be skeptical and keep asking questions. Use the checklist you made. Add to it. And stay far away from the edge of your Circle of Competence. And focus on well-established companies. You remember, I worked with Steve Jobs when he was developing a new computer company after he left Apple the first time. The NeXT."

"Yeah, that boxy black computer that was going to be the next big thing. The NeXT big thing."

"I invested in a software document management system for the NeXT that was really good. It was a huge hit. But, in this case, I bet on a new operating system, and when NeXT went down, the software company decided to port the product to Windows NT. That turned out to be quite difficult and was nearly a train wreck. Another venture capital partner and I brokered a sale of the software company to a public company, except a month later, that company's CEO admitted to manipulating their financials and the company's stock price crashed and took my investment with it. What a mess. Twenty million dollars went to two million dollars almost overnight."

Oh my gosh. I could imagine. Working like a dog for years building a company, only for the company to fail because of an operating system. That's the soul-destroying side of entrepreneurship that nobody talks about.

"In that case, I knew I had the right product in the right industry, but two bad choices for the platform that it was on wrecked the investment. These mistakes convinced me to stick with established businesses to cut down on how much I had to know."

"You've got to know enough to know what's up—and to know when what's up has changed."

"Exactly, and with the NeXT computer, I did not know that the NeXT was doomed, and I did not know that the software engineers were overestimating their abilities. I should have stuck to what I first started investing in because I knew them backwards and forwards: guns and motorcycles."

I cracked up laughing. Of course my father chose guns and motorcycles to invest in. While everyone else was spouting off about oil futures and obscure companies that were supposed to be the next big thing, he chose Smith & Wesson and Harley-Davidson. They say write what you know; he invests in what he knows.

"I'm serious!" he protested. "Understanding an industry is key. You have to understand it like you understand that condo of yours. It has to be that easy. If someone works in the digital-storage industry, they almost definitely know way more about the digital-storage industry than you or I do right now, and for them, digital storage is as easy as a condo. We can go learn about digital storage, don't get me wrong. But that person who has experiential knowledge knows a lot more about it than we do right now, just by virtue of their job."

"Or, you know, shooting guns and riding motorcycles for fun can provide that experiential knowledge that is so utterly vital and surprisingly useful for investing purposes," I teased.

He chuckled. "Yup. I knew for sure that, in the 1980s, Harleys were the best motorcycles."

"For people who like Harleys."

"Well, it turns out there were a lot of people like me who like Harleys."

"Turns out wandering around the world and being in the army is a little bit useful," I replied. Then I couldn't help myself from throwing out a barb: "Wandering around seems to be your thing, even when it means not seeing your daughters for a couple of years to do that NeXT computer stuff. Or maybe especially when it means that."

Surprised, my dad said, "What?"

"I think looking at what people actually do under pressure is the best way to decide if they're trustworthy."

My words surprised us both.

Dad didn't say anything for a moment. I took a deep breath and realized the nausea was back. I couldn't keep talking to him right then. "Dad, I need a break. Sorry. Can we pick this up again later?"

"Sure, honey," he said dejectedly. We hung up and I sat there holding the phone.

Well, that had taken a weird turn. Maybe this emotional stuff was partly why I wasn't totally connected to my Investing Practice.

After all, there were lots of ways I wanted to be like my dad. He was a rather extraordinary person. He was generous, kind, incredibly loving, and supportive of me beyond how anyone should be, really. He was a wonderful dad.

Still, I let the thought sit in my stomach, trying not to judge it or push it away. If there was ever a time to unknot this, this was it. I let the nausea sit, breathing through it. What, I asked myself—what was I avoiding?

And the answer came back with the speed of an online stock purchase order: *Untrustworthy. I do not want to be untrustworthy.*

Immediately, I felt horribly guilty and ashamed for thinking such a mean thing about someone I loved and adored. It was uncharitable, unkind, and unloving toward this loving father who was helping me with my Investing Practice.

Justified or not, those deep childhood feelings were hurting me now by keeping me from helping myself, and that was very real. I had to face them. I didn't want to be untrustworthy, like how the eleven-year-old version of me remembered my father. The nausea disappeared once I had named that feeling, though. It was like the very act of thinking it and thereby putting a name to that which could not be named, Voldemort-style, lit up the thing I was afraid of, and it had less influence once it was illuminated.* *Well fine, then.* "Voldemort. Voldemort, Voldemort, Voldemort," I said out loud to the empty room. Nothing bad happened, so I switched from the Dark Lord to my own darkness.

"Untrustworthy," I squeaked out loud. The word stuck in my throat, like a bad cliché. I grabbed a sip of water and tried to say it out loud again. "Untrustworthy." This time it came out, reluctantly. "Untrustworthy, untrustworthy, untrustworthy." I said it louder. I said it a few more times, for good measure. Each time, it hit me like an insult, but each time, the hit was slightly less painful. Each time, I was a little less afraid of admitting it: I hadn't trusted my dad to help me with money because I felt he'd used money as a weapon against me when I was little. It didn't matter that we'd gotten through it, that he'd taken care of us in every way since then. I had the deep and automatic distrust and disengagement of a child thrown into an adult-level situation and was, naturally, incapable of handling it. When it came to working with my dad around the issue of money, I was still back there sometimes. I was stuck between deep feelings as a child and my adult understanding.

When it came to investing, my dad was unassailably trustworthy. His work was backed up by strong sources. His opinions were matched by other heavyweight investors'. He was positively peer-reviewed when his books were published. He called the bloody 2008

---

* If you don't get this reference, then book publishing is not in your Circle of Competence. Also, how have you not read any of the Harry Potter books?

stock crash, for goodness' sake. There was no question in my mind that he was legit in the realm of investing. But it was still hard, on a personal level, to trust him, even after all he had done for me.

In hindsight, I realized that I had attempted to face this before. I had tried the day-trading thing. I had tried working for my dad one summer to get closer to understanding him and his methods, and it did help in the trust department. I saw how much and hard and intelligently he studies companies. I hadn't gotten to the point of totally accepting him yet, though. So I tried a third time: now. Third time's the charm.

My feelings about money had nothing to do with money. They had to do with the mess inside my head. I wanted to sort out the mess.

Right then, Nuno called, and I was still sitting in the same spot holding the phone. I answered without thinking. He could immediately tell something was wrong. "Oh, I just was kind of mean to my dad. He was talking about his work when he left us during the divorce, and finally I just couldn't help myself from saying, 'Uh, yeah, you sure did leave us!'"

Nuno didn't say anything for a moment, and then he responded, "He seems to be with you now, and for quite a long time, no?"

It was infuriating. He knew almost nothing about what had happened, but he was defending my dad?

"There's no way I have a clue what happened," he admitted. "But what I do see now is that he is there for you, and he's spending a lot of time and energy with you to help you learn to invest—by the way, other people pay huge amounts of money for advice like that, if they can even get it from someone who has their best interests at heart. He's giving you the best gift he can. I'm not saying anything more than that effort has got to count for something good. No?"

I sighed. He was right. I hadn't succeeded in letting the old pain go, but I could at least notice what my dad was doing now. He was being around, the best way he knew how. He had been showing up not only for the podcast week after week but also as a dad for many years since the divorce. And now, he was showing up for our Investing Practice.

"Yeah." I sighed again. "I should probably call him back."

"Good luck, sweetie," Nuno encouraged me, and we hung up.

I could feel in a millisecond that little girl wondering what she had done to make her dad not come back. I had come out of it with a wound that healed but left a twisted mess of a scar—a scar that mostly is no big deal but, if it's hit just the wrong way, sends pain reverberating down to my bones. There was no escaping it—talking about his job, his absence from my life, was complicating all this talk about investing and, most of all, money.

I wasn't sure what I would say—or what he would say—but I took a long breath, imagining the air coming in through my head and traveling all the way down my body and out through my toes, and called my dad back.

"You're making it sound like I abandoned you. Is that what you think?" he asked incredulously. "That I abandoned you? That I left you on purpose?" He was half concerned, half incensed.

We had never spoken so frankly about it before.

"Well, isn't that what happened?" I ventured. "You left and went to California, and now you're saying it's because your business needed you, which I can understand. It was a crazy time in your personal life and for your business."

"No!" He flipped. "My investment wasn't in California, it was in Iowa. NeXT was in California, so I needed to be there some of the time, but no, I would never have left you voluntarily."

Was that true?

"Danielle, I would die for you and your sister. I would do anything for you. I would never, ever, ever abandon you."

"But you left," I said flatly. "That happened."

"I wasn't there a lot," he acknowledged, "but I did not abandon you. At all. You've got to know why I wasn't around."

He told me his side of the story, about how horrifically bad it had been between him and my mom after they split up: the cruel accusations, the murderous lawyers, the blame, the . . . well, the war. Nasty Divorce 101. I knew my mom had her own side of the story, but until that moment, mine was the only side I'd experienced or really known. Listening to what my dad had gone through in the divorce years was hard, but I heard him. I really heard him. There were a few things I hadn't known, and for the first time, I deeply empathized with him from a new perspective. Maybe on the surface it had seemed to me, the little kid with no clue about what was happening between the adults, like he had gone off to live the high life, but my father was also a man who had done the best he could in the moment, for, not despite, his children.

"Me being around your mom in a little tiny town was not good for me, for her, for you. It was like rubbing salt in the wound—my wound, your wound. It seemed like I was making things worse by being there, and I wanted desperately to work out our divorce settlement so that I could spend as much time with you as possible. I decided the best thing to do was to remove myself from the situation until it cooled off. I thought taking you to cool places would ease the pain a bit. I'm sorry it came across like I didn't care. I thought keeping at a distance for a short time was the best way to make sure I could be with you long term."

That actually sounded like a smart response. Mature.

"It seemed like it took forever, but once we did cool off, we ditched our lawyers and settled things with an arbitrator in about an hour, and I moved a few doors down from you and we saw each other all the time, right?"

"Yes"—I nodded—"we did."

"So how can you say I abandoned you? I left for a while because I thought it was the best way to get back to you. I didn't abandon you at all. I hate that you think that."

I . . . I could see that. Understanding his intention changed everything for me. What mattered to me was knowing that he had not left me on purpose, and he was always going to return. Abandonment is not the same thing as being physically away. He knew he would come back—but I hadn't known that. I had felt abandoned, but he had never abandoned me.

"I didn't know that stuff," I responded. Tears came. I couldn't stop them. I cried, "This is hard. It's all really hard, and complicated, and it was all such a mess. People do stuff they don't even remember, or they get confused about what happened, and it's just a total, horrific mess. For everyone."

"It was, honey," he said sadly. "Absolutely."

It was different to view those years from my current perspective as an adult. I could feel the adult me understanding his situation better. Identifying with him was a new feeling for me.

"Danielle, what happened happened, no matter how much I want to go back and do it over. At the time, I did what I thought was best, but I had no idea you felt abandoned. Obviously, what I did was so completely wrong. Knowing how much it hurt you, I should have just stayed, no matter what."

A soft spot in my heart flinched and made me cry again. "I hear you that you didn't abandon us. That helps a lot, actually."

Dad was silent. I could feel my heart pounding in my chest, but I managed to go on. "That's life. Things happen. Crappy things. Lots of worse things happen to lots of people. But I can have you in my life now—and I want that," I said.

He jumped on the opportunity.

"So do I. I will always be there for you, no matter what. I would do anything for you." He thought for a moment. "What I do know is that I can teach you how to make money."

I laughed, in spite of myself.

"I can!" he protested. "And I'll always be here for you whatever else you need. I promise."

"Dad, I know you will. You have been. You *are*. What matters is what people do, remember? Here we are; somehow, against every prediction I would have ever made, I am sitting here talking about investing with you for an entire year. I love you. We're doing pretty good."

He started laughing. I could feel his relief.

"And I'm enjoying it!" I laugh-cried. He was cracking up. "I think you've got a miracle on your hands, Dad. I don't know how you did it." I wanted to thank him, but it didn't seem quite right. "And you're sticking with me through it. You haven't quit on me yet."

"No way will I quit on you, sweetie. I will prove that to you."

Achieving freedom, it turned out, was about way more than what was in my bank account.

Diving In

As Dad and I got back on track, I felt closer than ever to him. We agreed that after the success of my Investing Intensive reading of the news and the Buffett Bible, I should use this month to delve more deeply into companies. The only way to do that was to kick things up a notch and attack the annual reports.

Annual reports are boring. They just are. But they are the best way to learn about a company. Maybe I could make them part of my bedtime routine, I mused. Forget warm milk and Ambien—I'd be nodding off to the melodious words of a lawyer describing the company's greatly detailed risk factors. Then, I thought, if I could get through a bunch of them for two days, I would know how to read them efficiently from then on. Any company I wanted—two days of the same company, or several different companies. My goal was to read eight of them, no matter what.

When you live weekend to weekend—and most of us do—a month gets shortened to four sets of two days that are useful, and those eight days have to fit in the errands, the laundry, the household fixer-upper tasks, the spillover work from the week, family time, and friend time. And now, for me, a long-distance boyfriend. Remember when weekends were for waking up with a hangover after taking too many shots the night before and then mainlining *Friends* reruns? That was fun.

Using a weekend to start the journey that would support me the rest of my life was not actually hard. It was a matter of prioritizing it over commitments I had already made, over household work that genuinely needed to be done, over my desire to see someone other than my coworkers, and over genuine rest. The only thing I could not prioritize it over was my actual job and doing some sort of workout to stay healthy, however limited. I resolved to treat my Investing Practice like what it was: the single best way I could possibly direct my time.

I thought about my resolve to put myself first, and that no one else was going to take care of me but me. This was the time to take action, rather than continue to think about investing. It had been an intense month already, and I wanted to get back to the basics by focusing on investment research. I had been spending parts of my weekends on my Investing Practice since the beginning of the year, and now I would focus one entire weekend on my practice.

On Friday night, I was ready to carry out my commitment to myself and my practice, and then a not-unusual thing happened: an urgent work matter came up and couldn't be pushed off. By the time I finished my work that Friday evening, I was so tired that all I wanted to do was take a hot shower and crawl into my bed and sleep for a hundred hours. I went straight home.

Saturday, I got up early and groggily decided that I read better tucked up in bed. At least I'd be comfortable while bored. I happily drew my covers up around me, wiggled my toes in pure comfort, and dove in. I got out my checklist and opened up the Whole Foods 10-K PDF on my computer and saved it in my "Investing Practice" folder on my desktop.

Sixty-one pages. Here we go. (Following are my live notes as I read through the PDF.)

▶ It's a Texas company! I didn't know that.

▶ I'm learning a lot about what qualifies food as organic.

▶ Whole Foods has a lot of programs and natural food initiatives that I didn't even know about. This is much more interesting than I thought.

▶ They seem to be growing a LOT.

▶ They capped salaries at nineteen times the average wage of full-time employees. That's rare. Very cool.

▶ Wow, the whole top management team has been there a really long time.

▶ What is a basis point? I feel like I know, but having a feeling about it seems inadequate. Should look it up. Probably won't.

As I read, I remembered what I love about legal documents. They are precise and they are complete. They go deep and wide into their topic. Annual reports literally tell us, the public, the risks the company faces. Which is a rather extraordinary thing in a competitive environment.

Also, I could see, once I got a few of these full annual reports under my reading belt, that I would get faster.

It turned out that the explanatory part of the 10-K was only the first half of the report. The other half were the financial statements, which I left to read later. Charlie would agree, I thought—find out if I thought I was capable of understanding a company first, which for me meant reading their words and understanding what they did, to give me good context, and then review the financials once I knew how.

Overall, my impression of Whole Foods was that it was a company with a real focus on conscious capitalism. (Duh, its CEO literally wrote the book *Conscious Capitalism*.) Whole Foods' Mission was fantastic. I couldn't support its Mission more if it were my own company. The company had some interesting ways it incentivized employees, and I wondered if those methods really worked. I had heard rumblings in the Boulder Whole Foods stores that employees weren't so happy with the scheduling of their shifts. So, overall, I loved the company, but I wanted to look more into its growth plan and its employees. Also, its executives— John Mackey famously gets $1 per year, but how were the others compensated? Was Mackey expected to stick around for a long time to come?

I listened to the most recent quarterly investor call while I did yoga in my living room. It wasn't ideal, but it was a way to squeeze both in. I read two more of the annual reports, and I did a lot of Internet searching for the company and its executives. "The Internet is the best scuttlebutt machine in the world," my dad had anachronistically proclaimed.

After the weekend, I switched to researching other companies. As my dad had predicted, I threw out a lot of companies without finishing their annual reports. Ten minutes or an hour into it, I decided I wasn't capable of understanding the company, or the report was too boring to keep reading, and I'd rather watch C-Span than keep reading about this company. I then ditched the company and moved on. "Too Boring" is a pile too. A very important pile.

I kept a list of companies I had rejected and the reason why I rejected them. Most were Too Hard, but some were Too Boring. Any articles or other research I had found about a rejected company, I saved in the "Too Hard" folder on my computer. I wanted a record of what I had rejected so I didn't repeat the process.

A few companies were potentially interesting and seemed understandable, but I wasn't excited about them. For those, I made a "Watching" category. Maybe I would come back to them after doing this a bit longer.

And I made a list of companies I loved. That was my "Wishlist," and I wanted to buy them.

Wishlist	Short Story
Whole Foods (WFM)	Love the Mission, love the values Brand Moat is good ROE, ROIC, and debt are good Mgmt is very good
Costco (COST)	Love the values, best in class Price and Broad Moats are great Great in a recession ROE, ROIC, and debt are good
Seritage (SRG)	Location Moat Potential upside in ten years is huge Buffett in at $35 for 10% Sears risk of bankruptcy
Amazon (AMZN)	Bezos is extraordinary and disruptive CEO Tough values—love the "providing everything to everyone," but hate the destroying small stores and issues with employees Cash flow machine
Berkshire Hathaway (BRK)	Buffett best CEO but what if he's not there Safe and steady diversification Growth—about 9%
Chipotle Mexican Grill (CMG)	Best of breed Ethical food ROE, ROIC, no debt Great founding mgmt team Fresh-food safety problem

And I decided to do something my dad had not recommended.

Fantasy Investing

My friend and fellow corporate attorney Ilana is a baseball nut. She knows every statistic that exists in baseball, and more amazingly, she makes it an interesting topic when she explains them. I actually love going to baseball games with her because she gives me a whole new understanding of the players, the strategies, the game itself. When a guy walks up to the plate, she'll go, "Oh good, I'm glad he's back in the lineup tonight. Since he's a switch-hitter and isn't as strong power-wise from the right side, he sat out the last two nights, because both starting pitchers were lefties." And suddenly, the game just got really interesting.

As a statistics geek, she was interested in my Investing Practice. One Friday after work when she was over at my house for a glass of wine, she looked kind of sheepish and said, "Well, I'm sure everyone knows about this, but I have a question about beginning investing."

"Please," I laughed, "I know nothing, but I'll do my best."

"Okay." She sighed. "Well, I just feel ridiculous about this. It would be great if you would describe how to buy a stock. Like, really. What website do I go to, and what information do I need to have ready to . . . I mean, I don't know, give them my bank account information or something to buy stock?"

Indeed—why should anyone know how to buy stock? They don't teach us this stuff in school, and buying stock is not exactly a commonsense process. We were both corporate attorneys, and we didn't know. Lots of smart people have no idea what to do. I also had no idea until I did it.

Here's what you do: you open what's called a brokerage account with a stock brokerage company, like Interactive Brokers, TD Ameritrade, TradeStation, Schwab, Scottrade—you know, the ones with ads you see on TV that emphasize either their service or low price. This is similar to a checking or savings bank account in that you will put money in it, but the money in that account is only used for the purpose of buying stock through the stock brokerage company. Some people with a high net worth will have this kind of account with their bank because the bank gives them advice and planning services to keep their account with the bank—this is the kind of thing Nuno works on for his banking clients—but the rest of us will probably use a stock brokerage that is online. They're easy and cheap.

Each time you buy or sell a stock, they charge a transaction fee. I believe most online brokerages charge about $5–10. Which means, if you're only working with a few thousand dollars, those transaction fees eat away any gains extremely quickly. For people trading many thousands or millions, they don't really notice them, but for me, transaction costs would be an issue. Just one more reason value investing is good for people with little money like me—the whole plan is to buy and sell very rarely.

Pick one of the brokerages based on whether your priority is more service or lower transaction prices, then click on the button to open an account with them. They'll ask all the typical credit questions to verify that you're you, such as your old addresses and former employers, and they'll ask how you want to move money into your new account, and you'll choose a username and password, and then, presto, change-o, you'll have a brokerage account.

I just hadn't done it yet.

"Ilana," I warned, "I haven't opened a brokerage account. I'm not buying stock yet. I think I might only paper invest now."

"Paper invest?"

"Paper investing means fake investing. Think of it like fantasy baseball. When you have a fantasy baseball team, obviously you're not actually running a baseball team, but it's a virtual version of that, right?"

"Right."

"So paper investing—and I have no idea why people call it paper investing, or paper trading—is a virtual version of buying stock."

The light bulb went on for Ilana, and I realized paper investing *was* just like fantasy baseball. Except it was much more boring. For long-term value investing, there isn't much to do when it comes to Fantasy Investing. All I was going to do was choose a few stocks, and wait.

I made an Excel spreadsheet with four columns: name of company, date purchased, price, and number of shares. That's it.

I knew no one would ever see this spreadsheet unless I showed it to them, but it still felt a bit serious to put the name of a company on that spreadsheet. It felt like staking my claim, and even though it was only for me, my claim mattered to me. I took a moment to notice what was going on with me. My chest got a little tight, and my feet were tingly and antsy. It was the "get up and run" feeling. This is what fear of investing feels like, I reminded myself, and took notice so that when I staked a claim for real, with real money, I could recognize the feeling as a general fear, rather than a serious, Enclosed Concrete Stairwell instinct to avoid the company.

I took a deep breath and grounded my feet into the earth, imagining them growing roots like a huge redwood. Unshakable. I typed the information into each column.

Then I locked the spreadsheet with a password, and closed it, putting it deep into my investing folder.

Once I was done, I felt comfortable with my choices. Staking a claim was just hard to carry out. But once my claim was staked, it was mine, and I could move on.

I rolled along quite well with my Investing Practice for a few weeks. I read my *WSJ* every day along with my celebrity gossip. I read some annual reports. I continued to notice companies in plain sight during my regular day that had previously been invisible to me. Carpet companies! Shoe companies! Construction companies!

In late June, my dad and I finally launched our podcast with a bunch of episodes we had recorded over the last few months, beginning with episodes about Charlie's Four Principles of Investing. Shockingly to us, the podcast went to the top of the iTunes Business charts in its first few days. We couldn't believe how many people wanted to learn about investing with me. It gave me such a lovely boost to keep trying to understand this stuff, because I knew if I could do it, anyone else following along with me could too.

To my surprise, the podcast had become a safe space with Dad. He showed up every single time, with humor, love, straightforwardness, humility, and intellectual honesty. When recording, I could ask him anything I wanted, and to his extraordinary credit, he did not shy away from it. At all. He leaned in. He took my challenges like a man and usually completely turned my opinion around. Sometimes he accepted that I had another way of looking at an issue. Those were the best moments. Hour by hour, episode by episode, argument by argument, practice by practice, he showed up for me every time. Proving himself, over and over, in both practice and action and in thought and academic rigor. My safe space was going out to thousands of listeners who also found it to be a safe space, and there was something wonderfully comforting about that.

I tried again to conjure an image of myself as a successful investor. This time, instead of blankness and nausea, I instantly saw an image of myself. That alone was progress. In that image, I saw a certain amount of ease in my carriage, a veil of stress having been whisked away.

During our next Investing Practice phone call, I realized I probably wasn't the only one with weird, complicated issues around finances and money, particularly the messages around money we receive from our parents and loved ones. "This money stuff can bring up a lot of family stuff," I mused.

"It's utterly intertwined with family," he agreed with a knowing chuckle. "Somehow I was able to escape my family's money tradition. I grew up in a family with people who thought that rich people got there by hurting other people," he said nonchalantly.

My eyes widened in shock. *What?*

My dad seemed very comfortable with his money-making efforts, so I had never considered that he might have his own issues, until now.

"Oh yeah," Dad went on. "I got a lot of messages like that and got a twisted picture of being wealthy. My uncle—my mom's brother—made money, but he hid it so people didn't know. He never did anything that would indicate he had any money, because he didn't want to be one of *those* people. My mom had those same feelings he did, and yet wanted to have money and success so badly, and she found that impossible to reconcile in her life. She made the adobe house all on her own, and it was just beautiful."

"The adobe house" was a now-legendary house in our family that my grandmother, after she retired from running her own restaurants and raising kids, had designed entirely on her own. It was built out of adobe bricks almost exclusively by her and my grandpa with their own hands. Dad went on. "I was so impressed with it after it was built, and I knew a developer who was looking for capital to fund the development of two hundred adobe homes, with great thick real adobe walls, for a budget. My mom knew exactly how to do that and could have done it for the budget, and she would have been great at it."

"She would have loved it," I agreed. She is a take-charge kind of woman, and I could imagine her barking orders at the workmen and arguing with the contractors and loving every second of it.

"Yeah," my dad agreed. "Well, I told her I'd back the deal if she wanted to take it on as the designer and she backed away from that idea like I had just stuck her fingers in the fire. She couldn't handle taking it to the next level."

"You think it was too much for her?" I asked. I couldn't imagine it being too much for my pushy grandma.

"No, she could have done it, and she would have loved doing it. But she couldn't see herself actually doing such a big thing. It wasn't the work—she was an incredibly hard worker. But she couldn't take the mental step that was necessary to actually take charge. She couldn't see herself as a successful, wealthy person because that was too scary, or something. I'm guessing here, right? What I know is that she dreamed about it and when the opportunity came, she buckled; she couldn't see herself being in charge of her own money and her own life, and I think, on some deep level, she didn't feel comfortable being wealthy. She said, 'Oh no, I could never do that,' and wouldn't discuss it further."

Good Lord. She was exactly like me. Or I was exactly like her.

When the opportunity came to dig in and create wealth and success, I couldn't imagine myself doing it—truly taking charge of my own money and financial freedom. I couldn't envision what it would look like. I hadn't buckled, so there was some hope for me yet, I figured, but I hadn't exactly taken the bull by the horns either. Well, I thought wryly, I had psychological resources she did not and lived in a very different time for women. I could either straighten up and deal with my demons in the way my grandmother had not, or I could repeat her mistakes. She has dementia now, and she spends a lot of her days packing her things and telling her caregivers about how she was building a house and needed to be ready to move in as soon as it was finished. My poor grandma, born in the wrong era.

I asked my dad if he had any negative feelings about wealth. I couldn't really imagine that he did—in my lifetime, he had always made money and felt great about it. He told me about how he had always been skeptical of rich people, just like his mother, but hadn't really realized it until he grappled with becoming wealthy himself. As a river guide, he felt like he had no skills that would get him out of the Grand Canyon, but he wanted out, so he felt he had no choice but to just make money. He put his preconceptions aside, out of pure necessity, and with his back against the wall zigged and zagged into wealth. Once he had made some money, he realized that he wasn't evil or obnoxious, and he hadn't gotten there by stepping on anyone else. He let his judgments about other wealthy people go.

I had to decide how I would face my own preconceptions with finances, wealth, and money. Here is the procedure I came up with:

STEP ONE: FACE IT. Face the preconceptions that I've got and acknowledge them, and by doing so, reduce their power. Connect to the tradition I come from and accept that it affects my life today positively and negatively—that coin is double sided. My preconceptions influenced my openness to changing my life and creating financial freedom. They were affecting my wellness by creating deep stress that I hadn't even known was there. I felt like I was tearing open my chest with my fingernails and hitting raw heart to acknowledge how the eleven-year-old version of me had lost trust in my dad and gotten so afraid of money that the stress had been bleeding into my Investing Practice, but by facing it, its power waned. Facing my memories had given me the knowledge that my dad had planned to come back and, most important, did. He was trustworthy and he was there for me. And I did, actually, want to be exactly like that. I resolved to remember, in the back of my mind, the emotional journey I had gone through, and that my experience might still color my Investing Practice in times of stress.

STEP TWO: *MARO*. Be thankful for my family tradition with money. I took the positive examples my grandmother had set for me to heart: her strength, her tenacity, her zest to make something of herself; I left the fear behind. My family tradition was also the tradition, through my father, that gave me the Investing Practice I was getting ever more deeply into, and it had been painful to face my childhood feelings, but that's life: crappy things happen. Much worse happens to many people, and I was an incredibly fortunate child and adult in a million ways.

STEP THREE: TRANSFORM. Transform my own life into the abundance that I want it to be. I had to remember to notice whether my scars were influencing me and making something worse or scarier than it actually was. And do that over and over, each time it comes up, and each time lessening its power because I would now be aware of its influence on my thoughts and decisions. Create the tradition I want going forward.

I tried a third time to visualize myself as a successful investor. What would I look like? This time, it was markedly different. I saw myself feeling grounded, steady, and very secure, with the knowledge that I had enough money in the bank to not ever worry again. I saw myself, but better: more secure, more grounded, more settled, happier, because that worry about money was, quite simply, gone.

That version of me was adept in the financial world, knew what to do, and handled her finances confidently. It was a good vision, and it felt free of old baggage. I liked it and I liked the feeling it created in my body.

"Where we come from, our family history, really matters to what we do in a way I didn't really realize before," I observed.

"Absolutely. I see it all the time in my students," Dad explained, "people trying to do better than their parents did, but struggling with the very idea that they could. It's easier if your parents are into money. Buffett came from a stockbroker father who owned his own stock brokerage."

"Oh, so it wasn't a strange world to him," I realized.

"Not at all," Dad replied. "Lots of other investors we talk about—the Gurus—come from families with investors or people involved in the financial world."

I had a flashback to one of my first days of class in law school, when the professor asked those in the room with a family member who was a lawyer to raise their hands. About 75 percent of people's hands went up—but not mine. "I didn't realize until law school that a lot of people who go into law have family members who are lawyers. No one in our family is a lawyer, so I just never thought about it. But it makes sense that if someone in your family does that, it makes it real and available to you." As I said it, I realized ironically that I had the same thing in investing, but instead of going into it because it was familiar, like Warren Buffett had, I avoided it. I was afraid of it. I had wanted nothing to do with it.

Until now.

Now I was going for it. I wasn't going to buckle, and I wasn't going to let my preconceptions around money take me down. I decided to let my family tradition lift me up.

"Like me," I told him. "I have a parent in investing. And now it's becoming real and available to me."

"That's right," Dad said, and I could hear him saying it with a smile. "So let's get to it. Next month, we're going to move on to something a little harder for you. Ready?"

I was ready.

JUNE PRACTICE: This month was really hard for me, but because I was willing to go through the emotional turmoil, it was also the month that I broke through my boundaries to become a true investor in myself and my financial freedom. Commit to your own breakthrough by facing, being thankful for, and transforming your family history with money—either by talking to family members or remembering your past—and be kind to yourself if you discover your own Voldemort.

CHAPTER 7

Charlie's Fourth Principle: Pricing

| July

This Month

▶ Pricing Using Whole-Company Numbers
▶ Ten Cap Pricing Method
  • Owner Earnings
▶ Payback Time Pricing Method
  • Formula for Free Cash Flow
  • Windage Growth Rate

I WAS HORRIBLY JET-LAGGED, BUT IT DIDN'T MATTER. I HAD FLOWN TO Zurich from Denver for a four-day weekend—an insane trip that, with the time difference, left Nuno and me only three actual days together. It was totally worth it.

And now I was spending some of those precious days awake at 4:00 A.M. looking out at the streetlights and listening to the occasional steadying *whoosh* of a Zurich bus going by in the dead of night. I had always been a night owl by nature, but my job had forced me into ever-earlier hours. I had started to love waking up early to watch the sunrise outside my picture window, so I didn't particularly mind being on jet-lag hours. There's promise in those dark, still nights when everyone else is asleep except you, when the hours are gratuitous and doing anything at all is a pure bonus.

Even while in Zurich, I wanted to do my Investing Practice. I would have patted myself on the back if I hadn't been too stiff from sleeping upright on the plane. On demand, now, I could picture myself as a successful, happy, confident investor. That twisted scar of mine hadn't magically disappeared, but good Lord if it didn't feel like a marvelous balm had been put on it. Crème de la Mer for the soul. What would I wear when I became that investor I saw in my mind's eye? Chanel, I thought. No, on second thought, only people like me six months ago, who didn't understand compounding, would throw money at Chanel. (Words I planned to eat when I got to a certain number of zeros in my brokerage account and could spend whatever I wanted without making much of a dent in my Number calculations. A girl has to have something to look forward to.)

Being in the dark gave me the courage to try out what my dad had promised would be a little tougher, and which I had been dreading since the beginning of this endeavor: the math. It appeared in my head as "MATH"—block letters preventing me from seeing past them.

I had called my dad before my trip. I wanted to get back into my Investing Practice. Bring on the MATH, I loudly declared inside my head. Then, on the phone to my dad, I declared it out loud.

Well, first, I slid in that I was going to Zurich to see Nuno, to let him know that I would be out of the country and that I was serious about this man. When Nuno came to Boulder, I had mentioned his existence to my dad, but it was clear now that we were getting more committed. My dad thought it was great, was totally supportive, and didn't ask a lot of questions. He knew that if I was serious about this guy, this guy was worth being serious about.

Then we moved on to discussing the task at hand: Charlie's last principle.

Charlie Munger's Fourth Principle of Investing: A Price That Makes Sense and Has a Margin of Safety

Charlie says, as his final criterion in the list of his four principles, not to pay an infinite price for a company. Find the price that is reasonable, and then, still don't buy it—in other words, wait till the price is even lower than reasonable. Pay a price that, first of all, makes sense, and second of all, is a price on sale, which builds in a margin of safety. That way, if I was wrong about the price that makes sense—*ahem*, a likely scenario—I'd be saved by the extra margin and hopefully still not lose money.

I felt protected by this principle, which was, of course, the point. Charlie was as conservative about pricing these mysterious entities as I was.

When I looked at the stock price of a company, I heard Charlie's drawl in my head: *Well, we're not going to pay an infinite price . . .* like, *How much do they want for this bucket of bolts?* Exactly, Charlie. Exactly. I came at it from the same perspective as buying a used car: suspiciously. It's possible I could get a deal, but I've really got to kick the tires first and know what I'm looking at. Not to mention, I needed to see through the spotless job the seller did detailing the car so I wouldn't see the sawdust in the engine. (I sound like a 1970s mobster. Can sawdust even go into an engine anymore?)

But what Charlie only implied when he stated this fourth principle is that, in order to pay a price that makes sense, I'd have to know how to calculate a good price. He, and my dad, seemed to think that was no problem. I wasn't so sure.

"Will you walk me through a quick valuation exercise so I can see how you do it?"

My dad drooled a tsunami of numbers at me. "Sure, honey. Okay, let's look at this company. Its EPS is $4.50 and the analyst growth rate is 13 percent but, historically for this company, that's really high so let's make it 8 percent because who are these analysts kidding, and then, using the rule of 72, that grows to about $10 in ten years."

"What?"

"Ten dollars in ten years."

I sat there, blinking. "Ten dollars of what? The share price?"

"No, of future earnings."

"How the hell did we land on future earnings—aren't we trying to find a share price?"

"Yes, of course. Sorry. I lost you. Okay, let's start over."

To him, it all made sense, and doing it the way he did was fine because it was clear to him what he was driving at. I didn't even know what questions to ask so I could try to understand. You know you're lost when you can't formulate a question to describe something that would help you be less lost, and there was nothing in the mess of words he had just used that would help me be less lost.

I remembered and understood the Big Four Numbers.[*] I even understood ROE and ROIC and debt.[†] I had thought I was ready. This language, though, I didn't yet speak. I gave up and ended our call, and didn't come back to it until I was in Zurich.

Valuation, as a subject, is not easy. In my practice, I discussed company valuation with clients occasionally, but always from the legal perspective. A venture capitalist who had taught one of my law school classes breezed over valuation of a company like it was dotting an *i* in an agreement. A student asked him to go into more detail about how he values a company before investing, and he answered that it was an alchemy of factors and an imprecise science often based on the investor's previous experience in that area and how much had already been invested. Basically, he wasn't going to go into it in a law class if he didn't have to, because he didn't have a great answer. Valuing a private company startup with no financial history is a different beast than valuing an established public company with

---

[*] The Big Four Numbers, which I learned in our discussion of Moats in chapter five, are (1) net earnings (also called net income or net profit), (2) book value (also called equity) + dividends, (3) sales, and (4) operating cash.

[†] I learned these terms during our discussion of management in chapter five.

many years of financials, but still, as I had learned already with my Moat and management analyses, past performance is no indication of future results. In some ways, established public companies can be just as unpredictable as a startup.

Absent a good explanation from my dad, I had brought the next best thing with me to Zurich: his book *Rule #1*. I read the price chapters and drank coffee as the city woke up, then re-read the relevant pages again until they blended together into a mush of numbers and words about numbers. I couldn't decipher a formula out of it. I did not know what to actually do. I shook my head, trying to make the numbers inside line up in the proper order. I was so frustrated that my anxiety started to turn into panic.

Charlie had said it was all so simple and so obvious. I guess he hadn't met me.

When Nuno woke up, I wanly told him that I had failed at MATH, and when he stopped laughing, which took longer than I would have liked, he tried to help. He knew I was starting to lose it. "I've got something for you." He grinned. *Ooh!* A little love gift. So sweet. He jumped up and came back with a four-hundred-page book that said "Valuation" on the cover. "You're on to pricing and valuation now, and I used this book in business school. I think it'll help."

I breathed in some calming breaths, and squeezed out a thanks, and refused to cry from frustration. There was no way this book was going to help.

I sat down in Nuno's living room with the valuation book and him, a numbers enthusiast, reading his own book across the room, just waiting with excitement for me to get my *aha!* moment from the enormous valuation book. I waded through the mud of the first few chapters and steadily battled the valuation theory. There I had been, going so confidently into the value investing party with my not-Chanel dress on and feeling like I belonged, and it turned out I was being mean-girled the whole time. I couldn't do this. I couldn't do any of it.

I caught Nuno looking at me every now and then, trying to see if I was getting it. I kept at it, and my head swam. I just needed useful information, I thought despondently. Straightforward, unvarnished information about what to do to decide what price makes sense. *A little help?*

So I did what I often do when I feel like I've failed at life. I put the book down, and I did the dishes. While my hands were busy, my brain could zone out and I could at least feel good about accomplishing something tangibly useful.

I turned the problem over and over in my mind. How would I figure this out? My dad couldn't even explain the most basic version of valuation to me. The books were no help. I was up a creek without a paddle, and had been since 4:00 A.M.

Nuno came in from the living room while I was washing pots and kissed me on the cheek. "Doing good, sweetie?" he asked.

"Fine," I muttered. And then I lost control, and started crying.

He was, reasonably, completely flummoxed. He turned off the faucet and hugged me and asked, "Did I do something?"

"No," I cried into his shirt. "I can't value a company! I've spent hours on this. Hours! And I can't sit down and know what those formulas are and use them. When I think about what to do, my head spins."

He paused. "I think you're getting so worried about this because you're trying to remember formulas instead of truly understanding them. You know my memory. Do you really think I remember all these formulas?"

When he was working from my house while visiting me in Boulder, I had seen him write down and use the most complex formulas from memory. "Yeah, I definitely think you remember all the formulas. You pull them out of your head like they're nothing."

"No!" he protested. "I don't remember them. I think about the problem and use logic to determine the tool I need to get my answer. I don't actually memorize the formulas. You have an extremely logical mind, so if you think the process through with logic, rather than thinking about the formula, you don't need to remember them. The formula will come automatically when you need it."

I pulled away from his wet shirt. "I could do that."

"Yeah." He was warming up to his own idea. "Forget that this is even about math or a formula. Use logic to get from where you are to where you're going, and then you won't need to get all worried over the math. You just need to understand it, and then it will come."

I suddenly remembered how I learned math in school. I was always confused while in class, but once I figured out that I should pretty much ignore the class, take the textbook home, and teach it to myself, I did fine. I taught myself all of my high school math that way. Nuno was saying that I should look at a valuation method as pure logic. That way, when I get the eventual answer using that method, I'd know if the answer was correct or if something went wrong in the process.

Valuation would not beat me. I would teach it to myself, somehow. So I got back to Charlie. Fourth Principle. *We're not going to pay an infinite price.* So simple and so obvious? *Foin.*

I would turn this current six-foot bar into a six-inch bar. I would teach myself valuation and I would buy a company.

Hell, if my dad could do it, surely I could do it.

I had to believe that, for me, my dad could translate his numbers brain into a words brain. I left Nuno happily typing away on work stuff in the living room and sat at the kitchen table. Later, I videocalled my dad. "My confidence is at an all-time low on this. Can you show me the easiest way to value a business that exists on the planet? If you can do that, I will figure out how to teach it to myself."

He said, "Great minds. I've been rethinking how I should teach novice investors a different way to find the right price to buy the business."

"Really?" I squeaked.

"Yeah, I've sort of realized I'm so familiar with the process of running numbers through my formulas that I forget it's intimidating if you're not comfortable with that language. I've thought of a much better way to explain it. Let's go to the feet of the master."

I felt my body involuntarily relax. "Wonderful."

My dad started recapping Buffett's 2013 letter to his shareholders, in which Buffett spelled out the simplest possible way to put a price on a business. Buffett is fantastic at explaining business concepts to us Normals, and this was what I needed. Nothing complicated. No toaster-size book on valuation. Commonsense methods.

In his letter, Buffett said to think about pricing a business like pricing a real estate purchase. I know—not exactly in the same category as the public companies I had been researching, or the public companies Buffett was buying. But the real estate business rents space in a building. It requires only a few numbers, all of which I had used when I bought my condo: purchase price, maintenance costs, how much I would have otherwise had to pay in rent, taxes, insurance. Even if I don't exactly find them fascinating, I can connect real estate numbers to something tangible. I know why I'm using those numbers, where to get them, and how to tell if they're off from where they should be—just like I can understand why a Toyota costs less than a Lexus and why lululemon yoga pants cost more than leggings from Target. The same is true for some public companies, says Buffett.

I appreciated my dad so much for finding Buffett's "real estate" explanation and offering it up. I had missed it the first time I read the Buffett Bible. I used Buffett's example to start to learn my dad's three ways to price and value companies.

Yes, *three* ways. I wasn't happy about it either, initially.

At that moment, one method was all I needed. One was all I wanted.

"Having three different ways to get at the price forces you to understand the company better, and the better you understand the company, the easier it is to choose the right price to pay," my dad explained. "You should be able to see any manipulation in the financials by understanding and comparing them. Three methods make you safe."

Well, that was an excellent answer. I like safe.

"All right," I acquiesced. "Let's do it."

Three Methods of Pricing/Valuation

1. Ten Cap price (based on Owner Earnings)
2. Payback Time price (based on free cash flow)
3. Margin of Safety valuation (based on earnings)

A NOTE ABOUT MATH

Remember, if I can do this, you can do this.

To make learning the math easier, I offer you three examples of businesses: (1) a real estate example of a rental house (the Rental House), (2) a private company example of a lemonade stand (the Lemonade Stand), and (3) a public company example of Whole Foods. The Rental House and the Lemonade Stand numbers are clearer, less complicated, and more accessible than going straight to public company numbers. Each sample business's financial statements are also available in full in the appendix.

Early in my practice, my dad emphasized that I should think and act as though I were going to buy a whole company, and in pricing we take that literally by pricing the entire company as a whole. Yes, I know public companies are traded in shares and I'm not really going to buy the whole company. I don't care—and, actually, I might buy a whole house, or a whole private company, someday. Laying the groundwork of understanding these whole-company examples will make it a lot easier to understand how to know what to pay for one share of a public company, so please bear with me for a few pages. This is how I learned to be (relatively) comfortable with accounting and financial statements. Then, once we have the concepts, and only then, we will discuss purchasing a fraction of a company using publicly traded shares of stock.

Pricing Method #1: Ten Cap

In that 2013 letter to his shareholders, Buffett described how he determined what to pay for two of his businesses: a Nebraska farm and a building in New York City. Buffett used a pricing method that real estate investors call capitalization rate, also known as a "cap rate." Buffett and my dad *love* using cap rates because they think they are simple. Here's how I understand them.

Essentially, a cap rate is the rate of return the owner of the property gets each year on the purchase price of the property—the rate of return being the money the owner puts in her pocket. For example, if I buy a house for $500,000 and get $50,000 in my pocket at the end of the year, the rate of return on my investment is 10 percent. That's my cap rate: 10. If I get only $25,000 in my pocket at the end of the year, then my rate of return is 5 percent, and that's my cap rate: 5.

Basically, the higher the cap rate, the higher my rate of return (and the less I paid for the property). A higher cap rate is better. Capitalization rates can vary, often from a 4 percent capitalization, or four cap (a 4 percent return on the purchase price each year) to a 15 percent capitalization, or fifteen cap (a 15 percent return on the purchase price each year). Buffett and Munger require a ten cap rate—a 10 percent return on their investment per year—and therefore, my dad calls this pricing method the Ten Cap.

Warren Buffett makes his calculations based on a financial number he defined: Owner Earnings—the amount of cash that can go into the business or real estate owner's pocket every year without affecting business operations.

We'll get to calculating Owner Earnings soon. First, the farm.

In the 1970s, crop prices were rising with inflation and midwestern farm prices exploded upward. There was a feeling among farmers that if you didn't buy a farm now, the price would be insanely high in a few years and you'd never be able to buy one. So prices kept going up. Small midwestern banks made loans on these farms as the farm prices continued to rise. Then, in the early 1980s, the Federal Reserve Bank raised interest rates extremely high, which made it more expensive to pay a mortgage, so farm prices started to fall. The high interest rates also brought inflation down to earth and crop prices started falling. In a couple of years, the price of a farm dropped by 50 percent. Farmers started having trouble making payments on their high-priced land investments, and foreclosures skyrocketed. The small banks all over the Midwest that had provided the mortgages started failing, and eventually hundreds of them, along with their foreclosed-on farms, were taken over by regulators. The regulators operated the farms marginally while they tried to sell them. So here we had a major Event going on that was crushing the price of a farm. This went on for years.

From his prime location in Omaha, Buffett noticed. He found a four-hundred-acre farm that had a Moat: it was located in a unique area—Nebraska—where the combination of soil type, rainfall, and sunshine created a kind of durable competitive advantage over other farms in the world by providing the conditions for a reliable yield of corn and soybeans. He knew that he could hire professional farm management who would increase the farm's output back to its historical, pre–bank takeover days. He knew that the farming industry was going through an Event: the corn and soybean prices in 1986 were the lowest in multiple decades and would very likely be higher in the future. In other words, he knew that in ten years or so, this farm would likely be more productive and making more money than it was that year and would likely be worth quite a lot more in the future. He calculated the farm's current (not great) revenue, subtracted the expenses of growing and harvesting the crop, including replacing equipment as it got old (maintenance capital expenditures), and got the resulting Owner Earnings. In this case, it was about $28,000 per year, pre–income tax.

"So, what price did he think made sense?" Dad asked me. "You're gonna like this math. He was willing to pay a price that would give him a reasonable return on his money. He simply multiplied the annual Owner Earnings of the farm, $28,000, by ten: $280,000. If he got the farm for that price, the $28,000 of Owner Earnings meant he would get a 10 percent return on his investment in the first year. That's a good, solid return, and he was likely to get a much higher one in the future as Owner Earnings grew with higher crop prices and better production. So he offered $280,000 for the farm. And he bought the farm—not figuratively, literally."

The formula for the Ten Cap then, I reiterated to make sure I had it right, is: Owner Earnings times ten. It tells me the price I can pay that will get me a 10 percent return from my first year of owning it.

About buying that farm, Buffett wrote:

I needed no unusual knowledge or intelligence to conclude that the investment had no downside and potentially had substantial upside. There would, of course, be the occasional bad crop, and prices would sometimes disappoint. But so what? There would be some unusually good years as well, and I would never be under any pressure to sell the property [since there is no debt to force a sale in a bad year]. Now, 28 years later, the farm has tripled its earnings and is worth five times or more what

I paid. I still know nothing about farming and recently made just my second visit to the farm.*

Buffett was saying you should feel confident you can make a rough estimate of future production, and if it will be higher than today, then buy the entire house, farm, company, whatever, for a price that is ten times the current Owner Earnings. You should get a 10 percent return on your investment to start, and if you're right about the business having higher production in the future, you are very unlikely to lose money on that investment.

Dad then described Buffett's second example: the rental building. In the mid-1990s, Buffett found a building in New York that had gone into foreclosure during the savings-and-loan real estate debacle, and no one wanted to buy it because the previous owner had leased its space well below market rates. He did the MATH. If he could buy it for a Ten Cap price, he would get a 10 percent return until he could raise the rent, after which the return would go through the roof. He made the offer at the Ten Cap price and got it; then, after just a couple of years, he was able to re-lease and then refinance the building, taking out 150 percent of his investment and leaving the building revenue to cover the mortgage. Today, that building is worth many millions more than he paid for it.

All right, I thought. I see how this MATH works. This method will determine a sensible price to buy the company, a price that is very likely to be substantially lower than the real value of the company.

Wait a minute—a 10 percent return the first year? That's a great deal. How often do Ten Cap deals come around?

"Yeah," my dad answered wryly, "that is the catch. You could literally wait thirty years to have a Ten Cap rental building in New York or a farm-buying opportunity like Buffett got in Nebraska."

---

* Warren Buffett's Berkshire Hathaway annual letter, 2014.

"What is the point of this pricing method, if Ten Cap deals are so rare?"

"Two points: One, they do come along, and I've done some of them. You may not realize this, but the house we built in Iowa, where you saved my legs, was on a large farm I bought in 1986—at the same time that Buffett bought his farm in Nebraska. And I bought it for the same reason—it was super-cheap. Then I split it up and sold it off in lots that paid for our house."

"I did know that, actually—I figured it out when people started building houses all around us. I didn't know you had gotten a great deal like that, though. But if it's true that the deals don't come along very often, then how am I supposed to ever find deals that I can actually buy at a Ten Cap price?"

"Well, Ten Caps might be hard to find in real estate and farming, but in Buffett's 2013 letter he goes on to tell you why looking for Ten Caps in the stock market is a lot easier than finding them in your local real estate listings." He then turned my attention back to this passage from Buffett's letter (emphasis ours):

There is one major difference between my two small investments and an investment in stocks. Stocks provide you minute-to-minute valuations for your holdings, whereas I have yet to see a quotation for either my farm or the New York real estate. *It should be an enormous advantage for investors in stocks to have those wildly fluctuating valuations placed on their holdings*—and for some investors, it is. After all, if a moody fellow with a farm bordering my property yelled out a price every day to me at which he would either buy my farm or sell me his—and those prices varied widely over short periods of time depending on his mental state—how in the world could I be other than benefited by his erratic behavior? If his daily shout-out was ridiculously low, and I had some spare cash, I would buy his farm. If the number he yelled was absurdly high, I could either sell to him or just go on farming.

Buffett was saying that the stock market moves based on other people's valuations and the resulting price they're willing to pay varies so much—it is "liquid"—because trading is much more susceptible to short-term emotions like fear and greed, and that creates many more buying opportunities based on your own valuation. Just because of that, investors who are not swayed by emotion can capitalize on regular opportunities to buy wonderful businesses at great prices. The Ten Cap price was an anchor for me to know what an exceptional price for a company would be. Deals show up like Nordstrom's semiannual sale—you're never really sure exactly when it's going to happen, but when you get the e-mail, you know it's worth checking out. Companies are not on sale at a great price all the time, but there are regular times when they *are* a deal: when there's a recession every five to ten years, and when there's uncertainty in an industry or company. Whenever an industry is out of favor or an Event happens, prices drop, fear builds, and sometimes really good companies go on sale for a Ten Cap price. This is the advantage Buffett is talking about—the mere fact that there is massive trading going on daily in the stock market makes the prices go up and down much faster and with much more volatility than ever happens in the real estate market.

Dad summarized: "It's the nature of the market itself that makes it possible for us to find Ten Cap deals regularly, instead of once in a lifetime."

The seemingly incomprehensible movements of the market that I had been so worried about, and afraid of from the very beginning, were actually what would create a perfect opportunity for me to buy.

"Apple was a Ten Cap deal for a few weeks recently, for example," my dad cited.

"Did you buy it?"

"Yup. And so did Buffett."

I really got it, in that moment. I got how this whole Rule #1 investing is supposed to work.

There's a certain remove from the insanity of the marketplace that the Rule #1 investor has, and suddenly, I felt it. That sense of remove felt pretty good. I was separated from all the petty speculating and ups and downs that characterize the financial-industrial complex.

I felt kind of above it all.

"The second reason to use the Ten Cap pricing method," my dad went on, "is Owner Earnings."

Owner Earnings

It is not provided on standard financial statements, but it is made up of numbers from those statements, and it is an extremely useful number. It is going to give you the closest approximation to the funds you have available to you, as the owner of the business, without adversely affecting business operations. Owner Earnings is very important for Buffett because he owns a large number of private businesses that produce a huge amount of it. Owner Earnings is allocated by the CEOs of Buffett's companies to maximize the amount the company can send to Buffett to invest. This is where he gets so much cash to allocate each year.

I have found that Owner Earnings is very important to me too, for a couple of reasons. Crucially, it is much harder for bad actors to fudge the numbers in Owner Earnings than it is in net profit because there is nothing projected, expected, or anticipated in them. Owner Earnings is about the cold hard cash that the business is producing right now, not in some foggy future. When we base our buy price on the Owner Earnings, we avoid the problem of precisely figuring out how the business will be doing in ten years. As long as it will be doing better than now and we can get a Ten Cap deal, we're good to go.

I liked that. A lot.

In his 1986 letter to Berkshire shareholders, Buffett said Owner Earnings is *"the relevant item for valuation purposes—both for investors in buying stocks and for managers in buying entire businesses."* Since Buffett thinks this is such an important number, and because my dad feels all the feelings about the perfection of Buffett's formula, I'm going to put his definition down verbatim:

> [Owner Earnings] represent (a) reported earnings plus (b) depreciation, depletion, amortization, and certain other non-cash charges . . . less (c) the average annual amount of capitalized expenditures for plant and equipment, etc. that the business requires to fully maintain its long-term competitive position and its unit volume.*

Excuse me, Warren, while I go scream. Where is Uncle Charlie when I need him?

However, it's not as bad as it sounds. My dad simplified the formula for me and showed me on which lines of the financial statements to find the numbers. The formula in real-life words is on page 194.

On a typical cash flow statement, net income is the very first line, under "cash flows from operating activities." Depreciation and amortization, which is a non-cash expense to account for the declining value of certain assets, like the depreciation of a car, is the next number down.† Still in that same section, there will be a line or a group of lines about net change in accounts receivable (A/R) and accounts payable (A/P) from the previous year. Accounts receivable is when the business is owed money by its customers, and accounts

---

* Warren Buffett, 1986 annual letter to Berkshire Hathaway shareholders, February 27, 1987.

† A non-cash expense is an expense deducted from income that did not require the payment of any cash that period.

payable is when the business owes its suppliers money. As these numbers change year to year, the change either puts money in the owner's pocket or takes it out; that is, it can be positive or negative. Each number indicates only that change.

FORMULA FOR OWNER EARNINGS

Net Income*
+ Depreciation & Amortization
+ Net Change: Accounts Receivable*
+ Net Change: Accounts Payable*
+ Income Tax
+ Maintenance Capital Expenditures**
= Owner Earnings

*Watch out. These numbers could be positive or negative but you always add them.
** Negative number.
Yes, this does say to add a negative number. It's not a typo. It's like that because of accounting standards.

We also add the income tax that we find on the income statement because we are valuing a business the same way we value real estate—with Owner Earnings *before* we pay our income tax bill.

Maintenance capital expenditures is the tough number here, because, maddeningly, companies are not required to separate it out from total capital expenditures (usually called "purchase of property and equipment"). Maintenance capital expenditures represents the money spent on the long-term stuff that has to be replaced just to keep the business going. In the Rental House, it's stuff like the roof shingles and HVAC every fifteen years, the appliances every seven years, and exterior painting every five years. In a business with well-kept financial statements, the number for maintenance capital expenditures will be described in the "cash flows from investing activities" notes to the cash flow statement. However, since many companies do not break out maintenance capital expenditures in their notes, we have to understand the business well enough to estimate the average annual cost.

"I look for notes that describe the capital expenditures and purchase of property and equipment expenditures for growth—things like new restaurants or a new production facility—and separate those amounts out," my dad explained. "We're just focused on what it costs in cash to keep things running. Worst case, I use the full purchase of property and equipment number, and take note that it is a larger number than it should be and that I may not understand this company as well as I should."

I tested Owner Earnings out on the Rental House, which, like the Lemonade Stand, is an example my dad and I invented, because it is easy to understand. The Rental House is a house bought with cash—there is no mortgage on it—for the purpose of renting it out.

Owner Earnings	The Rental House
Net Income	$28,000
(plus) Depreciation and Amortization	N/A (Don't have any)
(plus) Net Change: Accounts Receivable	N/A (Don't have any)
(plus) Net Change: Accounts Payable	N/A (Don't have any)
(plus) Income Tax	N/A (Didn't pay it yet)
(plus) Maintenance Capital Expenditures	($4,000)*
OWNER EARNINGS	$24,000

* If a number is in parentheses, it is a negative number from the financial statements. Parentheses are used exactly like having a minus sign, but they are easier to see. It is correct to add the negative number to reduce the amount of Owner Earnings by that amount.

Owner Earnings from the Rental House is easy to calculate because we're using cash accounting. I subtract all the normal expenses of a landlord from the rental income to get net income and then subtract the average annual cost to replace the major stuff. What's left over is Owner Earnings in my pocket to pay off student loans or buy more real estate.

Now let's do this for the Lemonade Stand. The only maintenance capital expenditures for this company is replacing the juicers every three years. In the following table, I note where I found each number in the Lemonade Stand financial statements in the appendix.

Owner Earnings	Lemonade Stand	Where to Find Numbers
Net Income	$2,000	Income Statement or Cash Flow Statement
(plus) Depreciation and Amortization	$1,000	Cash Flow Statement
(plus) Net Change: Accounts Receivable	($300)	Cash Flow Statement
(plus) Net Change: Accounts Payable	$100	Cash Flow Statement
(plus) Income Tax	$500	Income Statement
(plus) Maintenance Capital Expenditures	($500)	Cash Flow Statement Notes
OWNER EARNINGS	$2,800	

Once you know which numbers to use and where to find them, the calculation of Owner Earnings is simple. Just look them up on the Lemonade Stand financials and plug them into the formula.

Owner Earnings are the owner's money, pre-tax, which the owner can spend on the company to build the business, buy other companies, distribute to herself (in a public company, in the form of a dividend), buy out partners or shareholders, or leave in the company as a nest egg. If I owned the entire Rental House or the entire Lemonade Stand, I would get to decide what to do with the Owner Earnings. If I shared a company with someone else, we would decide together. If I owned a small part of a company, I would leave it up to management to decide what to do with the Owner Earnings. That's what happens in public companies, as we learned in chapter three— the shareholders, as the owners of the company, technically own the Owner Earnings; but shareholders, by voting for the board of directors, appoint management to run the company on their behalf; the board then decides, on the shareholders' behalf, what to do with the Owner Earnings at the end of the year. We'll spend an entire chapter on how Owner Earnings are typically used by public companies; for now, what we need to know is that the concept that the owners get the Owner Earnings is the same for every company, real estate property, or farm, whether it's public or private, and regardless of how much of the company an owner owns.

My dad treated every company as though he were going to buy 100 percent of it—even if he wasn't—because it gave him simplicity and clarity of thought. He had been teaching me to think of a public company as if I would buy the whole thing, and pricing was no different. Price the whole company, then decide later how much of it you want to buy. This method worked for me and brought me to the point of Owner Earnings—pricing the business. That math I could handle.

I took the Owner Earnings for the Rental House and the Lemonade Stand, and multiplied each of them by ten. The Lemonade Stand was a steal at $28,000 and the Rental House was a bargain at $240,000. Got it. Nuno had been right about internalizing the logic of the formula. Once I understood the logic of it, I could summon it at will.

Lemonade Stand: $2,800 × 10 = $28,000
Rental House: $24,000 × 10 = $240,000

Once I got into doing the work of calculating Owner Earnings and using them in pricing a business—any business, including real estate deals—I understood why the great investors like Warren and Charlie do the work of calculating these numbers themselves.

I closed the video call with my dad and sighed, happily, with deep relief.

I flew back home to Boulder a few days later. It was deliciously comforting to walk into my home, in my own beautiful space, with my investing office laid out on the dining table. It was Sunday, and it was blistering hot. I splurged on an iced coffee from the expensive coffee shop down my street before coming back to sit at my investing office. The artisanal coffee definitely helped me steel my brain for what was to come—practicing pricing all by my lonesome.

I tried figuring out Owner Earnings for Whole Foods. This was the test, I realized, to know if I had studied the company well enough so that, when I read the footnotes to the financial statements, I could confidently come up with my maintenance capital expenditures numbers. If it was too hard, that meant I didn't understand the company well enough; in that case, it would be officially Too Hard, and it would be time to move on to the next one. Here are the relevant numbers from Whole Foods' 2015 financial statements. (2015 was the most recent 10-K when I researched Whole Foods.)

Owner Earnings	Whole Foods	Where to Find Numbers
Net Income	$536,000,000	2015 Cash Flow Statement Line 2
(plus) Depreciation and Amortization	$439,000,000	2015 Cash Flow Statement Line 4
(plus) Net Change: Accounts Receivable	($21,000,000)	2015 Cash Flow Statement Line 14
(plus) Net Change: Accounts Payable	$20,000,000	2015 Cash Flow Statement Line 17
(plus) Income Tax	$342,000,000	2015 Income Statement Line 10
(plus) Maintenance Capital Expenditures	($335,000,000)	2015 Cash Flow Statement Line 24: "Other property and equipment expenditures"
OWNER EARNINGS	$981,000,000	

Once I had the formula from Dad, finding the right numbers was easy. They were right there. To find maintenance capital expenditures, all I had to do was to search for "capital expenditures" in the Whole Foods 10-K, and I found what I was looking for in an obscure note called "Non-GAAP measures" on page 22 and on the cash flow statement. It took four clicks and less than thirty seconds. And that was the hard part.

I plugged the numbers in just as I found them on the cash flow statement and income statement, positive or negative, and then did the addition and got $981 million for the 2015 Whole Foods Owner Earnings.

Once I knew the Owner Earnings, the Ten Cap was simple. I multiplied the Owner Earnings by ten to get the price to pay. Ten times $981 million is $9,810 million, or $9.8 billion. That's my buy price for the entire business.

$$\$981,000,000 \times 10 = \$9,810,000,000$$

Whooohoooo. I can do this!

As my concern that I would never learn to price a company subsided, my Missions came to the front of my mind. I wanted so badly to vote with my money, but I wouldn't do so blindly. If I voted with my money for a poorly run company, my investing funds would eventually disappear and I'd be stuck without any votes (or retirement) left. The struggle I had just gone through to learn Owner Earnings would get me to a good price, for a wonderful company, with a worthy Mission.

I dialed my dad and exultantly yelled my results into the phone. I understood this pricing language, which out of the entire language of investing was the most difficult for me to wrap my mind around. He laughed happily.

Then he upped the ante. "With the Ten Cap method we assumed the Owner Earnings would at least stay the same each year and give us a minimum 10 percent return pre-tax, a ten capitalization rate. It keeps the math simple for finding a good price to pay. But, we only buy businesses we understand well, with great Moats and management, that—crucially—are going to grow."

Oh dear. I saw where he was going with this. Growth. My friend the Windage Growth Rate was back.

While we can put a price on a great company with the Ten Cap, there are two limitations to that method. The first is just that Buffett's definition of Owner Earnings is, obviously, pretty ambiguous in spots and determining the appropriate number for maintenance capital expenditures may, for many companies, be only an educated guess. So good investors may come up with slightly different Ten Cap numbers.

The second limitation is that the Ten Cap doesn't take growth into account. Buffett would probably argue that that's a strength, but using the Ten Cap, two businesses with the same Owner Earnings, whether they are growing faster or slower than each other, would be priced exactly the same. Growth wouldn't matter at all. But we know that, all else being equal, a company that is growing its cash faster will produce more cash in the future and is therefore worth more today. The Ten Cap, in its conservative glory, does not take that into consideration.

But, the Payback Time pricing method does.

Pricing Method #2: Payback Time

The Payback Time method is used by investors to put a price on a company that they're not going to sell for a long time. What they want is a fast return on their investment so their risk of losing money disappears, rather like a gambler taking his money off the table and playing with house money. What my dad calls the Payback Time is just what it sounds like—the number of years it takes to get your whole purchase price back. In this pricing method, the purchase price comes back to the buyer from another non-GAAP view of cash flow called free cash flow. We'll explain soon, but first, the Payback Time formula:

Free cash flow, grown by the compounded Windage Growth Rate for eight years

It's clearer with an example. I practiced again. This time, the Rental House.

The Rental House is in a nice spot, probably by the beach somewhere, where more and more people want to live. Rents typically go up in growing towns 3 to 4 percent per year, while my expenses would roughly stay the same. I wanted to be conservative, so I made its Windage Growth Rate 3 percent per year. I multiplied each year's free cash flow by 100 percent plus the Windage Growth Rate, going out eight years, and found the Eight-Year Payback Time.

The Rental House's Payback Time

Year	Free Cash Flow	Growth Rate	Expected Growth in Free Cash Flow to Be Applied to Next Year	Cumulative Free Cash Flow and Payback Time Buy Price
0 (the year I bought it)	$24,000	3%	$720	---
1	$24,720	3%	$742	$24,720
2	$25,462	3%	$764	$50,182
3	$26,225	3%	$787	$76,407
4	$27,012	3%	$810	$103,419
5	$27,823	3%	$835	$131,242
6	$28,657	3%	$860	$159,899
7	$29,517	3%	$886	$189,416
8	$30,402	3%	$912	$219,819 Eight-Year Payback Time Buy Price

The price I can pay for the Rental House is $219,819 and, if it grows as expected at 3 percent per year, I will have all my money off the table in eight years.

Why is eight years the magic number? Uncle Charlie thinks a fair price is about half of what the same company would sell for as a public company, and public companies sell for about twelve to twenty years of free cash flow, about sixteen years on average. Half of sixteen is eight.

The difference between public-company price and private-company price is liquidity—a measure of how easy it is to sell ownership of a company. It can be hard to sell off a piece of a private company. That investment is "illiquid." Public companies, by definition, are trading on a stock exchange and are much more "liquid" because of the high volume of trading, the regulation of the stock exchange, and the largely reliable financial reporting enforced by the government. Fund managers don't want to own a public company's stock for very long. Their need to trade quickly means liquidity is extremely important to them; they have to be able to sell off a big chunk of stock, fast, and they are willing to pay quite a lot more for that. About double, in fact.

Warren and Charlie don't need liquidity, though, and aren't willing to pay up to get it. A Payback Time of eight years, or less, is a sensible price for a wonderful private company, and I shouldn't pay more than that for a public company if I want to invest like Warren Buffett, Charlie Munger, and my dad.

I would have already figured out the Windage Growth Rate for a given company earlier in my company research. "This is where the work you did on understanding the business, the Moat, and the management comes in," my dad explained. "If the business has a big Moat, with a durable competitive advantage that protects the free cash flow from getting cut down by fierce price competition or loss of customers to some new product, then by definition the future should look quite a lot like the past. And if the business is run by talented, honest management, then they probably won't screw up the Moat.

From your understanding of the business, you're going to estimate how much it will grow its free cash out for eight years. If I can theoretically get my money back from free cash flow in eight years, that's a pretty good deal for a wonderful business."

The key was that I choose businesses that are easy to understand, skip the ones that are Too Hard, and apply my Mission, Moat, and management analysis to this price calculation. It was really nice to connect back to the non-math parts of this practice, especially when they could support my understanding of the mathy bits.

Now on to free cash flow.[*]

"Free cash flow has certain advantages," Dad started. "There is no subjectivity in determining the free cash flow numbers, some companies include it in the notes to their cash flow statements, it has growth capital expenditures baked in, and stock research websites show it so you can check your number against theirs."

Well, that sounded fantastic.

Compared with Owner Earnings, free cash flow is crazy simple. Here is the formula:

FORMULA FOR FREE CASH FLOW

Net Cash Provided by Operating Activities
+ Purchase of Property and Equipment (*a negative number*)
+ Any Other Capital Expenditures for Maintenance and Growth (*also negative numbers*)
= Free Cash Flow

---

[*] Dad wrote an entire book about the concept of Payback Time that became his second number-one *New York Times* bestseller. In that book, he used net earnings in the Payback Time calculation because it was more easily available. But now we are using free cash flow instead because it is more accurate.

About one-third of the way down on the cash flow statements is a bold line called "net cash provided by operating activities." Below that is the section titled "cash flows from investing activities," and in that section is usually a "purchase of property, equipment" line. On almost all cash flow statements this number includes *all* the capital expenditures, maintenance, and growth. Occasionally, as with Whole Foods as we will see later, there are two lines, one for growth capital expenditures and one for all the rest of the capital expenditures, which we can assume is the maintenance capital expenditures. The good news is that I will have already read the notes to the cash flow statement when calculating the Owner Earnings, so this calculation simply builds on that work. Remember, these capital expenditures numbers are negative, so we add them as negatives to the "net cash provided by operating activities" number. The result is called free cash flow.

Back to that paragon of capitalist excellence, the Lemonade Stand. Here is its free cash flow calculation:

The Lemonade Stand's Free Cash Flow

Net Cash Provided by Operating Activities	$2,800
(plus) Purchase of Property and Equipment and Other Capital Expenditures	($1,300)
FREE CASH FLOW	$1,500

Since we last checked, the Lemonade Stand has been investing in its growth: it bought new lemon-squeezing equipment and opened a second stand across town, and the second location was doing even better than the first. There's always money in the Lemonade Stand. Its free cash flow grew by 16 percent for each of the last two years, and I confidently project that that growth rate will continue because the Lemonade Stand's Brand Moat is killer. Exclusive street corners and just the right amount of tartness in the lemonade—no one can beat it. A 16 percent Windage Growth Rate is defensible.

So, starting with the free cash flow of $1,500, I ran my numbers, year by year, to find how much cumulative free cash flow the Lemonade Stand will give me in eight years: the Eight-Year Payback Time. I multiplied $1,500 by 16 percent for each year, cumulatively going forward for eight years.

The Lemonade Stand's Payback Time

	Year	Free Cash Flow	Growth Rate	Expected Growth in Free Cash Flow for Next Year	Cumulative Free Cash Flow During My Investment	Payback Time Buy Price
	0	$1,500	16%	$240		
My Investment Period	1	$1,740	16%	$278	$1,740	= My 1yr - Payback Time Price
	2	$2,018	16%	$323	$3,758	= My 2yr - Payback Time Price
	3	$2,341	16%	$375	$6,100	= My 3yr - Payback Time Price
	4	$2,716	16%	$435	$8,816	= My 4yr - Payback Time Price
	5	$3,151	16%	$504	$11,966	= My 5yr - Payback Time Price
	6	$3,655	16%	$585	$15,621	= My 6yr - Payback Time Price
	7	$4,239	16%	$678	$19,860	= My 7yr - Payback Time Price
	8	$4,918	16%	$787	$24,778	= My 8yr - Payback Time Price

The Payback Time price I could pay for the Lemonade Stand was $24,778.

Jeez Louise, 16 percent per year really grows quickly. That's also a nice illustration of the power of compounding.

For the Lemonade Stand, I had the Ten Cap price of $28,000 and the Eight-Year Payback Time price of $24,778. I saw what my dad was talking about in the beginning when he described the three methods of pricing: with these multiple prices, each a data point, I was getting a good sense of the range from which I could choose what my buy price would be.

I then practiced the Ten Cap and the Payback Time on the real thing. A real company. Whole Foods.

Whole Foods' 2015 Free Cash Flow

Net Cash Provided by Operating Activities	$1,129,000,000
(plus) Development Cost of New Locations	($516,000,000)
(plus) Other Property and Equipment Expenditures	($335,000,000)
FREE CASH FLOW	$278,000,000

Note: Whole Foods is one of the few companies that calculates free cash flow in their financial statements. See page 22 of their 2015 10-K.

Whole Foods' Eight-Year Payback Time buy price: after looking at its growth rates, which were a bit all over the place, I checked analysts' projections and saw they were around 14 percent. I went with it, grew the $278 million of free cash for eight years by 1.14, and came up with an Eight-Year Payback Time price of $4.2 billion. (See "Whole Foods' Payback Time" in the appendix.)

The Ten Cap for Whole Foods was $9.81 billion. The Eight-Year Payback Time price was roughly $4.2 billion—lower than the Ten Cap because of the major expenditures for new locations. With this huge difference, how would I decide?

"Remember our three points of data that will keep you safe?" my dad asked on our Investing Practice call. "Time for the third: Margin of Safety."

The Margin of Safety would value the entire company, not only put a price on it as the first two methods had done. I wanted to learn it, but I still had not touched valuation since putting down that giant valuation tome Nuno had given me. The valuation of an entire company was a beast of a different color, and remembering that, I felt a bit shaky in my solar plexus. Complexity around math was where my dad and I sometimes had, shall we say, communication issues. At the same time as the shakes, though, a new feeling of confidence emerged from somewhere deep, and it soothed me. We had made it through two methods of pricing. I smiled to myself as that sank in. Only one method to go.

JULY PRACTICE: Make practicing pricing as easy on yourself as possible: choose three companies you like and calculate the Ten Cap price and Payback Time price for each one. Reward yourself by bragging to someone who will appreciate it that you just used Buffett's special calculation of Owner Earnings to price a company.

CHAPTER 8

Charlie's Fourth Principle: Value

| August

This Month

▶ Margin of Safety Valuation Method
- Earnings Per Share
- Windage Growth Rate
- Windage P/E Ratio
- Minimum Acceptable Rate of Return (MARR)

THE AIR CONDITIONER IN MY HOUSE WAS TRYING VALIANTLY TO FIGHT the heat, blowing without a break, but even it wasn't quite up to the challenge posed by August in Boulder. I was tired of the heat, tired of work, tired of all the back and forth travel, and I was really tired of missing Nuno when we were forced to be apart. It felt like a chunk was ripped out of my chest, then Band-Aided back in when we were together, then ripped right out again when one of us got on the inevitable airplane. And I was flying, again, to Zurich for a ridiculously short weekend. It was getting silly.

Worst of all, it was the worst month of Investing Practice with the worst MATH. I wasn't afraid of it anymore, but I was tired. I wanted to skip this month of the worst part of my practice. Even putting my hot laptop on my legs was annoying.

I rolled my eyes at myself.

Just get on with it, I thought. I would have paid money to avoid it, but when you are waiting to see if someone shows up for you, you have to show up for yourself. That's just how it works. I wanted to be that successful investor self that I could see in my mind's eye, and I knew now that I could do it after probing the dark fog of a few months earlier. I had found companies with Missions I adored. I had faced my preconceptions around money. I had faced pricing. Now, learning this month's math was required, I reminded myself. Get up and get on with it. It's math. It's not brain surgery.

I *wanted* to learn how to value the whole business, I told myself, très convincingly.

I noticed, suddenly, that the way I was thinking about my Investing Practice had changed. It was no longer something terrifying and unknown and filled with dire implications; rather, this month's practice was simply something to be learned and internalized, by doing the work. I did not feel the Enclosed Concrete Stairwell feeling at all. It was a little bit less of MATH and a little more of . . . math. Plain old math.

I smiled to myself. Yes, there was some fluttering in my chest when I thought about the math. But I also felt confident that I would learn it. That investor chick in my mind would know the math, obviously, and my job was to become her.

I wanted to learn how to value an entire business. I really did.

My dad and I jumped on our video call in the evening Zurich time, midday Atlanta time.

"I now have two ways to put a price on the business but I still don't know how to find the real value of the business." I opened the floor. "Lay it on me. How do you value a whole company?"

"Remember Charlie's fourth principle?"

"A price that makes sense."

"You might have missed that he also used the words 'Margin of Safety.' Buffett says that those are the three most important words in investing. We only buy when the price gives us a Margin of Safety. The Margin of Safety is a price below the company's value that will protect us from most mistakes. Not all. But most."

A Margin of Safety is key, just in case I got my price analysis wrong. The business lawyer in me was hyperaware that public companies may have a lot going on that little-guy investors like me don't know about. People make mistakes. People do bad stuff. People lie— especially when there is big money and a good reputation at stake. Executives can have motives that are different from the motives and aims of public shareholders. No one can be completely certain about any company's future production. An inherent risk of investing is the information asymmetry between a company and its investors.

"All investors can do is try to invest in businesses we understand. If you're as comfortable with the business as you are with your condo investment and buy at a price with a Margin of Safety, you'll be okay."

"Do the Ten Cap and Payback Time have a Margin of Safety?"

"That Margin of Safety is built into both. The Ten Cap requires a return that is very high. That means the buy price must be very low and therefore has a big Margin of Safety. The Payback Time price gets us our money back in eight years, roughly half of what the same business would sell for if it was public and therefore about a 50 percent Margin of Safety."

So, the Ten Cap and Payback Time were pricing methods with a Margin of Safety built in. Now I would learn a *valuation* method with a Margin of Safety built in.

A NOTE ABOUT PER-SHARE NUMBERS

WHOLE-COMPANY NUMBERS ARE DIFFERENT FROM PER-SHARE NUMBERS. I still treat the Margin of Safety method as though I'm buying the whole company. However, as we saw with Whole Foods, public company numbers are huge—often in the billions—which makes the math unwieldy. To alleviate that problem for public companies, and because in practical reality potential investors (not us!) generally only care about the shares they are buying, the financial-industrial complex divides the whole-company numbers into *per-share numbers*. This is helpful, but be aware always of whether you're using per-share numbers or whole-company numbers. Either one is totally fine, as long as you're consistent within your formula. Financial people often switch back and forth between whole-company numbers and per-share numbers, which is really irritating, and it can be really confusing. I try to always make sure I know which one I am working with. Going forward, for all the examples in this Margin of Safety method, I will use per-share numbers.

Pricing Method #3: Margin of Safety

"We've used Owner Earnings and free cash flow, and now in the third pricing method, we're switching to earnings. The Margin of Safety (MOS) method calculates what I'd pay today to get years of future earnings and my risk of actually getting the money in the future. Let's start to understand the relationship between time and risk by thinking about what it's worth to you to put your investing money to work. The most obvious option is to put it somewhere really safe. What's the safest place you can think of?" Dad asked.

"Under my bed?"

"It could get stolen or burn up. Someplace safer than that."

"In the bank."

"Okay, pretty safe. But there is an even safer place. The safest place it can go is into a U.S. government treasury bond."

"Oh yeah. T-bills! That was my hoarding plan."

Dad laughed. "Right, and they represent the risk-free rate of return. If we're putting our money to work somewhere else, which is not risk-free—in the Lemonade Stand, for example—we need to be paid more than the risk-free rate—or else you might as well keep your money and enjoy using it instead of tying it up in an investment."

"So how can I figure out how much I need to get so that making the investment is worthwhile?"

"There is a clever way to figure this out."

Of course there is.

"I'm going to teach you a simplified version of what the financial industry calls Discounted Cash Flow Analysis," my dad started.

That giant valuation book Nuno gave me? It was mostly about Discounted Cash Flow Analysis. I was not thrilled.

The biggest problem with this method of pricing is figuring out the amount I'd invest today for money I'm going to get in the future. It would be silly for me to invest $100 today to get back the exact same amount in ten years, right? My nemesis, inflation, had destroyed that genius hoarding idea: with it, that $100 won't buy as much in ten years. Plus, there is the risk that I won't get paid back at all. To handle the declining buying power of my money and the risk that I won't get it back, I have to invest less than $100 today to get $100 in ten years. The question is: By how much? That's what the Margin of Safety valuation tells me. And yes, it is indeed a simplified version of Discounted Cash Flow Analysis—which I drop into casual conversation as much as possible to sound fancy.

We need to use readily available mainstream numbers for this pricing method so we can compare our results with how the rest of the world values the company, since we'll be buying from others and selling to them. The important thing here is: (1) know that we're making a change from Owner Earnings or free cash flow to earnings, (2) we're making a change from pricing a company as a private company to valuing a company as a public company (which, if you remember, typically doubles the price), and (3) therefore, our results may be a bit different from the Payback Time and Ten Cap methods.

"The easiest way to think about it," Dad started, "is to figure out the rate of return you need to get each year on your money to make the risk worthwhile. Over many years, I've found a good, solid rate of return for stocks is 15 percent per year. In other words, a 15 percent compounded return rewards me well for doing the work and taking the risk."

Dad calls this 15 percent return his Minimum Acceptable Rate of Return, or MARR. We use the MARR to figure out how much to invest today to get some higher amount in ten years. The higher I set the MARR, the lower my investment will be. Fifteen percent is high enough for the risk of investing but low enough to find reasonable value. I went with it. I got my MOS valuation by estimating what I expect to sell the company for in ten years, then worked backward using a 15 percent MARR and basic algebra to arrive at the price I'm willing to pay.

Summary of Margin of Safety Method

Purpose:	Calculate what I expect to sell the company for down the line in ten years, then work backward using basic algebra to arrive at the price I'm willing to pay.
Required Numbers:	Earnings Per Share (EPS) Windage Growth Rate Price-to-Earnings (P/E) Ratio Minimum Acceptable Rate of Return (MARR)

New numbers, again. These MOS numbers, though, are easily obtained, and having been through the crucible of deciphering and calculating Owner Earnings and free cash flow, I learned these numbers quickly. They don't require reading footnotes on the financial statements! The MOS numbers were like a vacation.

Here is how to prep them:

Numbers Needed to Calculate Margin of Safety Price

Number	Definition	How to Find It	Example: The Lemonade Stand
Earnings Per Share (EPS):	Earnings Per Share is the whole-company earnings number divided by the number of shares outstanding.	Provided on the income statement	The Lemonade Stand, as a company, has $2,000 of earnings per year, and has 100 shares, so its Earnings Per Share is $20. $2,000 / 100 = $20 per share.
Windage Growth Rate:	The growth rate expected for the company, chosen by reviewing the Big Four Growth Rates and understanding the business well enough to be comfortably certain of the future.	We know this one already—yay for having to decide it way back when we were working on Moat! Doesn't that seem like a simpler time, when taking an educated guess at a growth rate was intimidating? *A growth rate!* We've come a long way, baby.	The Lemonade Stand's Windage Growth Rate is 16%.
Windage Price-to-Earnings (P/E) Ratio:	Price divided by earnings; or, the ratio of how many times the earnings go into the price. Like the Shiller P/E, which indicates if the whole market is under- or overpriced, the P/E ratio of a single company describes the relationship between the price and the earnings of the company. Because it is a ratio, it will be the same number regardless of whether it uses whole-company numbers or per-share numbers—as long as they're consistent.	Use the lowest of these two options: 1. Multiply two times the Windage Growth Rate number (lose the percent symbol—this is a straight number) 2. The historical highest P/E of that company of the last ten years (readily available online)	1. $16 \times 2 = 32$ 2. The P/E of the Lemonade Stand in the past has been 19, 22, and 20. Therefore, the highest historical P/E was 22. Windage P/E: The lowest of those two options is 22.
Minimum Acceptable Rate of Return (MARR):	How much annual return we require for every year our money is tied up in this investment	It's always 15%.	It's always 15%, even for the Lemonade Stand.

Margin of Safety Formula

	Plain English Version	MATH Version
Step One	First, work forward in time ten years. What should the price of this company reasonably be in ten years? We know that the price will be a multiple of the Earnings Per Share, so let's find out what the Earnings Per Share will be in ten years. Grow the Earnings Per Share by the Windage Growth Rate each year (getting the Future EPS for that year) for ten years = Future 10-Year Earnings Per Share	EPS × (1 + Windage Growth Rate) [repeated ten times] = Future 10-Year Earnings Per Share Can be done manually year-by-year or on a spreadsheet
Step Two	Multiply the Future 10-Year Earnings Per Share by the Windage P/E = Future 10-Year Share Price. Now I know what the price of one share will be in ten years.	Future 10-Year Earnings Per Share (multiplied by) the Windage P/E = Future 10-Year Share Price Remember, the Windage P/E is the lower of 2X the Windage Growth Rate or the high historical P/E
Step Three	Now, work backward to find out what the price should be today (not what it is actually selling for on the market—we'll check that later), with a 15% return each year. To find out what the price should be today, with a 15% return each year, use this formula: Future 10-Year Share Price / (1.15)^{YEARS} = Sticker Price. With a 15% MARR, the bottom portion of that formula with the numbers plugged in is 1.15 to the number of years. With ten years, that makes it 1.15 to the 10th power, which equals 4. Always. It always equals 4. So as long as we are using a ten-year period and 15%, my bottom number is 4. That's what a reasonable price for this company is today. Yay! But wait, what about Charlie's Margin of Safety?	Future 10-Year Share Price / (1.15)^{YEARS} = Sticker Price Or: Future 10-Year Share Price / 4
Step Four	The Margin of Safety is half the Sticker Price. Sticker Price / 2 = Margin of Safety buy price	Sticker Price / 2 = Margin of Safety buy price

There's a long-standing relationship between the growth rate of a company and its price-to-earnings ratio, and they usually end up being about double in public companies. My dad has, through experience, found that twice the Windage Growth Rate is an accurate and easy stand-in for the P/E ratio.

So that is the Margin of Safety Formula, step by step, for us manual mathematicians. My dad has also laid out his Excel process on the next page.

Once I broke it down into steps, bringing the math forward in time and then back in time to today, I had a logical picture that made sense. That's what Nuno meant when he told me he doesn't remember equations or formulas. I wouldn't remember this one, exactly, but I could summon it by thinking about the process.

I ran it through the Lemonade Stand:

Margin of Safety Method Example: The Lemonade Stand

Numbers Recap:	
Earnings Per Share (EPS):	$20
Windage Growth Rate:	16%
Windage Price-to-Earnings (P/E) Ratio:	22
Minimum Acceptable Rate of Return (MARR):	15%
Formula:	
Step One: EPS × (1 + Windage Growth Rate) *[repeated ten times]* = Future 10-Year EPS	Future 10-Year EPS = $88.23
Step Two: Future 10-Year Earnings Per Share (multiplied by) the Windage P/E = Future 10-Year Share Price	$88.23 × 22 = $1,941.06
Step Three: Future 10-Year Share Price / $(1.15)^{YEARS}$ = /4	$1,941.06 / 4 = $485.27
Step Four: Sticker Price / 2 = Margin of Safety Buy Price	$485.27 / 2 = $242.64

For a comprehensive view of the valuation examples, look in the appendix.

A NOTE FROM PHIL

It is easy to calculate the MOS for the Lemonade Stand using Excel. The equations are called "present value" and "future value," and in Excel it is =PV() and =FV(). When you type that in, Excel presents the formula and it tells you what to put in it. First, we grow the current earnings for ten years with the Excel formula =FV(): use the Windage Growth Rate, the number of years, and the EPS.

> =FV(16%,10,,-20)
> FV(rate, nper, pmt, [pv], [type])

(Note that we are not using the "pmt" part of the formula, so to skip that part, just type another comma. Also notice that I put a minus sign in front of the $20 for "pv." Excel needs that sign to know that the $20 is going into the business in order to tell us what earnings come out of it in ten years.)

The answer we get is $88.23. That is the EPS that the company should be making ten years from now if our estimate for growth is correct.

Now we can figure out what the business should be worth ten years from now. Just multiply the P/E ratio (22) times the future EPS ($88.23). We get $1,941.06. Excel calls that "future value"—how much per share the business should sell for if it earns $88.23 in that tenth year and is still likely to grow at 16 percent per year.

Now we can decide what someone would reasonably pay for the business today. It looks like this: = PV():

> =PV(15%,10,,-1941.06)
> PV(rate, nper, pmt, [fv], [type])

The "rate" is the MARR, the "nper" is the number of years back to today, skip the "pmt," and the "fv" is the future value of the business in ten years (don't forget to put in the minus sign). Hit "return." The value of the business today is $479.79 per share, a bit different than the manual calculations due to Excel's formula but close enough. Then, divide by two to get the Margin of Safety buy price: $239.90

And, crazily, I totally got it. Four steps and done. Four! I could do four.

For the Lemonade Stand, which has one hundred shares, the Ten Cap gave me a buy price of $200 per share, the Eight-Year Payback Time buy price is $247, and the MOS calculation put the sticker price at roughly $480 and the MOS price at about $240. Of course, the Lemonade Stand was not for sale: business was too good!

"Dad," I announced. "I am done. I can do the three valuations. This is completely amazing. Thank you, Dad. I didn't think this moment would happen."

He laughed and said, "I knew you could do it."

I side-eyed that one. *Had he really?*

"Yeah," he emphasized. "I absolutely knew that you could do it. You've learned so much, and you've shown me a better way to do pricing and valuation. The only option was to find a way through it together."

"Together," I repeated.

"Yup, together. No question. It's downhill from here."

We said our goodbyes. I don't think someone who finds this stuff easy can truly empathize with how difficult it can be, but that was okay with me. It was a feeling that I've had rarely in my life: I had conquered what seemed unconquerable. I felt powerful.

Charlie would probably be completely dismissive of my trials, but

I had managed to complete a formula for valuation, which I had partly figured out on my own, and I sent him a silent thank-you.

And I thanked myself.

I had had no thought of what it would be like to be successful at this, and I suppose I would have liked to have done a backflip or danced around the house. Instead, I sat in my desk chair and grinned. I just sat there and grinned. I grinned until my eyes were tiny and I could barely see out of them, and then I laughed out loud, alone, like a crazy person. All this joy from conquering a little old valuation formula. And then I realized it was late and I should go to bed, and I had a great night of sleep. The sleep of the mathematician. I highly recommend it.

In the morning, I practiced on Whole Foods. It was easier than I had expected. My calculations are on page 222.

For Whole Foods, I had calculated whole-company prices using the Ten Cap and Payback Time methods. To compare the per-share result in the MOS method, I had to divide those whole-company prices by the number of shares Whole Foods had outstanding.

The number of shares is another Windage number, unfortunately, because the number changes all the time. The 10-K showed Whole Foods share numbers had been dropping: 360 million shares, then 349 million, then the introductory note in the 10-K said 341 million. I searched online, and my dad's website and Yahoo Finance agreed, so I went with 341 million shares. Using that Windage number, I got the following prices for Whole Foods:

Ten Cap (total $9.82 billion): about $29 per share

Eight-Year Payback Time (total $4.2 billion): about $13 per share

Margin of Safety: about $19 per share

I purposely rounded my numbers to remind me that this was not a precise science—there was a lot of Windage, and what I had was a range from which to decide what price made sense.

That was all I could take. I would decide later how those prices shook out. I was going to call it a day on my practice and buy myself a chocolate cupcake, I decided. It was so painful to read financial statements that I had to bribe myself with a treat afterward.

Then I remembered that I was in Switzerland and cupcakes didn't commonly exist there. Still, in that moment, no matter. I was going to celebrate my achievement. I wandered into the kitchen and opened the fridge and saw champagne. Yes. I deserved champagne—equation champagne! I looked at the bottle. Fine, it was prosecco. I deserved prosecco! "Noons!" I yelled. "I'm opening the prosecco!"

"It's eleven A.M.!" he yelled back.

It was already popped open. Done-With-Financial-Statements bubbly. Nectar of the gods.

After about half a bottle, I was feeling pretty good about myself, so I started bragging to Nuno about my mad math skills. "And then, I just logically—as you suggested!—figured out how the Earnings Per Share relates to the future share price, and I can tell you all about it." I started explaining the three valuation methods to him, because if I could help someone else, I would. I was giving back, just like Oprah tells me to do. But each of my explanations broke down about halfway through, trailing off into confusion and mixed-up numbers. I was going to have to practice more to really ingrain the equations into my head, I realized. At that thought, I drank more prosecco. Then I fell asleep.

Napping. I highly recommend it. It's another good self-bribe— zero calories and zero dollars.

After I woke up, I mentally reviewed my Investing Practice status. I had learned three valuation methods. Suddenly, like a brick wall had landed in front of me, I mentally stopped short. Each method had given me dramatically different results.

I called my dad in a hungover semipanic. How would I decide what price made sense?

"Yup," he proclaimed, "you will sometimes get dramatically different results from those three methods, because they're all measuring

Margin of Safety Method: Whole Foods

Numbers Needed	
2015 Earnings Per Share (EPS):	$1.48
Windage Growth Rate:	1. Historical growth rates during 2009–2015 averaged 16.7%. 2. Analyst average five-year growth estimate: 14%. 3. The lower of 16.70% and 14% is 14%. Therefore, the Windage Growth Rate is 14%.
Windage Price-to-Earnings (P/E) Ratio:	1. 14 × 2 = 28 2. Whole Foods had a range of P/E ratios of 10–46 over the last ten years. The high was 46. Windage P/E: The lower of 28 or 46 is 28. Therefore, the Windage P/E is 28.
Minimum Acceptable Rate of Return (MARR):	15%, because it's always 15%.

Formula:

Step One: EPS × (1 + Windage Growth Rate) *[repeated ten times]* = Future 10-Year EPS	Future 10-Year EPS = $5.49

Year	Future-EPS	1+Windage Growth Rate
0	$1.48	1.14
1	$1.69	1.14
2	$1.92	1.14
3	$2.19	1.14
4	$2.50	1.14
5	$2.85	1.14
6	$3.25	1.14
7	$3.70	1.14
8	$4.22	1.14
9	$4.81	1.14
10	$5.49	

Step Two: Future 10-Year Earnings Per Share (multiplied by) the Windage P/E = Future 10-Year Share Price	$5.49 × 28 = $153.72
Step Three: Future 10-Year Share Price / $(1.15)^{YEARS}$ = /4	$153.72/ 4 = $38.43
Step Four: Sticker Price / 2 = Margin of Safety Buy Price	$38.43/ 2=$19.21

different things. Payback Time is often the most accurate and most useful because it is based on free cash flow and it includes the potential of the business to grow that free cash flow larger and larger into the future. But in Whole Foods' case, they're spending a huge amount of their cash on growing the business by opening new stores. That is likely to add a lot of free cash flow in the future, but it is reducing free cash now, and that means the Eight-Year Payback Time buy price is going to be lower than the other pricing methods. If you want to know if you're really stealing it, the Ten Cap based on Owner Earnings works quite well. If you can buy a wonderful public business at ten times Owner Earnings, that's a really good deal because it doesn't require future growth to be a successful investment. And the Margin of Safety Formula gives you a conservative public company value."

The Margin of Safety Formula gives us the value of the business as a publicly traded business and then discounts it by half to protect against, as Charlie said about his fourth principle, "the vicissitudes of life." These three ways of getting to a buy price are another form of Windage Growth Rate situation. I had to make a judgment call.

And now I had to add to my checklist that I had started earlier and finally create some points for Charlie's fourth principle:

4. Reasonable Price with Margin of Safety
- ❏ What is the Ten Cap buy price?
- ❏ What is the Eight-Year Payback Time buy price?
- ❏ What is the Margin of Safety buy price?

It was now up to me to practice and correctly apply all the pricing formulas.

I let the thought float, without judging it. I noticed how it made me feel. Rather than making me feel the Enclosed Concrete Stairwell feeling that it would have only a few months earlier, it made me feel powerful. I knew what I was doing, for goodness' sake. I was in the investor party with an Old-Fashioned in hand, feeling comfortable. Okay, foin, a lot of other people had been there a lot longer than I had and knew a lot more. Big deal. I knew enough to be there, and not as a wallflower anymore.

I suddenly felt curious about buying stock for real. I started to feel like it was going to be time, very soon, to actually put serious money into the stock market. I knew my dad had told me I wasn't to buy stock during this year, but surely just opening a brokerage account wouldn't hurt, right? I'd use it eventually. I hadn't seen one in a long time, and I wanted to see what the real thing looked like now.

Opening a Brokerage Account

I searched online for "brokerage account" and one came up that was a company I had heard of before, so I figured it was fine and went with it. I answered the questions over about fifteen minutes, and voilà, my account was open. I transferred some money into the account, and the site said it would be available the next day. Easy peasy.

It was so easy, I was a little surprised. Shouldn't there be a minimum-competence exam or something? I wasn't even sure how to buy a stock.

Indeed, the site's home page was not so easy peasy. It was a mess of information, news, numbers, stock symbols, and research tabs. I could see my money was provisionally there, in the account. Probably to encourage me, they showed the money as "available" but I wanted it to stay put. I did not want to accidentally press the wrong button on this messy home page with real money and real stocks and commit to buying $8 million of Apple and have Tim Cook coming after me for the money. I was not good for it.

Actually, that would probably barely pay for their free employee lunches. Apple wouldn't even notice such a paltry stock purchase. Shniiiikies, I thought, as I looked at the stock symbols and buttons on the home page. Stuff was getting real, real fast.

Practice, I told myself. This is a practice. Breathe. Don't buy anything, don't touch anything, just breathe.

I felt like I did the first time I ever picked up a small handgun. That was also under my dad's watchful eye, when I was about fourteen. There was a small indoor shooting range in our town in the basement of a downtown office building, and my dad took me there. I suppose—like thinking I'd better have a good argument under his Socratic-method questioning—he thought it was time I learned to be comfortable with a weapon. The gun was unloaded, and I knew it was unloaded because my dad had showed me the empty chamber, but when I picked it up I was afraid of its power. Maybe we missed seeing a round in there, I thought. He showed me again that it was unloaded. I got a little more comfortable with it. Then he laid down the rules. "Never, ever act like a gun is not dangerous," he emphasized. "Treat a gun at all times as though it is loaded. We do that because it is easy to forget to check for bullets, easy to get nervous and overeager and make a mistake, and it is easy to pull the trigger. A deadly weapon demands respect."

There, with my newly opened brokerage account, I made sure not to hover the mouse over any BUY buttons. I felt like the gun was loaded, even though I could see that it wasn't. This was investing safety. I respected investing's power to move money to change my life in the right direction or the wrong direction, and treated it accordingly.

I didn't tell my dad about Fantasy Investing or opening the brokerage account. I didn't think he'd understand taking these baby steps. He had also said he didn't want me to buy any stock this year, and I wasn't sure if the brokerage account qualified as being part of the verboten category.

Still, I felt like I was making progress, not just mentally but physically as well. That month, I had felt so much better in my body that I stopped taking my stomach medication. I had wanted to get off it ever since starting, and not being attached to those little pills every day felt like freedom all by itself. I should still be sick, I thought, with flying across the world all the time and my Investing Practice taking up my minimal free time. But those extra nonwork things made me so happy that my body seemed to be responding to that rather than how busy and overscheduled I still was.

Not that everything was all lightness and rainbows. Just before leaving for the airport at the end of the weekend, I checked my Fantasy Investing spreadsheet. Four of my five companies had gone down in price on the market. I blinked and looked away. My heart sank. I felt so disappointed. Suddenly I realized that I had expected to be secretly and magically good at this investing hullabaloo. I had expected to be a wunderkind, to be able to say, "Oh golly, I just chose what looked good to me, and it worked out!"

It hadn't. My companies were down. I suddenly felt a visceral fear of making a mistake with real money. I remembered the Emotional Rule of Investing—everything goes down once you buy it, and it's because you bought it. It was funny at the time. It was less funny now. I knew that short-term volatility was not relevant in long-term value investing, but what if this dip was indicative of a larger trend? What if I had really made a mistake?

I let that sink in. I always wanted to get an A+ instead of an A, and asked for extra homework in first grade.

Nope, I was not ready to invest real money in this harebrained idea of mine to learn to invest by myself. I was scared—again.

I had to find out where the holes in this practice were.

AUGUST PRACTICE: Calculate the Margin of Safety price of each of the three companies you have already valued. Compare the three prices you have calculated for each company and decide on your buy price. Most important: reward yourself with a treat.

Inverting the Story

| September

ALL RIGHT, SO I HAD SCREWED UP AND MISSED SOMETHING. I COULD live with that.

I mean, I couldn't, at all, but whatever. The sun would come up tomorrow morning and I would debate whether I should commit my own money to my own judgment.

What had I missed?

As with people, falling in love with a company doesn't happen very often. So when it does happen, it is so tempting to dismiss or explain away negative impressions. Behavioral economists call this "confirmation bias"—when we tend to believe people in our environment who have views that agree with ours, without even realizing it. In fact, it's so tempting to dismiss anything negative about the company we love that researchers have found we actually avoid doing so on a subconscious level. Having to admit that my dear company has flaws is painful, and I find myself clapping back with the immediate thought: "They just don't get it."

My own views when researching a company are, at first, naturally skeptical. However, I want to find wonderful companies badly enough that when one looks promising I switch sides pretty quickly to believing in that company. Their Mission suddenly is fantastic, I can understand the company, their management looks strong and principled, it has a good Moat, and even the financials look pretty good. I start getting excited: *Company X might be a winner!* I check the price: *Holy moly, it's on sale!* I read and read, and everything I find says that the company does great things in the world; it's a cool company. At that point, I love it. I want it. I'm all in.

Was I allowing myself to be unconsciously emotionally swayed away from the facts? For the success of my Investing Practice, it was vital that I stay aware of my own confirmation bias. I had to be able to figure out a way to know what I didn't know.

Buffett and Munger combat their confirmation bias by keeping each other around to shoot down investing ideas. Buffett has said many times that one of Charlie's joys in life is to tell him no, and he treasures Charlie for that, reiterating the point recently in his 2016 Berkshire Hathaway shareholder letter, writing, "I will commit more errors; you can count on that. Fortunately, Charlie—never bashful—is around to say 'no' to my worst ideas."[*] When he lived in New York, Guy Spier regularly met with a group of other investors he called "the Posse" to debate investing ideas, which saved him from missing some holes in a company he otherwise would have probably bought.[†]

I'm a lawyer, I reminded myself. I love to find the holes in an argument. If I could find the holes, I would find my mistakes. That's how I would not lose money.

I was flying to Atlanta to record a block of podcasts with my dad over the weekend. Nuno and I were on a crappy stretch of too many weeks apart due to work and airplane tickets being expensive, and

[*] Warren Buffet, 2016 annual letter to Berkshire Hathaway shareholders, February 25, 2017, 15.
[†] Guy Spier, *Education of a Value Investor* (New York: St. Martin's Press, 2014).

I was in a bad mood about it, so I wanted to at least use the time well and focus my energy on work. It would also be nice to have a few quiet days with my dad, grilling salmon on his Big Green Egg barbecue and getting to grill him during our podcasts.

I wanted to ask my dad how he handled his own bias against finding the holes when he loved a company. Socrates was pretty good at making arguments—did he try to argue against his own argument for a company?

"Oh yeah!" my dad said. "Wanting a company to be awesome is a huge problem! It's probably the biggest problem I face."

"It's called 'confirmation bias,' Dad. It's pretty well researched."

"Very cool. Well, here's what I do to avoid it. I have a checklist of expensive errors that other investors and I have all made. I have to answer every question on this checklist and I don't get to cut corners."

"I've already worked on a checklist," I confirmed happily.

"Yeah! Let's research a company together and see how this works."

I sat next to him at his desk in his little office attached to his house so we could look at the computer screen together. The plan was to start with Tesla, Whole Foods, or lululemon, but before we sat down we both grabbed cans of La Croix sparkling water from the fridge. All of a sudden, it occurred to me: *Everyone I know has La Croix water in their fridge. Kamala drinks it like . . . well, like water. Pamplemousse water.* Sparkling water was nothing new, and even fancy sparkling water like Perrier was certainly not new. La Croix had been around for a while. But for some reason, everyone I knew was buying La Croix. Dad said, "Let's look it up," so I guess we were starting with what was right in front of us at the moment: La Croix.

He searched online, found their website, and it turned out that they were owned by a public company called, ever so brilliantly, National Beverage Corp. He pulled up their most recent annual report, and we learned that they own a number of beverage companies and brands, but La Croix is the only one we'd ever heard of. We looked at the Moat and management numbers and the company's reports, and he ran a quick valuation to discover that he thought they were pretty overpriced.*

I had always thought of people who do this professionally, including my father, as being very different from me. They must have some secret sources of information that I couldn't access and probably shared them in dark speakeasies. At that moment, though, our initial research plan was exactly the same. Dad was much faster at it than I was—probably by a factor of about ten—but it was the same review: check the company's website, get the basic information about what they do, review Moat, review management, and determine what would be a good price. And I discovered that all of a sudden we had this process in common.

I realized, sitting side by side at the desk together, that we shared the same language—at least a rudimentary version of it. I was speaking some business. I could travel a bit through that country now. I could ask where the bathroom was.

He turned to me and smiled. "This is pretty cool." I smiled right back at him. It was.

Expensive Errors Checklist

"All great investors have made mistakes," my dad went on. "What matters is not the mistake itself. It's easy to get caught up in regret and all sorts of feelings about it, but that's not useful for the future."

"What should we do, then? I don't want to make the same mistake twice."

"That's exactly the right way to think about it," Dad agreed. "Avoid regret, but ruthlessly assess why you made that mistake. Harder than it sounds. A lot harder. What did you miss? What did you learn? Not the easiest questions to answer."

---

* National Beverage Corp. was overpriced according to its past performance, but since we ran that analysis together, National Beverage Corp.'s stock price has gone up dramatically. We weren't the only ones to notice we drank a lot of La Croix and no other competitors were touching it. But the company didn't have the track record to make it a Rule #1 company. C'est la vie.

In *Risk Intelligence,* which analyzes how people can more accurately determine risk—*spoiler:* we humans are terrible at determining risk—author Dylan Evans noted that expert gamblers, who win or lose based entirely on assessing the odds and risk, were brutally honest with themselves about their strengths and weaknesses by keeping notes and reviewing what worked and what did not. I was trying to do the opposite of gambling in my Investing Practice, but the methodology still applied—I still had to assess the risk of buying a given company using incomplete information and be ruthless with myself about my own errors of judgment.

"What's the best way to look at my own screw-ups?" I asked my dad.

"The best way is to not make them in the first place. Stick to what I'm teaching you so you get the benefit of eighty-five years of expensive mistakes that our family of investors already made. I keep a list of screw-ups that I cross-check companies against."

He called it his Expensive Errors checklist. Between himself and other smart investors, including even Warren Buffett, a lot of errors have been made and, in hindsight, clear and basic facts were ignored by them. Instead of making these expensive errors myself, I could learn from them. Mohnish Pabrai keeps his checklist to only seven questions. Dad keeps his list longer than that, but still short; he's afraid if it's too long that he'll skim it and miss something critical. Here's my dad's list of warning signs—basic errors that were there before the investments failed and caused expensive problems:

Expensive Errors

▶ Meaning
  • On edge or outside Circle of Competence
  • No Gurus buying
  • Not a business I enjoy studying
  • Industry or company or product is not easy to understand

- Did not do inversion
- Industry on the decline
- Unfriendly union
- Demand for the product in ten years is uncertain
- Uncertain the company will be more productive in ten years
- Industry rate of change is high
- Did not read ten years of footnotes in 10-K

▶ Moat
- Moat is not intrinsic
- Moat is not durable
- Moat is not being widened
- Big Four Numbers are not growing
- Book value (plus dividends), in particular, is not growing
- Owner Earnings and free cash flow not predictable
- Cheap foreign competition getting stronger but hasn't reached U.S. industry yet

▶ Management
- ROE & ROIC are going down
- CEO does not act like an owner
- CEO puts self first
- CEO glosses over problems
- CEO selling too much stock
- Company buying back stock well above value
- CEO recently replaced
- Debt more than two years free cash flow
- Debt increasing
- Loan to expire soon
- Loan covenants close to being breached by company

▶ Pricing
- Can't confidently calculate Owner Earnings
- Pay more than the Ten Cap price, *or*

- Pay more than the Eight-Year Payback Time price, *or*
- Pay more than the Margin of Safety price
- Temporary issues making earnings and/or free cash growth/losses abnormal
- Earnings-Per-Share growth engineered via buybacks
- Future growth rate and future P/E estimates not realistic
- There is no Event and no price drop
- Price dropped but not enough of an Event to go on sale
- Event produces significant fear but may not resolve itself in one to three years
- Event may permanently damage the business
- Can't understand the Event—too complex

I noticed that pricing errors were way down on the list.

"Remember," Dad admonished me, "price is actually least important, because time will fix errors on a wonderful business. If you buy a great company but pay too high a price, if it stays wonderful it will eventually be worth more than you paid for it; you'll just have to wait longer."

I laughed. "You're telling me that one of my foibles is to get too hung up on price."

Dad shrugged. "Obviously, a great price is very important as a cushion against mistakes. However, if you get the business right, price becomes less of an issue."

"Probably true," I realized, and added it to my own checklist. "What else do you do to protect yourself from confirmation bias?"

"I also talk through my argument for a company with other investor friends whom I trust and respect. We don't say whether we buy or sell a company, only the argument for it, and it includes the Inverted Story—the argument against a company.

"The idea is to change the Story from a focus on buying, and flip it to a focus on selling. You can't trust yourself to find the holes in an argument while you're making the argument. The only way is to flip it on its head and try to prove yourself wrong. Take your best three reasons to own this business and make each one a reason not to own it. For example, if I said Chipotle has a great Moat, then the inversion is that Chipotle's Moat is broken."

So that's how he finds the holes and prevents his own confirmation bias. I confirmed, "Cross-examine my own argument by proving the opposite."

"Exactly. It's harder than it sounds, because you just spent days or weeks or months getting excited about this company, building your interest, finding reasons you like this company a lot. Set your mind for this by agreeing with its opposite. Tell yourself: 'I should sell. Why?'"

"Can we try it out?"

Story

First, write the Story. I got out my checklist, worked through it, and then I wrote my first complete Story on Whole Foods.

1. **The Principles of Investing:** Let's take each one and apply it to Whole Foods.

   ▶ *Understanding*—This is a short overview of the company. What they do and how they do it. How did I find them? (Preferably from a Guru starting to buy them.) If I can't explain it in one paragraph, I don't understand this company well enough. It's Too Hard.

   • <u>Whole Foods</u>: Grocery industry. Whole Foods is the number-one organic grocery store chain in the United States, which I found by shopping there. I love buying groceries at Whole Foods. They offer their own branded products and lots of products from small and large retailers, all vetted to meet their high standards of food sourcing, ingredients, and sustainability.

▶ *Mission*—Why I like it. The company's Mission and the values they express in how they do business.

- Whole Foods: Their Mission is to do good by doing well, to provide food products that support the planet to customers who want such products, and even to stay ahead of demand by educating customers to raise their standards. For example, Whole Foods' seafood sustainability rating system raised the industry standard, and customers came to expect to be informed about the source and sustainability of their seafood before buying.

▶ *Moat*—Who are their competitors? What intrinsic characteristic protects them from competitors?

- Whole Foods: Competitors have historically been other organic grocery stores because conventional grocery stores competed on price rather than quality, but Whole Foods has been so successful that conventional grocery stores have become their main competitors. Whole Foods' Moat is a Brand Moat, and it remains one of the strongest Brand Moats in companies today. It stands for ethical food. Anyone who wants a great grocery shopping experience, absolute confidence that their food is consciously sourced, and products they can't get anywhere else will go to Whole Foods, and that will not change with conventional grocery stores offering organic food products.

▶ *Management*—Who is running the company, and my opinion of their integrity and talent.

- Whole Foods: John Mackey is Whole Foods' founder and CEO, the man who led the organic food revolution for the last forty years and now runs the company for minimal money. Whole Foods is his baby. He now has a co-CEO to bring the company into better competition with conventional grocery stores.

▶ *Sensible Price*—Does it have a margin of safety?
  • Ten Cap buy price (based on Owner Earnings)
    <u>Whole Foods</u>: $29
  • Payback Time buy price (based on free cash flow)
    <u>Whole Foods</u>: $13
  • Margin of Safety buy price (based on earnings)
    <u>Whole Foods</u>: $19

2. **Three Reasons:** Three great reasons to own this company that relate to Moat, management, or price.

> *Whole Foods Reason 1*: I trust the management implicitly.
> *Whole Foods Reason 2*: The Brand Moat will continue to provide high margins, as consumers prefer Whole Foods above all other product providers.
> *Whole Foods Reason 3*: The industry will continue to grow fast and Whole Foods will be worth more in ten years.

3. **Event:** Describe the Event that has put this company on sale. Will it come out of it in not less than one and not more than three years?

> *Whole Foods Event*: It is being attacked by conventional grocery stores on product prices and competitive products, and investors have freaked out about it, driving the price down from its high. Whole Foods is universally recognized as such a well-run company that it's unlikely that its price will get any cheaper. Whole Foods will come out of it within three years by restructuring its operations, reducing its prices, and, most important, slowing its expansion. They were putting crazy amounts of cash into opening new stores, and once they pull back from doing so, they will have a lot of extra cash to fight this threat.

Dad explained further: "Now take the reasons to buy, and see if we can prove the opposite is true. Describe why it sucks and you don't want to buy it."

"Honestly, it's going to be difficult," I said. "It's no fun to try to find holes in the argument I've made, after I've already tied it all up in a nice little bow."

"It's not easy, but I know you've got that ruthlessness inside you. You and Charlie Munger are both lawyers, and Charlie invented this idea of inverting the Story before deciding whether to buy a company. When asked by Harvard Business School to speak at their 1986 commencement, Charlie Munger said, 'It is in the nature of things, as Jacobi knew, that many hard problems are best solved only when they are addressed backward.' Jacobi is a famous mathematician who said, 'Invert, always invert,' as a formula for solving difficult problems."

I smiled. "The tradition of masters goes way back, no?"

"It does indeed." Dad smiled back at me. "Let's invert Whole Foods."

Way to kill my baby, Dad. I loved Whole Foods like George Clooney loves tequila—for a good time that would hopefully lead to a lot of money. But foin.

For Whole Foods, I had massive inherent biases. My bubble was very real. Boulder was the birthplace of Whole Foods' only legitimate competitor, Wild Oats, which Whole Foods bought out in 2009. I lived in a town where people regularly discussed where their food was sourced from and what kind of company made it. They discussed where a food company was formed and who ran it. They discussed ingredients in great detail. So, when I researched Whole Foods, I totally got their Mission, a Mission that was obvious, and successful, and spreading. I kind of perversely liked the idea of testing Charlie's inversion on the company that would be the hardest for me.

Inverting the Story

"The easiest way to get to a decent Inverted Story is to take each of the three reasons you want to buy this company and invert it," Dad explained. "Then rebut each inversion."

1. **Story Inversion:** Invert the three great reasons to own the company into three great reasons not to own this company.

2. **Invert the Inversion:** Rebut each reason not to own.

This is what we came up with for Whole Foods:

▶ *Reason not to buy #1*—Mackey is old and new management has already demonstrated they aren't Mackey.
  - Rebuttal: John is actually younger than my dad and Dad isn't going off to play golf any time in the next decade, because he loves what he's doing. Mackey loves what he's doing too much to let his baby suffer. He will not go away until Whole Foods is back on track and back on top.

▶ *Reason not to buy #2*—The Brand Moat is unsustainable, because organic food is rapidly becoming a commodity sold at Costco, and the Whole Foods experience will suffer as the company tries to compete on price.
  - Rebuttal: Organic food cannot become a commodity, because it is too specialized. I trust Whole Foods to deliver quality and choice I can't find anywhere else. Their Brand Moat is secured by how difficult it is to replicate their people, care, choices, suppliers, industry impact, and values at a price-driven enterprise.

▶ *Reason not to buy #3*—The industry will continue to grow fast but Whole Foods' profit will shrink to conventional-grocery-store size and will be worth less in ten years than it is today.
  - Rebuttal: The global organic grocery market is expected to grow at 13 percent compounded annually.* Whole Foods will continue to open smaller 365 brand

---

* Duff & Phelps, *Food Retail Industry Insights*—2016, 3.

stores and regular large-format stores in select markets. In addition, it has started to offer delivery services to reach more customers. Even with lower profitability, its increase in size and continued growth of same-store sales point to a significantly larger and more valuable company in ten years than today. Even at the Ten Cap price, it is highly likely that this investment will make money over time.

"Wow. Serious cross-examination."

"Absolutely. You've been worried about trusting yourself with your own money. This is how you become certain. It's not by magic. It's by ruthless examination."

"This is fantastic, Dad."

He looked surprised, then grinned. "Really?"

"Yeah. I've been wondering how to protect myself from myself, and this does. I know I can argue anything away, so if it convinces me, it's probably a good bet. Inverting is totally doable, and I'm into it."

"You are genuinely excited about investing," Dad reflected. "It makes me really happy. I want you to feel comfortable and safe with it, so you can go out and start getting those 15, 20, 26 percent returns."

Really, my dad was the one who prepared me to make an argument, and to invert an argument. "Plus," I half teased him, "you trained me to do this from all those car rides you put me through." I realized that, back then, he had been trying to help me the best way he knew how. He had been trying to prepare me for college and life by pushing me and prepping me to be pushed.

"Ha!" He laughed, taken aback. "I don't know, honey. I probably just scared you off. But you are doing a great job learning this, so I did something right."

"You did lots of things right, Dad."

He cleared his throat. "And now, I'm going to add one more protection for you."

"Cool."

"If, after inverting each part of the Story, this one becomes too hard to be certain, then it goes into the Too Hard pile. Just move it over from your Wishlist to the Too Hard list. Done."

"After all that research? Seems like a waste of time."

"No time spent on investing research is ever a waste of time. If there's one thing I can impress upon you, it's that. Even if Whole Foods is Too Hard, the education you got from researching it can never be taken away from you. You'll use it for some other grocery store company in ten years, or to see if a similar industry like retail meets your liking. It's research you can use to ruthlessly review your wins and losses by looking back in a few years when you know what happens to Whole Foods, and determine if you missed something or you got it right. It's never a waste of time."

I'd save my research and take my education and go forward: *Never mess around with something that's Too Hard.*

"But," Dad went on, "if, after the inversion, you've actually become more certain about your analysis of the company—if inverting failed to convince you that it's not a wonderful company to buy—then you have finished your work and it goes on the Wishlist. If the price is right, you could buy it now."

"Okay, I'll try it on my own."

"You actually don't really ever have to come up with an inversion entirely on your own."

"I just call you?"

Dad laughed. "Totally, yes, of course. But even more help is right on the Internet! There are plenty of people who think that buying that company is a stupid idea and write about why."

"Oh, that's true," I realized. "Analysts write articles about companies and put them online, don't they?"

"Yup. Seeking Alpha, The Motley Fool, and other websites like those, plus news articles, have plenty of inverted arguments about companies: what's wrong with them, why you shouldn't invest in them. Read all of it and use other people's research to make the argument against the company."

"The questions the analysts ask on the quarterly phone calls are also a good indication of holes in the company's Story, I would think."

"Sometimes," Dad hedged. "Analysts on those calls soft-pedal everything and hardly ever really grill the CEO. Too bad. The calls would be so much more interesting if the analysts would push. Still, sometimes they do ask pointed questions that can highlight an inversion of the Story. Ask yourself: If you agree with this person's point of view, how would you support it?"

"I can see how I could get swayed right back, to become totally against a company I was just in love with." I was starting to think I had unwittingly jumped on a pendulum of opinion, never to land at a final decision about a company.

"Here's the important bit, though: companies are like horses—if you look deeply enough, there is something wrong with every single one of them."

I laughed. *Oh no.*

"But is that problem enough to sink your Story?"

Ah, I saw it then. *I have to do both: try to show that it's wonderful enough, and try to tear it down.*

I would write down the inversion, just like I had the Story. I think in words and express myself best in writing. Other people might do better talking it out to the wall, a mirror, or a friend. But I do better writing words on a page that I have to read and defend. I'd make the argument against the company in an essay. Then I'd see which argument was stronger. Writing out my inversion would force me to consider every point on my list and make sure I had thought it out fully. It would make the inversion seem more real. I was so resistant to the Whole Foods inversion that I knew I wouldn't quite make myself believe it until I saw the arguments on the page in black and white. Writing it down would force me to take the argument seriously.

Later, I sat down and I added to my "Investing Practice" folders on my computer. I love folders. In my "Investing Research" folder, I made a folder for each company. Inside the "Whole Foods" folder are:

▶ "Company Filings"
▶ "General Research"
▶ "Pro Opinions"
▶ "Con Opinions"

Doing the inversion was more painful than I thought. Playing devil's advocate on a company I love was like cross-examining my best friend—it's emotionally terrible, but I also know exactly where to find her weak spots. In the process of working on my fear of buying, I had become emotionally attached to my favorite companies, and that was a sign that the inversion process was vital to protect me from an irrationally exuberant decision. A company that survives an inversion has passed its cross-examination and made it into my "Buy It" pile.

Practice Shares

Later that week, I was on the phone with Nuno, and he casually asked if I was going to buy a company soon. He hesitated yet had some energy in his voice when he asked, while simultaneously staying super-laid-back about the question, because *who cares, man, just do whatever you want, but on the other hand maybe you should actually do what you've been working on for months. He's breezy!*

I said, "Yes."

I did not want to say "Yes."

I added, "Soon."

I did not want to buy anything soon. I had promised my dad that I wouldn't.

I wasn't sure exactly what scared me about buying shares. It was almost the inverse of the problem with day trading. With this Investing Practice, buying shares felt like a really big decision that would affect my life for years to come. This wouldn't be an action I took and probably reversed by selling the stock in an hour or a day or a week. This would stick around—maybe to haunt me.

Plus, I didn't know how to use the brokerage platform. Literally didn't know which buttons I should press and when. What if it asks me questions I don't know the answer to? I worried. What if I hit the wrong buttons and lose my entire tranche, or somehow buy way more shares than I meant to?

Plus, people will ask me which stock I bought. I'm identifying with and representing this company. I don't feel like I can just buy something.

Unless I could.

What if I practiced by taking a test drive? An emotional test drive?

I would pick a company I knew I liked and wanted to own, and I would practice buying a small number of its shares for a very small amount of money—an amount I would not miss. I would not care if it was on sale, not on sale, insanely overpriced, whatever. It didn't matter a bit. It was about the experience and—here is the key—it was *not* an investment. I would never expect to make a penny on this purchase, and instead would treat it as money that has been paid to buy the educational experience of buying shares, just like a tennis lesson. At the end of it, I would (1) own a company I love, which is always great, (2) maybe have lost that money forever, and (3) have practiced buying shares with awareness on my emotions rather than on the numbers. I could keep the shares or sell them the next day. It didn't matter. It was about practicing.

Later that month, once I was back home in Boulder, my dad and I had a video call. We did this regularly now. It was much nicer and more comfortable to be able to see each other. Quite a contrast to the stilted phone calls we had when I was a kid.

I thought my dad would think my idea for an emotional test drive was interesting. He surely knew by now how I operated and that it would give me some confidence.

Instead, when I told him about it, he cocked his head back like I'd punched him in the jaw. "You just ignored everything I have taught you. That's not investing."

I blinked. I didn't think he'd be insulted. "Exactly, it's not investing. It's practice, by buying an experience."

"An experience? What does that mean?"

"The point is to practice how it feels, so that when I do it for real, with real money, it's not as scary. I'll have been there before. I can see what emotions I go through so I can manage them when I put a lot of money on it."

"Well, how much are you going to spend?"

"It needs to be a small amount of money that I don't mind spending on an important experience, and it needs to be large enough that I notice it and have emotions about it. I don't really care about spending $20, but a few hundred is definitely a big deal for me. I have to think about spending a few hundred dollars. And I would spend a few hundred on something important. So yeah, I think about $250 to $300 will be an amount that I'll feel."

He snorted. He didn't get it at all.

"Okay. What company are you going to buy but not really buy, and waste your money on buying at a price that's too high?"

"Whole Foods."

He softened a little. "Well, at least that's a good one to gamble on."

"It's not a gamb— That's the whole point!" I stuttered. I left it alone after that. No point pushing something he really would not understand. I was going to buy the Practice Shares anyway.

Then it occurred to me that maybe he didn't empathize with my idea because he had never felt nervous about buying a company. I asked him, and he looked at me like I had asked if he had ever gotten nervous about brushing his teeth. "No, I've definitely never felt that." And then he got it. I saw the light bulb go on. "No, I've never felt that. But you feel nervous about it, huh?"

"Yeah, it's really scary. It's scary enough that I want to practice it."

"Well, okay. That's definitely different from me. Okay, try the experience thing. As long as you understand what you are doing is not investing, and it has nothing to do with what I do."

I laughed. "Don't worry, I get it. That's exactly the point. It's not investing. It's practice."

"It's practice. They're Practice Shares." He liked that. He still didn't really get it, but he wasn't against it anymore.

"I'll let you know how it goes."

I had not touched my brokerage account in so long that I had to reset my password. I typed in the stock symbol for Whole Foods: "WFM." There was a big BUY button, and a big red SELL button right next to it. I carefully avoided touching either one. It was awfully exciting to be on the page and buying real shares, but I did not want to do it wrong. I could imagine myself buying $5,000 of stock I did not want. So my mouse moved very slowly, very deliberately, and I typed in ten shares.

Still, it was fun. I could not imagine myself doing this months earlier, and here I was, freaked out and excited like I was about to step off a bungee jump.

A box came up asking what kind of order I wanted. *Oh no.* I had not expected that. *Order?* "Limit order" was the default, so I searched online for "limit order" and Investopedia told me it meant the seller would sell it to me at that price or less. I put in a bit more than the current price so that the purchase would be sure to go through. It was 9:07 A.M. in New York and I knew the New York Stock Exchange opened at 9:00 A.M., so I was ready. I clicked BUY.

Holy crap. Had I done it right?

It's an expensive experience, I consciously reminded myself, not an investment. I'm not investing, I'm experiencing. It's a test drive. Breathe.

A screen came up that said "Order Status," and beneath that it said "Open." Okay. That sounded promising. Did I have to refresh the screen? Did the stock price just jump up, making my limit order too low? As with how you're not supposed to refresh the screen after buying a plane ticket until the purchase goes through, I didn't want to press the wrong button and accidentally buy more shares. I breathed and thanked myself. Thank *goodness* I was practicing this and not dealing with serious money yet. I mean, this counted, but it didn't count much.

I was still waiting on the "Order Status" screen. It had been one full minute. Nothing had happened. *Shouldn't the market move a little faster than that? What the heck?* Why wouldn't mine have gone through? Had I done something wrong? The market opened at nine A.M., right? I searched for "ny stock exchange trading hours" and discovered the market opens at nine-thirty. Nine-thirty A.M. to four P.M., sports fans.

It was now 9:10 A.M. in New York. That would explain why nothing happened. *Okay. Breathe again. Twenty minutes to wait.*

Then I started rethinking the whole thing. *Should I change my order price? I should change my order price. Maybe I can get it at like two cents less, or five, or ten! Should I cancel the order altogether and start over?*

I heard my dad's voice in my head: *It doesn't matter what minor price variations are happening if you want to own that company. If you know you have a Margin of Safety and you want to buy it, that's all you need to know. As long as it's on sale, the actual moment-to-moment price doesn't matter.*

Foin, I thought. My teacher has spoken. I'll let it ride. Plus, I think my limit order will mean that if the price opens at a lower price than my limit order, I'll get the lower price anyway. Another thing to test out! I decided to leave my limit order where it was.

Eleven more minutes. I would be useful and fold the laundry.

I successfully folded laundry for four minutes and texted frustrated emojis to my group text with Kamala and our friends for six minutes. A good balance.

9:29 A.M.

9:30 A.M.

9:31 A.M. Nothing changed on my order status page, but I saw my account balance was down about $300. *Someone took my money. Did they give me Whole Foods ownership in exchange or am I going to have to sue them for breach of contract?*

Finally, after frantically searching the page, I spotted a teeny-tiny REFRESH button at the bottom of the screen. Seriously, this nub looked like it was stuck in the corner and forgotten about. I clicked it, and lo and behold, my order said "Filled."

There was no fanfare, no congratulations message from the online brokerage, no welcome e-mail from Whole Foods thanking me for becoming an owner. No one knocked on my door to deliver champagne. But I owned Whole Foods! I was an owner. A proper owner of the whole company, just like every other value investor. I wiggled with happiness. I was a conscious capitalist, bar none. *Let's do this thing. What happens now?*

The first thing I did was open my Stocks app on my iPhone and add "WFM" to check the price. I typed in "WFM" to the quote page and the stock price was eleven cents higher than I paid! My reptilian brain *loved* this. *Sorry, Phil Town.* I was a fan of stock I own going up. Straight up.

I looked away for a few minutes while I closed my brokerage account's website, and then looked at the stock price again—now it was lower than where I bought it. *What the heck!* That was not okay. Then it almost immediately ticked back up, and I immediately felt a pang of regret that I didn't make my limit order lower to catch that valley. Shouldn't I have known to wait a little bit until after the market had opened? I downloaded two other stock tracking apps so I would have the most complete information, and left the last app open on my phone. I watched it update itself constantly. *Crap. This could be addicting. And maddening.*

It's not an investment, I repeated in my head. *Itsnotaninvestment, itsnotaninvestment, itsnotaninvestment.*

This was making me crazy. I got so nervous when the price fell from where I bought. And so happy when it went up one entire penny. I have literally thrown away actual pennies in the trash because taking them to a coin machine is too much trouble. What was I doing? I deleted "WFM" from the Stocks app, and moved it and the other two stock-tracking apps to a spot way at the back of my phone, where they would rarely be seen. I kept them, just in case I needed them, but I didn't want to need them. I nested them all in a box I titled "Torture." No one wants to click on "Torture."

And I haven't, ever since that day.

I came to terms with the realization that I'm not going to catch the very bottom of a stock price, and I'm not going to sell at the very top. In fact, I've decided to assume that, going forward, I expect to leave some imaginary money on the table from poor timing. I'm not smart enough to figure out the perfect times to buy or sell, and I'm definitely not lucky enough to catch them by accident. I can't even choose the best line to stand in. That's okay. As I would tell my startup clients who called me panicking about investors taking some of their ownership in the company they founded with their blood, sweat, and tears: Owning 100 percent of a company worth zero dollars means you cash out with zero dollars, while owning 50 percent of a company worth $50 million means you cash out with $25 million. Which would you rather have?

Then I thought about what a value investor would do. Not look at the "Torture" box, that's for sure. In fact, Mohnish Pabrai has said he will never put in an order to buy or sell stock when the market is open so that he won't be influenced by the day's price fluctuations. Considering my experience trying to buy my Practice Shares, I see why that is. It's genius.

Still, a value investor would probably keep up on the company to some extent, right? We've got to know what's happening.

Wait, it occurred to me all of a sudden. What kind of regular commitment was I getting myself into? I'm not someone who likes checking stock prices. I hate having to be online every day. If I want to go on a device-free holiday for a week, don't I have to be worried about checking the market every day?

I called my dad and told him I had pulled the trigger. I had bought Practice Shares. And now I was practicing owning a company, and all the attendant worries. Had I gotten myself into a life of constant vigilance?

"No, no, no," Dad said. "It's not like that. I don't even want you to check stock prices every day; it would make you stressed and crazy about the ups and downs. You're looking long term at these companies. Knowing what's happening every day does you no good."

"If there's a market meltdown or something, I need to know about it, though, right?"

"Well, I guess if there's a massive crash you might want to buy some shares in the companies you've been watching for their prices to go down. But you wouldn't sell the companies you own unless the *value* is going down. You'd buy more shares of them, actually, because you know their value is fine and the price is a bargain."

Hmm. Okay. I can get behind that.

"It's strange that all of these questions literally just occurred to me for the first time after I bought the shares," I mused. "I mean, I did think about it beforehand, and yet as soon as I bought the Practice Shares I suddenly thought of all this research I needed to do."

Dad laughed. "It seems strange, but it happens to me too! Often, I'll buy a small position in a company I'm interested in, because as soon as I own some of it, I start to understand it in a completely different way than when it was just theoretical. All of a sudden, my name is on the line for that company, and it's real. My reaction to owning a few shares lets me know if I want to keep going with buying more of it, or if I should stop and wait. I know other value investors who do the same thing."

Wait a second. Did he just say he buys small amounts of shares to see how he emotionally handles it? "Hmmm," I teased, "it's almost as if—hear me out on this—you buy Practice Shares to see how you feel."

I let that sink in, then noted, "But wait, that's impossible, because you think buying Practice Shares is totally stupid."

"Uh, no, I mean . . ." he stammered, "I wouldn't say they're for practice exact—"

"No, just shares you buy to test your knowledge and emotions. Exactly like I just did."

He laughed at himself, knowing he had been caught. "Okay," he admitted. "It's like Practice Shares. It's a good idea."

There was something truly soul-soaring about making my dad admit that I was right and he was wrong. It felt like vindicating my eight-year-old self, stuck in the car being questioned by Socrates, and then coming up with the perfect retort.

Then he appropriated my idea. "I'm into it," he exclaimed. "Practice Shares. Cool."

I took my win and hung up the phone.

I was getting excited to buy for real. I wanted to get so solid on a company that I would, in my dad's words, "load up the truck." But I had no idea how much "load up the truck" meant.

SEPTEMBER PRACTICE: Pick your favorite of the three companies you've been researching, and write the full Story and Inverted Story of that company. Be mean in the Inverted Story. Try to understand why you should not buy this company. What can go wrong?

Compiling an Antifragile Portfolio

| October

"DAD, I DON'T WANT TO FANTASY-TRADE ANYMORE. I DON'T WANT TO do Practice Shares. I want to be a real investor. I'm ready to use serious money. I want to own something forever. What can I buy right now?"

We were on our investing video call: me in Boulder, and Dad in Atlanta. I was on a mission that month. I had my investing office set up around me, I was feeling invest-y, and I wanted actionable information about when to buy and how much.

Dad looked at me, hard, and even through the computer I could feel it. "Uh-oh. The year is almost up and you're starting to feel the pressure to do something. Welcome to the world of fund managers and the pressure to invest—that's why they can't beat the market. What do you think makes a great investor? Buying stock because you need to? Or waiting patiently like a hunter until the right company comes along at the right price?"

I stared at him. "You want me to stalk my prey?"

"Exactly. When you buy because you have to, what are the chances you're going to get a bargain on a great company?"

"Um, they're low."

"Exactly." He glared at me through the screen.

"I know, but people who know about my Investing Practice keep asking me what I own," I said. "I don't think I would even care on my own, but every time someone asks me about it, it's like a reminder that I'm not a real investor without buying a company."

"Hey, you own Whole Foods, no?"

"No, remember, I don't count buying the Practice Shares. I bought an experience, not the shares."

"Are you worried you're missing out?"

"Well, yes, that too."

"Actually, that feeling of being left behind is a serious issue for Rule #1 investors. There is a little voice inside us that starts worrying that we're missing out. It comes from the power of group consciousness. That's what we feel when we go to a sold-out concert or football game, the power of the crowd pulling at us to join in. Just recognize it for what it is and ignore it."

He was right, of course.

"Buying because you feel pressure is not investing. It's what all those typical mutual fund managers are doing in the market every day—speculating on the direction of the crowd in this industry or that stock. They are not investors."

"You're saying an investor waits?"

"Patience and knowing what you're buying are what separate investors from speculators. The secret to good investing is to wait. Try to remember that you intend investing to be a lifelong practice, and you've sacrificed to make the time and energy to do this practice so you can become great at it and have these investing skills your whole life. You really have sacrificed, honey. You've spent a lot of time and energy and brainpower on investing this year that you could have enjoyed spending on something else. That's really amazing."

I shrugged. "I don't think I had much choice. I had to do something toward financial freedom or I was going to be buried by my own life."

"And you have been doing great. It's good to pay attention to that pressure, though. Even the greatest investors can feel that pressure. Julian Robertson was a fund manager who had a 32 percent compounded return going to his investors for something like twenty years,[*] and he was so much pressured by his investors to invest as the market kept going up and up and up that in 1999 he finally just threw in the towel and closed his fund. And I think Warren Buffett did the same thing in 1969. Buffett doesn't describe his decision this way, but I think he was feeling pressure from his Buffett Partnership investors to invest when he wanted to wait, so he told them they could buy Berkshire stock or invest with Bill Ruane at the new Sequoia Fund or just take their money home with them. Like these great investors, you will feel pressure, but you must not bend to it—the market will come your way eventually."

Foin, Socrates, I get it. I'll stand down. "What you're saying is to slow my roll?" I teased him.

He chuckled, briefly. "If you don't have a company that meets our Rule #1 criteria, then you Do. Not. Buy." He was steely-eyed serious again. "That's the only way to protect yourself from making a wrong decision based on fear or greed."

"I hear you not to buy right away. What I need to know is how to prepare. When they get to my buy price, how much of each company on my Wishlist should I buy and in what order?"

---

[*] Nathan Reiff, "The Greatest Investors: Julian Robertson," Investopedia, October 27, 2017, http://www.investopedia.com/university/greatest/julianrobertson.asp.

Dad gave me an approving look. "Danielle, this is where the rubber meets the road for investing. Building an antifragile portfolio is what Rule #1 is all about."

Antifragile Portfolio

In his book *Antifragile: Things That Gain from Disorder,* Nassim Nicholas Taleb suggests that great results come from strategies that benefit from chaos to the point that they are "antifragile," a term coined by Taleb that means something that benefits from and is made stronger by adverse events. Mutual fund and index fund investors own portfolios that are fragile: their portfolios are badly damaged by "black swan" events: unexpected events that create chaos and shock the market into a state of fear. Such events can cause a massive drop in the price of all stocks, a disaster from which an ordinary diversified portfolio might not recover for a decade or two. Think 1929, 1941, 1973, 2000, 2008.

Even so, the advice I have always heard is to diversify among companies, industries, and even stock markets. *Diversify, diversify, diversify.* Have your investing money in all sorts of different things. Efficient Market Hypothesis (EMH) investment advisers, whose basic thesis is that you can't beat the market, are all about how to allocate capital. There's nothing else for EMH advisers to do, because they believe that the only way to get high returns is to take a lot of risk and get lucky. When I told my financial adviser friend I would hold no more than ten to fifteen companies at any given time, she looked at me like I was dumb as a post and basically said, "Oh, honey." But she didn't know about how buying wonderful companies with Missions and Moats when those businesses go on sale creates an antifragile Rule #1 portfolio in two surprising ways.

First, my dad said that companies with a durable Moat do not just withstand or barely eke through market chaos; wonderful companies generally benefit from Events. If there is inflation, their Moat protects them from competition and they can raise their prices as their costs of labor and material rise. If there is deflation, their Moat keeps customers coming back, and that protects them from having to lower their price. Even better, the companies with the biggest Moats have the highest profit margins, and can use major downturns to eliminate their weaker competition through mergers, acquisitions, price wars, and other aggressive tactics. Great businesses emerge from recessions and chaos stronger and with more control of their market niche. As owners, we get the benefit of that, as their stock prices will eventually follow the increase in their market share and cash flow.

"Let me make sure I understand this," I said. "The companies themselves are antifragile because even though their stock prices might go down with a recession or industry chaos, their Moats will ultimately make them more valuable after the chaos is over?"

"Exactly. Which makes our Rule #1 portfolios as a whole, by definition, antifragile."

"But isn't that also what happens with a nicely diversified portfolio full of mutual funds and ETFs?" I wasn't really seeing the difference—and there had better be a difference, or all this work was not going to be worth the trouble if all I had to do to be antifragile was buy the index.

"Good thought. That brings me to the second reason our portfolios are antifragile and index portfolios are not. We wait in cash for Events that bring the prices down; they don't."

I can buy all the best companies, but if I pay too high a price, as Charlie says, the "vicissitudes of life," those ups and downs that we call Events, will massively reduce my overall returns. I could get that 7 percent we talked about back in February in an indexed, diversified portfolio if I have twenty years to recover from a big recession—but if I wanted to get to financial freedom, I needed to keep my buy prices low, wait in cash, and be ready to take action when chaos hits. Buffett describes it by saying we want to be ready to run outside carrying a washtub when it's raining gold.

"To be ready with that washtub," my dad went on, "that means

258 | Invested

you have to make sure to have investing funds available when a recession hits. If you can do that, you'll eventually have a portfolio of wonderful businesses that you bought on sale in times of crisis that you can sell for huge profits when things go back to normal." That's the key to having a portfolio that is antifragile.

Passive-Aggressive Strategy

Dad went on: "Because here's what's going to happen in the real world. The market is going to regularly fluctuate and you're going to watch the prices of companies on your Wishlist come down. One day, one of your companies will go on sale below your buy price and you'll want to buy it. But strangely, you will also *not* want to buy it."

"What?" I exclaimed skeptically.

"Your effort to make a decision, because you are human, will be all wrapped up in emotions. One of the most powerful is fear. We've talked a lot about fear. That's the one that says, 'Don't do it.' But there will be another emotion kicking in as you start to understand this strategy—greed. You're watching this stock go down, right? And it will occur to you that if you wait and if the price keeps going down, you're going to make a lot more money when it goes back up. Greed starts to kick in and now you *don't* want to buy; you want to wait until the price drops even more. You want to buy and you want to wait. It's like you have two devils on your shoulders whispering opposite advice in your ears."

Ugh. I already knew he was right. I would totally get greedy and try to time it just right, and at the same time be worried that my original analysis was in error and it wasn't a wonderful company at all. When I bought my Practice Shares, I got mad at myself when the price went down one penny below where I had bought it. With Practice Shares! I could only imagine the angst with real money. The Emotional Rule of Investing says that the moment I buy a company, the price will drop—entirely because I just bought it. The price dropped as soon I bought Practice Shares, so it had to be true. And that meant that I would never time it just right.

Dad noted, "Trust your work. You did the work so that your emotions don't screw up your decisions. The only real mistake you can make, when you have a wonderful business on your Wishlist and the price is below your buy price, is to do nothing. You've got to understand that. We wait and wait and wait and do our homework, but when it's time to buy, we've gotta get aggressive."

I started laughing. Hurry up and wait. "So this is a passive-aggressive investment strategy, right?" I asked.

Dad smiled. "Absolutely. Passive, and then suddenly aggressive. Laziness bordering on sloth when it comes to hitting the BUY button, and then suddenly we're the most aggressive investors in the world. Believe me, buying just a little bit of a company is almost a bigger disaster than buying none. You'll really hate yourself later when this company makes you a 1,000 percent return and you didn't put a lot of money into it. It's a human frailty to be totally certain and then fail to act on that certainty. You will probably go through that process anyway, but, hey, at least I warned you."

Something important clicked for me. "I get why you don't get too worked up when the market is moving around. If it moves downward, you know you're going to benefit because you're a buyer. And if it moves upward, you also benefit from the prices of your portfolio going to the moon."

"Exactly," he said happily. "In March 2009, when I told Maria Bartiromo at CNBC that I was getting back into the market, it wasn't because I was trying to call the bottom of the crash; it looked like it was still going down. I started buying in because the best couple of companies on my list at that time were priced as if they were cheap private companies instead of public companies. They were on sale big-time but their stock prices were starting to move up. That's all I needed for justification to buy. If those two stock prices had continued going down, I'd have been happy to wait longer. If, after I bought in, the prices stopped going up and started going down more, I would have been happy too, because now I could buy more even cheaper. I told her I didn't know if the market was going to go down to a Dow of 2,500 but it didn't matter to me; I was loading up the truck now."

It was the same experience, from a different angle, I had had when I was learning how to price a company. I felt like I was witnessing the market, and utterly removed from its emotional ups and downs. I could see the fear and exuberance other people felt and acted on, but I was able to stay removed and calm because I had perspective on what was happening and a plan to benefit from it. That's antifragile in action.

I wanted to be like Buffett: ready with a washtub when it's raining gold. That would be a lot easier for me to do if I had a very specific plan ready to go, so that as my mind whirled and I freaked out about the market crashing, and all the yelling guys on CNBC yelled even more than usual, I could open up my Wishlist buying plan and follow it. It would be an "in case of emergency" plan, and I was expecting—and kind of looking forward to—the emergency.

The "In Case of Emergency" Buying Plan

My dad loves to say that I'm supposed to "load up the truck." But what did that actually entail? Should I literally buy everything on my list, or only certain companies?

"As a rule," he stated, "10 percent of your investing portfolio per company." Then, he backed off, immediately. "These are pirate rules. More like guidelines, really."

"What does that really mean, though? Don't put more than 10 percent into a company, no matter what? If there are less or more than ten companies I want to buy, how do I choose?"

He sighed.

"Here's the answer, and then I'll explain, because it probably won't satisfy you. You should buy what you like the best. The way I think Buffett would recommend is 'buy your favorite,' because he says to load up on what you've really thought about."

I laughed. Of course that was the answer. Always Windage. But

I understood what my dad and Buffett meant—I had spent time researching, choosing, and falling in love with my Wishlist. I liked all the companies, but of course I had favorites. It's natural. Buffett was saying that if they're all below my buy price, then I get to buy my favorite ones. I thought another judgment call would annoy me, but I actually kind of loved it. Easy peasy. Just buy my favorites. I could do that.

"If everything goes on sale, it's a great situation to be in! Remember to be thankful for that problem. Massively, hugely, generously thankful. It's a great problem to have."

"True, true, true." I smiled. "That's what I have you around for—to remind me to be thankful when that happens! Because I'm going to be freaking out."

"Nope, you're not going to freak, you're going to know exactly what to do. Here's the question I ask myself: If I can only buy one, which one is it going to be?"

"I have to make that choice?"

"It is a good discipline to recognize that these businesses are not all equal in all regards. One might be *way* under its buy price, while the others are only slightly under. One of them might have a Mission you desperately want to support. One might be more certain to grow quickly or rebound from that Event. One might have management you trust a bit more. Ask yourself, 'If I can own just one of these, which one is it?' Then, ask yourself again, and again, and again, until you know your buying order if they are all on sale."

I remembered Whole Foods and Costco on my Wishlist. "I'd choose Whole Foods."

"Why?"

"Well, Whole Foods seems to me to be much more on sale. It has better Owner Earnings than Costco, which is why it has a better Ten Cap. I also like the values and the CEO more. If these were private companies and I were going to own the whole thing, I'd definitely pick Whole Foods."

"Great. Here's the point to remember: it jumped out at you that Whole Foods is your favorite. So this is your number-one choice."

My dad explained that my Wishlist should have two components to it: names of companies and the price at which you'll buy them. That Wishlist, not the market overall, was going to tell us when to actually buy.

I started to get it. "The Wishlist tells me what to buy. And the buy price tells me when?"

"Exactly."

"I just buy the first one on the list that goes on sale?"

"Basically, that's it. That's why we don't call it a 'watch list' like the rest of the world. We only put companies on the Wishlist that we really want to own, when the price comes down, and we pull the trigger and buy it."

If they all go down together (e.g., in a stock market crash), I should buy my favorite company first and then go down my Wishlist from there. If they don't (e.g., if a given company is undergoing an Event), then I should buy whichever company goes below my buy price first. That made sense, because who knew what would happen with any of the others? Gotta make hay while the sun shines.

Wishlist Buying Plan

Priority	Company	Range of Prices	My Buy Price	Online Alert Set Up for the Price?
1	The Lemonade Stand	Ten Cap: $200 Eight-Year Payback Time: $247 Sticker: $480 MOS: $240	I'll look seriously at $250 per share and below	No—I can't buy it online
2	Whole Foods	Ten Cap: $29 Eight-Year Payback Time: $13 Sticker: $39 MOS: $19	I bought Practice Shares and now I want to buy more	Yes

I made a first draft of my Wishlist buying plan.

Hmm . . . Whole Foods. When I shared the plan with my dad so he could check it over, he noticed.

"You used to be afraid of buying, and now you can't wait to buy. These twin emotions are dangerous. You've got to be steady when you're irrationally fearful, and steady when you're irrationally excited."

"Sometimes it's hard to tell the difference between the right amount of fear—the kind that protects me—and irrational fear."

"We all have a hard time with that. The greatest secret of phenomenal investing results is this simple axiom that I learned from Davy Crockett on TV when I was about eight years old: 'First be sure you're right, then go ahead.' I thought Davy and his coonskin cap walked on water. I would sit on the floor in front of that nineteen-inch black-and-white TV and think, That's how you behave like a real man—first, you get sure that you're right and then you just go do it. Warren Buffett must have been channeling Davy Crockett, because he came up with the inverse: 'If you are at all unsure of what to do, WAIT. Do not go ahead.' And that's why, to protect your emotions as a new investor, I want you to buy a bit differently than one chunk all at once. I want you to allocate four slices of money, or 'tranches,' for each company."

"Okay," I said slowly. *Tranches?*

Buying in Tranches

A tranche is a financial-industrial complex term for "slice" or "portion."

"Because you're buying a company in the middle of an Event, right? And we're not geniuses, so we're definitely not going to time things perfectly. We expect the price of a company to go down and to keep going down. If you buy in tranches, you can take advantage of the opportunity to buy stock in wonderful companies at ever cheaper prices."

"So your tranche system assumes that the price will go down, and lets me take advantage of the falling stock price."

"Exactly. The price going down," Dad noted, "creates an opportunity to buy this great business for an even better price. Think about it like this: If I sold you a $100 bill for $50, would you be upset at your purchase if you now can buy another $100 bill from me for $25? And would you be really angry at yourself if I then offered you another $100 for $10?"

"No, I'd be excited to buy the first one, more excited to buy the second one, and absolutely thrilled to buy the third one."

"Of course! The fact that the third one was a much better price does not take away from the fact that the first one was also a great price. That's the way you must learn to think about all investments. If you're nervous because you don't like the idea of the stock price going down after you bought the company, your intuition might be telling you that you don't understand the business well enough to own it. Pay attention to that voice inside and revisit your Story and inversion until you know you know. But if you know why the price is dropping and you're confident in your buy price and you're still nervous, perhaps on some level you still feel that the price has something to do with the value. Just remember: it doesn't. Price is just what you paid. That's all. It has nothing to do with the value."

By planning for the price to fall, I felt excited to think of buying, instead of feeling unnerved.

I imagined a layer cake with four layers. The cake is my entire investing budget for a given company, and each layer is a tranche—25 percent of what I want to spend on that company. I buy my first tranche of 25 percent, then wait for the price to go down another 10 percent or so and buy my second tranche. After another 10 percent drop, I buy my third tranche. With the last tranche, I just wait.

"Let the thing drop as far as it wants to drop. It might go down another 30 percent. Wait. And when you're pretty sure it's not going down any farther and it's starting to go back up, buy the fourth tranche."

"That's so much more work," I complained. *What happened to the nice, easy "buy your favorite"?* "If I want $10,000 of that company, why not just buy $10,000 of that company and call it good?"

"You can," Dad said, "but obviously you'll miss out on the lower and lower prices. This is a strategy to help you control your emotions, but if you don't like it, that's okay. You don't have to get it just right."

If the price starts to go up, I decided, I'd buy my full allocation and be done with it. I did not want to have to follow the price of my companies too closely or open the "Torture" box of apps on my phone. If the stock price popped up too high, over my buy price, then I wouldn't chase it. It might come down to where I could buy it, or it might not. No point in stressing about it.

"You don't have to get the tranches perfectly right," Dad reiterated. "Just be sure you load up all four tranches while the price is still around your buy price."

"I can see the value of tranching as a psychological comfort. I can tell myself all day that the price should go down after I buy it, but I know from my Practice Shares that when that happens, it hurts."

"If one of the companies on your Wishlist goes on sale and you don't have capital to invest, it does hurt! In one sense, it totally sucks. But rationally it is a great benefit if the price drops if we do have additional capital to allocate to this investment, because we can buy more at an even better price. So yes, this system of tranches is set up to help us handle the emotions of investing and to take advantage of not having perfect timing."

"Anything else to help with that?" I asked.

"Another thing I do to keep my emotions steady in times when the market is rocketing around and I'm being left behind is to keep my eye on two important pieces of information about what the overall market is doing: the Shiller P/E and the Buffett Indicator."

"Oh yes, we talked about them months ago."

"Right. Check those. They'll give you good perspective on the market overall. I actually even do one more thing, so automatically I usually forget about it. It's inconsequential financially, but it helps me."

"Great. I love details."

"When the stock price is getting close to my buy price I buy a small amount to test my resolve. The amount of money is important. It has to be small enough that losing a piece of it isn't a problem but large enough to make me nervous if I don't really know what I thought I knew. With real skin in the game, my perspective on the company changes. It goes from theoretical to real; some kind of unconscious mechanism goes to work in my nervous system and I quickly feel physically and emotionally stressed if I haven't done enough work to have a true sense of certainty. Does that sound a little crazy?"

He had told me about that already, last month. My Practice Shares idea must have really triggered him thinking about how he tiptoes into a stock.

"I've certainly made mistakes even after I got comfortable with my knowledge of the company. But I do think we know more than we can consciously access and I know this little trick is used by a number of good Rule #1 hedge-fund managers. What happens is that the stress stops me from loading up the truck until I dig deeply enough into what's going on that I realize that this one is either Too Hard or a solid yes. There is a huge difference between imagining owning a business and owning it. You might feel that difference in your body."

"That's so interesting. It's exactly like what I did," I pointed out, "by buying my Practice Shares. Buying a small amount to learn the emotions and find out, now that you have to defend being an owner of that company, if there's anything you've missed."

"It is similar and similarly useful. Another little trick I pull on myself is to tell someone whose investing judgment I respect that I'm looking at this company. I don't tell them I already own it because they might soft-pedal their criticism. Just looking. Then I give them what is essentially a one-minute Story about the company. Why it's interesting. I learned I can't say I like it again, because it sets up a change in how this person will respond. Of course, I've already run this idea past friends I do that with, but that was back before the price came down. Now it's almost time to really pull the trigger, and this trick is just a way to nudge the subconscious, to trigger any hidden unknowns."

I laughed. It was so true. Having to tell someone you respect about being interested in a company had crystallized my own opinion on it pretty quickly.

So had telling someone I needed to change my life. After Dad and I ended our long video call, I felt rather introspective. I called Kamala to say hi. Not only had she switched jobs since our rather desperate conversation in January, she had applied for a fellowship to a prestigious writing colony that pays artists and writers to stay at their cabins in the middle of nowhere and do nothing but be creative while they're there. There are so many applicants that the odds of getting in are tiny—but she was accepted. Now she was pondering using that intensive time to launch a freelance writing career. I could not have been prouder of my sweet badass friend, making it happen.

I knew Kamala knew that, when I was taking action in my Investing Practice, I thought back to whether I was living up to our January conversation. Neither of us had referenced it, though, until now. Going over the things happening in our lives, she said, "Remember our talk at the beginning of the year?" Of course I did, I told her.

"Well, it's crazy"—she laughed a bit incredulously under her breath—"but we've both kind of done it. Look at how different things are for both of us since then. And it's not even a whole year yet."

"It's kind of . . . amazing," I agreed. I laughed too. What else was there to do? I had gone from Unconsciously Incompetent to . . . well, I was definitely Conscious now, and, mentally reviewing my skills to date, I realized I felt pretty Competent. I was no longer Incompetent at investing on my own? Me? I smiled.

"We needed to change things, and we *did*. But I couldn't have predicted it would happen this way if my life had depended on it."

"No way."

That's the power of intention. And the support of a good friend, without having to say a word.

OCTOBER PRACTICE: Picking my favorite company puts a smile on my face. Pick your favorite, and write your own Wishlist buying plan for your antifragile portfolio. Then sit back and take a moment to appreciate that you have a list of companies you have researched on your own and want to buy—how different is that from just a few months ago?

When to Sell

| November

I WAS SO EXCITED ABOUT DOING THIS FOR REAL. I MADE A DETAILED Wishlist buying plan spreadsheet and kept it in my "Investing Practice" folder.

I was no longer afraid. I did not want to wait anymore. I was feeling a kind of Christmas-morning desperation to unwrap what's under the tree. I wanted to use what I had learned.

I knew patience was the key. But I wanted to get in there and do it now.

Buying Comes Before Selling

My dad had said from the beginning that I should not plan to buy anything this entire year and he hadn't been too happy when I brought it up again the previous month. I didn't know if my wanting to buy meant that things had gone better or worse than he expected, but I hadn't gotten this far by ignoring my own instincts. I would

wait for the right time and price, obviously, but I definitely wanted
to buy.

I thought about keeping my decision from my dad, but that went
against everything we had built together over the last months. We
had become something of a team, he and I. He had invested so much
in me, and I certainly wasn't going to leave him out of such a moment. Hopefully I could convince him. I called him up in Atlanta.
We would see each other later in the month for Thanksgiving, but I
didn't want to wait on this.

"Dad, I want to buy some shares of Whole Foods for real. It's the
right time."

I laid my pitch on him. "They have a huge Brand Moat and loyal
customers who think in terms of the franchise name. The price is
the lowest it has been in over six years! I love the company and I
understand its business. The debt is so low it can be paid off with the
cash they have on hand. It has great return on invested capital and
return on equity for a grocer. And the Owner Earnings is huge. John
Mackey, the CEO, is a genius with amazing integrity and values.
The price is just a bit higher than the Ten Cap price, but it's such
a popular company that the worries about it are already priced in,
and I don't think it's going to go much lower than this again. I don't
think waiting two months will help me any more than right now. I
think it's time for me to take a full position. All of it. Now."

He thought it over, leaving a long silence on the phone. I let him
sit with it, waiting. It was a big decision for him too. Was I ready?

He came back. "Yeah, okay. You practiced, and now you're ready.
It's time for you to go for it."

That was so much easier than I thought. He loved Practice Shares
now! And he agreed that I was ready.

I felt like a bird who wanted to fly the nest and had gotten a little
nudge to do just that. He trusted me to fly. It wasn't a small thing.
As my teacher, on some level he had his name on the line for my
investing choices. Though I would do my own thing, obviously, just

as I always had, we were inextricably connected in this endeavor. It felt like a graduation.

I was going to own this business for real. I bought Whole Foods at $30.85 per share.

And it was a breeze.

It was so easy for me that it was almost like a video game. I bought the shares, didn't panic, and ignored the price I bought at. It was so easy that I wondered if I had actually just spent part of my precious investing funds, or if I had imagined the whole five-minute experience.

As I logged out of my brokerage account, I wondered if I should do it over again just to make sure it was done. I leaned back in my chair and remembered sitting in that exact spot, quivering while buying my Practice Shares. I was so happy that I had practiced buying shares. The pendulum of emotions had swung so far the other way, I couldn't quite believe it even as it was happening. And I really did want the price to go down, not up, so I could buy another tranche even cheaper.

I was feeling pretty antifragile right about then. I guess that's what all my practice was for.

For Thanksgiving, my parents (they get along well enough now to have holidays together), my dad's wife, my sister and her husband, my sister-in-law, and I gathered as a family at my sister's house in San Diego. We had a guest there: Nuno flew in from Zurich to meet them. No pressure. They were eager to meet this guy I had been changing my life around for and show him what American Thanksgiving is all about.

After all the turkey and mashed potatoes and wine, we scattered around the house chatting, doing dishes, and watching football (American football, the real football, which the visiting European among us was smart enough to accept without comment). Dad and I collapsed on the side couch in the living room. Something was nagging at me that I needed to ask him.

Now that I was a real investor, how would I know when to sell? I couldn't just keep holding companies forever.

Sagely, slowly, like a Zen koan tinged with pinot noir, my dad replied, "Buffett says, 'The right time to sell a company is never.'"

Never? Had the Thanksgiving turkey's tryptophan gone to his head? I made him an espresso to perk him up, and then kept at it.

"In real life, though," I clarified. "In reality. When do you sell?"

"I'm serious," he insisted. "Unless the Story of the company changes, you should never sell that company. This is another mistake I've made, because compounding depends on holding on for the long haul. I bought a lot of companies in 2009 that I sold in 2015. I should have held on longer, because they're still going up. It's all in the attitude. You should have that attitude of never selling when you decide what to buy. A smart investor who buys a wonderful company at a good price should not be thinking about selling that company, ever. Doing less actually accomplishes more."

I took his point as a metaphorical one: have the attitude that I'm never going to sell this company, and I'll take buying it a lot more seriously. Just like our *Maro* thankfulness, planning to own a company forever would definitely put me in a serious-commitment frame of mind.

Still, I needed to know how a Rule #1 investor takes profits. In real life, in the real world. I wasn't going to lock up my money forever. "Buffett sells companies."

"Absolutely," Dad agreed. "Buffett routinely sells companies. And yet he says he never wants to sell companies. How do we reconcile that?"

I stared at him. Exactly my point.

"The reason is that he only sells when the Story changes. Only. Otherwise, he'd keep it. Why sell?"

I stared at him some more.

"Think about it like this: You're trying to find maybe twenty great companies you can buy on sale in your lifetime. What makes these companies great, by definition, is that they have big Moats that protect their profits, low debt, a lot of Owner Earnings and free cash flow, and they are led by great people with a Mission that matches your values. If you owned the whole company, you'd never, ever sell it."

"Definitely," I agreed. Especially if it had dividends coming off it into my bank account.

"However," he went on, "companies don't last as long as they used to—even wonderful ones. Now, new ideas replace old ideas faster than ever in history. One hundred years ago, the average life span of a company in the S&P 500 was sixty-seven years. Now the average life span of such a company is fifteen years. We investors have to be aware of how the Story is changing—most often by the Moat being breached by a sea change in the industry, brought on by a major shift in the way people consume. Look at what Amazon is doing to retail stores. Or what health consciousness has done to the center aisles of a grocery store. Or what the iPhone did to Nokia and BlackBerry. These changes in shopping or culture or technology are a form of creative destruction."

I had seen it many times in my startup and venture capital work. A new idea would come along and change the paradigm for how a given market worked.

As a society, it's fantastic for us to keep moving forward and innovating. As an investor, it meant I had to stay on top of my Stories.

Dad was on a roll now. "Look at the car rental industry today; they are on the eve of destruction from ride-sharing and driverless cars. The combination means that in a couple of years a Tesla will drive you to work and then spend the day taking other people around town and then it will come back and pick you up at work at the end of the day. You'll pay your car off with the income from ride-sharing or Tesla might just give you the car to put it in the ride-sharing pool; for sure people will need fewer cars. A salesperson at Neiman Marcus told me she moved to San Diego a year ago, didn't buy a car, and went from home to work and back with Lyft for $5 each way. No car

---

* BBC, "Can a Company Live Forever?" January 2012.

payments, no gas, no maintenance, no insurance, no parking issues, and only about $200 a month. And that's in San Diego, where you've always needed a car. Now you don't. It's a paradigm shift. What's that disruptive technology going to mean for car companies, ride-share companies, car rental companies, used car sales companies, and all the companies that service those companies with insurance, parts, parking, and loans? With all those garages empty, what happens to the storage industry? As an investor, you have an opinion on the answers to those questions, or that company is Too Hard. And there is nothing wrong with it being Too Hard."

I laughed. "I know!"

"Just keep focused on what is not Too Hard. Look at what Buffett and Munger own, for example. Buffett owns Apple and IBM, Wells Fargo and American Express, Coke and Kraft and Phillips 66. All of them have the required big Moat that makes it really hard for competitors to wipe them out. Even Kraft, with all of its total-crap food from the 1950s, will still be going strong in ten years—if only because their food is cheap and well known. That's Price and Brand Moats. Buffett's values may not be your values, but that's not the point—the point is to own companies that do match your values, resist change, and then never sell them."

"Buffett's statement never to sell really means 'Never sell as long as the Story stays the same.'"

"Precisely. For many companies, their Story will change due to new technology. For others, they won't be touched. Your job is to stay on top of it. Bill Gates once suggested to Buffett that he buy a computer (and by extension computer companies) because 'they're going to change everything.' Buffett replied, 'Will they change the way people chew gum?' Some businesses are much more exposed to a Moat breach than others."

"We sell if the Moat gets breached for sure. What about management?"

"If they've become traitors to the stakeholders, then we sell that company too. So, if debt starts rising, ROIC starts dropping, the CEO isn't telling us what's really going on, then yes, we might sell then."

"Okay, Moat broken, management turning into scumbags. When else?"

"Occasionally when the price gets way too high. But as a novice Rule #1 investor with an income from outside your investing that will provide you with a steady stream of cash to invest, if you love the company and the Story isn't changing, just stick with it and count on basis reduction to protect you from the ups and downs of the market."

Basis reduction? Was that like a lovely white wine reduction sauce to go on our Thanksgiving turkey?

"Explain, please."

Reducing Your Basis

"I use 'basis' to mean the adjusted investment capital you have in the stock. Remember planning out allocation in your portfolio? We used the example of investing a total of $10,000 into one company. So, your basis in that company is $10,000."

So it has nothing to do with wine or sauce. Foin.

"Reducing your basis means lowering the dollar amount of capital you have invested in the stock. This is one of Buffett's greatest secrets for lowering risk and raising the overall return. He buys companies that, over time, pay down the amount he's invested in them by sending him some of their free cash flow. The free cash flow coming to the owner year after year can reduce the owner's basis, and the lower the basis, the lower the risk of ownership. Buffett has a portfolio full of businesses that have already paid him back his original investment."

"Those companies didn't hold on to that money to try to grow?"

"Free cash flow—remember, that's cash left over after the company has already invested in growth—can be allocated to whatever the management and board want."

He went on. "To avoid the ROE and ROIC dropping from just sitting on excess cash, the CEOs of Buffett's companies can use the excess cash in a few ways. They could spend it on growing the business by investing in the next generation of products or on more aggressive marketing that might increase earnings and raise ROE. They could spend it on external growth by buying other companies—maybe a competing manufactured home builder or carpet company. Or, if those options have already been maxed out and the company still has excess cash, they could distribute it to the owners of the business—to Buffett for him to invest."

I noticed I completely understood all the terms he was using, and I smiled to myself. After just ten months, I had learned a lot. It was a nice moment of victory, made even sweeter when I realized Dad hadn't noticed my moment of victory in the slightest, because he, by now, didn't question that I understood his language. We were two investors, chatting.

"Oh, I see," I realized. "We're talking about dividends."

"Right, when a company passes on cash to the owner, it's called a dividend payment."

Dividends

Many companies pay out cash directly to shareholders quarterly. They literally put money in your brokerage account for doing nothing except owning the stock. Pretty cool. A dividend gives the owners a return of some of their investment capital and reduces their basis. If I have a $10,000 basis from my original investments and this company sends me $100, I simply subtract the $100 dividend from my original $10,000 basis and I now have an adjusted basis of $9,900. This dividend is my money coming back off the table.

"By the way," my dad went on, "most of the world looks at stocks only for the return they get upon selling the stock. The way I look at it is more like a private investor. I want my money back as fast as possible. I want a return *of* my capital before I worry about a return *on* my capital." Dad was channeling Mark Twain, who said, "I am more concerned about the return *of* my money than the return *on* my money."[*]

"You want all your money back from dividends?"

"Absolutely. That would be great." My dad gave me an example of Coca-Cola's dividend payments, which between 2005 and 2015 paid out a cumulative $9.21 per share.[†] The stock was selling for around $20 in early 2005, so the adjusted basis per share would have dropped to $11 after those ten years. That means that, even if the stock price went nowhere, the effective rate of return doubled.

The return doubled! Just from using dividends to reduce basis!

Was the power of dividends something everyone already knew?

"Oh, yeah. Shareholders can become addicted to the dividend and will scream bloody murder if they don't get paid what they were expecting," my dad noted. It was true, and I could see why. If I bought Coca-Cola for its dividend and didn't get it, I would not be pleased. Investors get locked in to those expectations, and even if it stretches their cash, companies keep that dividend going up to avoid worrying their shareholders. It's already happening now: Coca-Cola's free cash flow is down considerably from its recent peak in 2014, but they just raised their dividend, as usual, as if all is well.

Buying a company for its dividend seemed crazy to me. Why wouldn't I want a wonderful company, with management I trust with my own money, to handle the money as they see fit? With a recession, a market disruption, an Event, they could easily decide the company needs the money more than the shareholders.

"It's because, just like fund managers, these executives are judged on short-term results, quarter to quarter. They want to keep

---

[*] Mark Twain Performs, October 28, 2017, http://marktwainperforms.com/quotes.html.
[†] Coca-Cola Dividends, http://www.coca-colacompany.com/investors/investors-info-dividends. However, these dividend amounts have to be adjusted for subsequent stock splits.

shareholders happy, and since most shareholders don't bother with looking at their numbers, they can get away with it without being challenged. That's one reason. The other reason is that people really depend on that dividend. It's an important part of their retirement income, and if it doesn't come, it's a huge shock to their financial plans. The pressure to keep that dividend coming is intense, and unless there is something terrible happening with the business, they're going to keep it coming as long as they can. For example, BP cut its dividend when the Gulf well disaster happened, but reinstated it as quickly as it could because a huge percentage of British pensioners depend on that BP dividend to eat."

The power of dividends was sinking in for me. Having a steadily rising dividend attracts investors and builds trust in the company, but it puts the company into what is essentially an implied contract of expectations between the company and its shareholders that, once entered, the company can never breach: a Dividend Contract of Expectations. The agreement in a Dividend Contract of Expectations is that the company will continually pay an increasing dividend, and shareholders will interpret that payment as a sign of the company's strong financial health. If the company ever stops paying the dividend—even if the company was perfectly financially healthy and had made a managerial decision that it could use its funds better internally—shareholders would consider the Dividend Contract of Expectations breached, trust would disappear, and the stock price would likely dive.

Dad wrote in *Rule #1* about General Motors paying its dividend out of borrowed money because it knew that not paying it would cause a panic and crater the stock. As long as it paid its dividend, investors assumed everything was fine because, remember, dividends are supposed to be paid out of the company's extra cash. They paid their dividend right up until declaring bankruptcy in 2008. The dividend payment itself becomes the focus, not the good use of the money. Which is ridiculous.

Apple didn't pay dividends for sixteen years, because Steve Jobs believed the company could use that money to create more marketing or acquire even better products and do so with a continuously high ROE and ROIC, and, in fact, the company did so in spite of hoarding $100 million in cash. After Jobs passed away from cancer in 2011, his successor announced a quarterly dividend in 2012.* Since then, Apple has paid its dividend every quarter and raised its dividend amount steadily. Even so, as of this writing it has over $200 billion in cash, its ROE and ROIC have dropped dramatically, and shareholders are looking hungrily at that money. By choosing to pay dividends, Apple has entered into the Dividend Contract of Expectations that Steve Jobs wanted to avoid.

Companies know about the Dividend Contract of Expectations and use it to their advantage. When you're financially strong, you declare a dividend, right? So, they declare a dividend to make people think they are financially strong. "Dividends are a tricky thing," my dad mused. "Companies that are doing well and don't need their extra free cash should probably declare a dividend. But dividends being paid out do not automatically mean a company is doing well, and they do not automatically mean a dividend is the best use of money."

A dividend reduces basis, but isn't necessarily the best use of company funds. Company A pays a dividend; Company B does not. If they are exactly the same otherwise, which is the better investment? A lot of people would say the company with the dividend is a better deal because they want that check.

The answer is another Windage judgment call. There are so many options for using free cash flow that may be better for the company. It could buy other companies, it could do a ton of research and development, it could buy back its own stock, it could stockpile the cash and use it for a rainy day in the future. The only reason to

---

give it to the shareholders is if there's really no good investment it can be allocated to.

Which may be the case. An efficient public company that has already gone through its peak growing phase, just like an efficient private company, will probably (hopefully) have extra cash after having done all those things. It will choose to return free cash flow to its owners. Company A is only a better deal if they really are otherwise exactly the same, which of course would never exist in the real world.

My dad added, "The real-world answer is that no two companies are equal. You have to look at how much free cash they have and how they have used it in the past, then decide for yourself if the management is allocating the money well. What is the return on equity? Is it, like Apple, around 30 percent per year? If so, if they give you the cash instead, can you make 30 percent per year on it? If not, let them keep it. Don't fall into the trap of the Dividend Contract of Expectations. Forget the contract. There is no contract."

"The thing is, though, again in the real world, having money show up in my brokerage account sounds pretty good."

"I don't think that's a great way to look at it. You want to put your money into great companies because great companies allocate their cash in the best way. For some, it's paying a dividend. But don't buy companies based on whether or not they pay a dividend unless for some reason you need to live on that cash. If you focus on the dividend, you might pass up a much better company for one that pays a dividend, and that is not a great idea. Always go for the company that is the best company and let them decide where the cash goes. The most obvious example of that way of thinking is Berkshire Hathaway. It has been one of the best investments on the planet for about fifty years and it has never paid a dividend."

He paused and thought for a second.

"Okay, that said, if you have lots of money and you want to have an income from your portfolio to spend—as opposed to reinvesting the income—then investing in companies with dividends is one way to go. Get the quarterly dividends, live off that, and hopefully your stocks will also go up. If they don't, eh, you still have the dividends."

Errrr . . .

"That's great for people with lots of money," I began, hoping he would get the picture. "But for the rest of us . . ."

"Oh!" he exclaimed. "Yeah, for the rest of us, dividends are money that can get taxed and then has to be put right back to work in another investment. For investors trying to get to financial freedom, dividends are a bit of a problem."

I thought about that for a second. Was a dividend a problem?

"Keep it simple, silly," he answered. "Stay focused on the return on equity and the choices management makes. Stick with the basic principles of Rule #1 investing and don't be swayed by other influences like dividends. Invest in wonderful businesses and let them decide how to allocate the capital, not the other way around. I want you to understand dividends and buybacks as a way of reducing basis, but not as a way of determining what company to own."

Buybacks

Basis also goes down if the company buys back its own shares of stock from the open market, because then each stockholder owns a higher percentage of the company without doing a thing. It's not as direct a reduction of basis as dividends are, but buybacks do matter to the bottom line. Charlie Munger calls these companies "the cannibals" because they're eating themselves. The end result is that everyone who still owns stock in the company now effectively controls a larger per-share percentage of the company than they did before those shares were taken out of public circulation, and because the company's equity is reduced, ROE and ROIC often go up immediately. So does Earnings Per Share.

It's like when Ginger Spice left the Spice Girls and five beacons of girl power suddenly became four—but those four were still the Spice Girls (at least for a while). They each went from being 20 percent to 25 percent of the group without doing anything except sticking around. It's exactly the same process in the stock market, just harder to see because it is on a much larger scale.

IBM has been buying back its own stock for twenty years. Anyone who bought the stock in 1996 now owns double the percentage of the business that they owned then. Obviously, many investors know IBM has been buying and canceling their own stock, and have bought IBM shares because of that, which sent the stock price up. At its peak, that investment would have doubled three times in twenty years, for a compounded annual return of about 12 percent per year for two decades. Pretty good. In addition, IBM paid out dividends that, split adjusted, totaled $43, which reduced that investment basis to zero in under sixteen years.

One thing bothered me, though.

"You don't actually get paid for buybacks, right? You don't get the cash."

"You don't get cash, that's true. But often, like IBM, the stock price goes up in lieu of cash because buybacks increase Earnings Per Share (less stock, same earnings, higher EPS), and you get more dividend cash for each share of stock you own. But even if management has no better place to put our money, buybacks can be a bad decision for a company if management buys back stock at a price that is higher than the actual value of the business."

"Wait. Why does the stock price they buy it at matter?"

"They've got to buy it on sale, or it's a bad investment—just like us. If IBM is worth $200 per share and the company buys back its stock at $120, the remaining shareholders get the benefit of that differential of $80 per share. The company paid $120, and got a $200 value. That's a good deal by any standard."

"A buyback is kind of an imaginary gain, because I'm happy the stock price is higher, but it's not money in my pocket the way a dividend is."

"That's exactly right," Dad acknowledged. "It's money in your brokerage account, not in your bank account. You would have to sell shares to realize the gains. But that's the whole point of what we're doing here. We want companies that are doing the most they can with their dollars, and we don't care if it's money in our brokerage account or our bank account, because we're going to put it right back into the company anyway. Remember when I showed you the incredible power of compounding? Putting dividends back in the company when it's on sale makes those incredible compounding numbers happen."

"So I shouldn't take that dividend cash and buy the new Porsche 911?" I kidded him. Well, half kidded.

He laughed. "Do whatever you want, but know the consequences of giving up those compounded returns down the road."

For American companies, there is also a tax component to the choice to pay dividends or buy their own stock. "Don't forget the influence of tax incentives," my dad always cautions me. Of course. American corporations that pay out dividends are subjecting their owners to double taxation: the corporation pays taxes on its income, and then the dividend recipients pay taxes again on their dividend income that came from the company's net income after taxes. Same money, taxed twice. Buybacks avoid double taxation. Not the best reason for a company to choose buybacks, but important to keep in mind.

"Allowing corporations to deduct their business expenses distorts their decisions," Dad added, now on a rant about taxes. "They know if they buy a big jet that they can expense, a huge chunk of it gets paid with tax savings. Our tax system encourages these CEOs to spend, spend, spend, without worrying too much about it since a percentage is coming out of the taxes. With a tax system that rewards savings, our corporations would be much more profitable, and much more of those profits would come back to the owners in untaxed dividends and to employees in higher wages and more jobs."

"And the owners are mostly ordinary people who are saving for retirement," I noted.

"Yeah, they are, aren't they? Pension funds for firefighters, teachers, 401k savings, IRAs . . . these are the owners of most of the stock of American businesses. Hardly the fat cats that some politicians pretend they are. But people are so ignorant that they vote for people who help keep them down. If we can just get more people to understand how to invest, we're going to have a lot more better-educated voters, and a lot less crony capitalism."

Dad was on his rant and I'd heard it a hundred times. Didn't mean he's wrong. John Mackey is a reformed socialist turned libertarian who argues the same thing in his book *Conscious Capitalism*. If more of us voted our values and our own self-interest for our own financial freedom, we'd have a better country, instead of being captured by unethical CEOs and Wall Street exploiters who are doing everything they can to keep us ignorant about their compensation schemes, taxation schemes, and fund management schemes. That's why Mission is vital. I can't trust an unethical company to protect its stakeholders.

After I did my own research into buybacks, I discovered two areas of caution. First, don't trust buyback announcements alone. Remember that CEOs sometimes lie. Buyback announcements tend to make the stock price jump up, so sometimes they announce stock buybacks for that purpose. Then they never actually follow through with buying the shares. I know. It's so scammy. And scummy. Check to make sure the company bought the stock. Second, once a company actually completes the buyback, the Earnings Per Share go up immediately because there are fewer shares. That makes the company's accounting look better, which makes the CEO look better. Sometimes the CEO's compensation is tied to Earnings-Per-Share targets, an incentive structure that simply begs for buybacks that jack up the Earnings Per Share. They call this scheme "financial engineering," a game that makes earnings look like they are growing. I usually check to see if growing Earnings Per Share is connected to regular buybacks before believing the numbers.

Dad and I leaned back on the couch and listened to the pleasant sounds of people who were not us doing the dishes in the kitchen. Nuno was telling my mom about Lisbon.

"Here's what I want for you," my dad said quietly. "In ten years, you should have a portfolio of companies that you no longer have any basis in that are continuing to pay you a nice income every year from dividends."

"That would be fantastic." I tried to imagine that, with my successful investor self working at this practice until, someday, in not too many years—I couldn't remember my exact Number—the practice will be working for me and I can do whatever I want the rest of my life. Freedom.

"And down the road," he offered, "I'll show you how to use stock options to create even more cash flow out of your portfolio without any extra risk at all."

What? There was more?! I laughed, feeling pretty happy to keep practicing exactly what I had learned this year. Maybe eventually I would be up to learn some new tricks, or maybe not. Charlie never had. I wanted to stick with Charlie.

Still, he had not totally answered my original question. "I know the right time to sell is never."

"Unless the Story changes."

"So then, how will I know if the Story has changed enough to sell?"

When to Throw In the Towel and Sell

Dad said, "Knowing when to sell starts with the Story inversion. When you invert the Story, you determine those things that can wreck the company, that make it a not-wonderful company, that make it a not-on-sale company. Things like breached Moats and dishonorable CEOs and a soaring stock market. So, in a sense, once it's on the Wishlist, you've already begun the process of determining when to sell."

"Wait, I'm thinking about when to sell this thing I'm never going to sell, even when I don't own it yet?"

"Yup."

I cracked up. This guy. King of the contradictions.

Dad laughed and protested: "Because knowing when to sell is really about a change to the Story that says you should buy. We sell when the Story changes. That means inverting the story tells us what the business will start to look like when it's time to sell."

Inverting the Story already told me what could be wrong with the company. I'd plug the new information into my Inverted Story to see if it was getting worse.

Dad gave me an example. "Let's go buy Chipotle Mexican Grill in 2009 at $55. By 2014 nothing about its Story changed except its price reached over $600. That's a change in the Story, because it simply wasn't worth that much or anything close to that much. So now it's time to sell and lock in a 60 percent compounded annual return. The stock is now on the Wishlist because I want to buy it again if it ever goes back down. Much to our chagrin the stock continues to go up to $749 and then the news pops up in our e-mail that there is an *E. coli* issue. That's a big Event. We plug that into the Inverted Story. What does food poisoning do to the 'We're all about super-healthy gourmet food' Brand Moat? Bad stuff, right? It becomes an inverted argument: 'Don't buy this business, because its brand is busted and nobody is going to go to the stores anymore.' Is that true? Go find out. Ask at your local Chipotle. What's happening out there? Let's say we decide it isn't a long-term problem but it's still too pricey to buy, but just about then here comes another Event: another *E. coli* scare. Now the stock really drops down to $400. Is it time to buy more shares? Do the inversion: *E. coli* is killing the brand. Revenue and earnings are certainly going to go down. Then do the rebuttal—how long will the problem last? Two years, three years, ten years? How long have *E. coli* scares lasted with other fast-food places? You decide it's not a long-term Moat-killer, which means instead of selling, it's time to buy more shares. But at what price? Now plug in the two to three years of terrible earnings or adjust the Windage Growth Rate downward. What's the business doing for earnings ten years out if the first three years have zero earnings? You decide the right price to buy more is somewhere around $300. It goes on your Wishlist with a $300 target."

Whew. What had I gotten myself into, constant vigilance? "What does that even mean in real life?" I asked him. "How much attention do I have to pay to these companies?" Just keeping up with ten companies on my Wishlist was starting to sound like a full-time job.

"It's not that major," he reassured me. "You already did everything you needed to by researching the company before you bought it. First, you have people running the company whom you trust. Because they manage your company with integrity, they are going to tell you everything you need to know every quarter with their quarterly report filed with the SEC, and when they put that report out they also usually do a live report broadcast via webinars for about half an hour. The report is usually followed by an extensive question-and-answer period where analysts from big investment banks and hedge funds ask questions, all of which are transcribed, usually that day, and are available to read online."

"They deliver the annual report—the 10-K—also with a question-and-answer session."

"Yes, and when management delivers the annual report, it takes longer—often a couple of hours—and it is also available live and via transcript. There is also an annual shareholders' meeting. The total time it takes to review these reports is about six hours per year, per company, if nothing much is changing with the Story. Ten companies, sixty hours total, which works out to about an hour a week."

"Okay, I can handle that. What else?"

"Keep up on news and research. You should also continue to improve your knowledge about competitors and the industry by making it a habit to read the *Wall Street Journal*, *Barron's*, *Fortune*, and *Forbes*. Read the analysis done on Seeking Alpha."

I had already set up e-mail alerts for my companies. It put the news about them right into my e-mail, which was great, because I knew I would somehow miss it otherwise. I had also set up direct alerts from the SEC when my companies made a filing.

"Don't forget to keep track of what Gurus are doing with your company through the 13F SEC filings," Dad added. "The information is delayed by up to ninety days because of the SEC filing deadlines, but it is still really valuable to notice that Pabrai or Spier or Buffett is starting to buy or sell one of the companies on your Wishlist."

So nice to have Warren and Charlie tell me what they're up to on a quarterly basis.

"And just as in my Chipotle example, keep track of the difference between price and value. As Warren says, 'A simple rule dictates my buying: Be fearful when others are greedy, and be greedy when others are fearful.' He means we buy on the Events and we sell when the price gets too high.

"Now don't get too worried about the ongoing time commitment," he went on. "You're not going to have ten companies on your Wishlist overnight. You only have a few right now. You just get started learning about a business you like and can understand, and then go about following it as I've taught you. Go the right speed for you."

I smiled. "Okay, Dad." I remembered my idea to make this be a lifetime practice. I had to keep starting right where I was, just like with yoga, and not try to go any faster than I could right then.

"The actual practice is simple, just as Charlie said it is. But, as you've learned, simple is not the same as easy. Easy comes with mastery, and mastery comes with practice. What you've learned this year will apply to every true investment you make the rest of your life.

---

* Buffett famously wrote this in a *New York Times* op-ed, October 17, 2008.

These rules apply to real estate investments, limited partnership, buying a farm, buying your own business or franchise, starting your own lemonade stand, everything. With this knowledge, you'll avoid so many mistakes, and you'll only invest when you are certain it will turn out well down the road. You'll invest in wonderful businesses. Even if you get the price wrong, the right business will eventually make you money—time will cure all your mistakes as long as you buy wonderful businesses, just as it does with well-located real estate. And that's the key to sleeping at night—know what you own is awesome, and don't worry too much about the price you paid. Eventually, it will all work out much better than any other investment you can make."

"The only circumstances under which I should sell are if the Story of the company changes," I reiterated. "Otherwise, the time to exit is never. Keep on top of my companies with e-mail alerts and pay attention to the company filings. Any changing facts, plug them into the Story and the inversion to see if it makes me want to exit."

"Keep practicing, Danielle," he advised, back to his Zen attitude. "You've learned a staggering amount in the last months. I've taught you everything you need to be completely, consciously, confidently competent."

Everything?

NOVEMBER PRACTICE: Check to see if any of the companies you've been researching have issued dividends or done buybacks. It might or might not be almost time to buy, so set up a method of tracking your purchases, adjusted basis, and sales of a company so that you're completely ready. There's no more math!

CHAPTER 12

Living Thankfulness

| December

This Month

▶ Checklist for Ongoing Investing Practice
▶ *Maro*—Thankfulness

COMING INTO THE HOLIDAY SEASON IN DECEMBER, I SAT DOWN IN MY big chair before my typical weekend Investing Practice call with my dad. Things were getting busy with the end of the year and the holidays, so I consciously took a moment to relax. I noticed that my Year of Investing Practice was very close to being finished.

What a year it had been. I realized that the impact of this year on me was more about how I felt about my life than any tangible change *to* my life. I thought back to how I had felt in January—indeed, for my entire life until that January. Almost a year ago, sitting in that chair, panicking about my health and my job and my financial future, I had felt deeply shaky. Insecure. Unsettled. I had not known where to focus to make my finances better or where to even begin. More than anything, I felt afraid. I was afraid of the future, afraid of what would happen if I took action, afraid of making the wrong financial decision, afraid of losing money, and afraid of what it meant for my life that I did not have options.

But then, an extraordinary thing happened, which I could see clearly only in hindsight: I put my intention out there and asked for help from the universe. I did not realize what I was setting in motion, nor did I have a clue what help would even look like. I knew only that I needed it. I thought back to my conversation with Kamala, sitting in the same chair, in January. We had both despaired that anything could ever change for the better, because neither of us had any sense of what could realistically be different. Still, I thought about freedom, I spoke my desire for freedom out loud, and I asked for help.

I put my intention for freedom out into the universe. And when I did that, the universe helped me in ways I did not foresee. I did not foresee that putting that intention out there would—poof!—manifest options to help me almost immediately. I did not foresee that making the decision to act would initially be so difficult, or that the process of deciding what to do would result in one of the keys of my Investing Practice—my Missions. I did not foresee that I would feel more connected to the people and infrastructure around me after having an Investing Practice for less than a year. I was seeing the world through the eyes of an investor; simply by learning about valuing companies for the good things they do and by appreciating the good things they do, I understood my world better. I did not foresee that the fear I felt that made me avoid investing would become the real focus of this entire year, a fear that I massaged and kneaded when it did not serve me and learned to respect when it did. My fear and I were much closer friends than we had been almost a year ago.

I certainly did not foresee that my Investing Practice would force me to confront my childhood scars and, through the work, give my dad and me a much closer relationship. Actually, one of the fears I had was that we would clash during this year. I half expected that my dad would push me too quickly to take investing action that I was not comfortable with, and it would become a wedge between us. That never happened.

Instead, my dad, maybe for the first time in my life, respected my pace. I thought back to when we listened to Charlie's Four Principles of Investing. I did not think there was anything more to discuss and, on my own, I would have stopped there. He knew that I wanted a true education, though, and he trusted me to do the work he set before me.

Most especially, he trusted me to add my own ideas to this practice, and he was flexible enough to even change a few of his long-held ways of doing things. I mean, the guy changed the way he priced companies to help me understand it more easily. Neither of us expected that. When I needed to learn pricing and valuation formulas, he trusted me to make them my own. His faith in me was a communication of love that I will never forget. He trusted me to do this well, and I trusted him to do this well, and together, we developed a better practice than I think he even expected. The whole of our Investing Practice became more than the sum of our separate parts; it put my dad and me back together again.

My dad and I got on our Investing Practice call together.

"Dad, it's the official last month of my Investing Practice."

"Wait, what?" he exclaimed. "I've gotten so used to our practice together, honey."

"Me too."

I really had gotten used to regularly learning from my dad. He had become so good at teaching. He listened to my concerns and fears and actually heard them. He seemed to enjoy it too.

"It's been pretty cool to see you becoming a real investor. I've been doing it so long that I barely even remember learning it, but teaching it to you has brought some of that excitement back. Talking about investing with you has made my own investing better. I think about it even more carefully than I used to, because I want to make sure I'm teaching you the right things."

"I've learned a real way to take care of myself," I told him, "and that feels . . . extraordinary. I did not really expect it."

"No? What did you expect?"

"I expected to learn some basics and hoped we would get along."

He laughed. "I think we've done amazingly well at that, actually. It's been really special to get to talk so regularly, and I feel like you trust me a bit more now."

"Well, you know a thing or two," I teased.

"I know, I know, but I meant you seem to trust me more in a larger sense, and I hope that's true."

"That's true," I confirmed quietly. "You've stuck it out with me, and did so even when it was hard."

"Of course I did, and even though the year is ending, our Investing Practice together won't end. There's still a lot to practice."

"I know there is. Remember when you told me that a huge part of learning and investing well is knowing what you don't know?"

"Yes, of course."

"Well, I'm very aware of how much I don't know. Don't get me wrong, I know I've learned a lot. I expected to learn about how you invest. I did not really expect to internalize it and make it my own. Especially in the midst of feeling so utterly incompetent for months."

It had been so frustrating to feel completely, torturously, frustratingly incompetent. Not my favorite period of this year. For a while, I wasn't convinced that it would ever change. It was scary to be acutely conscious of my own incompetence—at something I actually wanted to be good at too. Only my dad's knowledge and his confidence in me assuaged that fear, and it took a lot of baby steps to make my way out of that fog and into a clearer view. I was an Unconsciously Incompetent investor for most of my life, and as soon as I became Consciously Incompetent, the first thing I was conscious of was my fear. It took a few months to develop enough knowledge to work with my fear in a way that would support, instead of hinder, my Investing Practice.

Now I followed the news and regularly looked for my Missions in companies. I noticed the multitude of companies I encountered every day and I kept notes of the people running them. I observed larger market and macroeconomic shifts and knew enough to have opinions about them. I knew about how to develop my own antifragility in my portfolio and in my own emotions. I had a plan about what to do when there was a downturn in the market. That incredible fear I felt in January? Knowledge is truly the great equalizer. I now felt strong—no—I felt antifragile. A crash in the market terrified me before; I wanted my money under my mattress. Now I knew exactly what to do when that happened. I even, antithetical to all normal emotions, hoped it would happen. Not because I wanted anyone else to lose money. Simply because when a market gets overheated with prices being higher than values, it is dominated by greed and is not a healthy place to leave hard-earned money. And it needs to come back to earth for me to be able to invest.

Months into this practice, I knew that I could select a wonderful company at the right price. That's an extraordinary thing. I can research a company from the comfort of my couch, decide if I trust the management, calculate three different methods of price, use my own judgment to decide what the right price is, and decide how much of my portfolio it deserves.

And now I know I can be wrong and be okay. This antifragile practice has built-in safeguards like a big Margin of Safety on the price, investing in multiple companies, and well-vetted checklists, and it requires that if I'm not sure about any part of it, I should wait.

How could I be more thankful? There wasn't anything else to add. I had all the ingredients.

And, I knew there was a lot I still didn't know. I saw how easily and naturally my dad evaluated a company. When we sat together and researched La Croix a few months earlier, it was a big moment for us. The next level was for me to get faster in my research and evaluation, with more internalized information and perspective on industries and companies, with more background on well-known management, and with more confidence in pricing. I could stand to learn a lot more about accounting, if I could stomach it. Conscious

Competence was going to be a long practice in itself, I could tell. There's always a next level, even for the masters.

"I've noticed how much more there is I can know," I told my dad, "and that makes me feel like a beginner all over again."

Dad guffawed. "Just like yoga! That's the practice, honey. It gets easier and you will get a lot better at it, to be sure. But on the inside, it's always a process of fine-tuning and careful practice. There's always something to be better at. There will always be the occasional new warning sign to add to that checklist. That's why I loved your idea of treating Rule #1 investing as a practice so much. That's just how a practice goes. It's a perfect attitude about lifelong learning and work toward mastery."

"It's nice to think of this practice as mine now. It's a little different from yours. And yours is different from mine."

"It is," he agreed, "and that's been a real education for me too, to see how Rule #1 investing looks when done by my daughter. I thought everyone doing this kind of investing would do it like I do, but you definitely put your own spin on it, and I love it. I love seeing you have your own flavor of this practice. It's the same, but it's yours, somehow."

"Like Practice Shares?" I teased him. He laughed.

"I was doing Practice Shares and didn't even know it! So yeah, exactly like that. And how much you think about the structure of companies, management, voting power, how indexes work, how stock markets work. I knew those things but I do not think about them in detail the way you do, and it has made me a better investor for sure."

That was so nice, I didn't know what to say. I reminded him, "Luckily we have the podcast, so I can keep bugging you about all these things. Our practice is definitely not over."

"Nope," he said, "but you are so much more free than you were before. Do you feel it? Because you certainly seem like you have a sense of freedom about you."

I did feel it. He was right. I had not dealt with the Enclosed Concrete Stairwell feeling for months.

"I think a lot of that, actually, is living without that constant fear of the future," I mused. "It's been a roller coaster of a journey, and I'm sure it's not over, but honestly, life without financial fear is freedom in a very real way. It's so real, I don't think I would be able to go forward into investing without having dealt with it."

Dad heartily agreed. "Plus, let's talk about literal financial freedom—the numbers—one last time. Now that you're ready with investing, the dollar figures and years we estimated seem more real, right?"

"To be honest," I muttered, "I don't remember my Number. And I don't want to! It's depressing."

Dad was silent, speechless.

"It's such a big Number that it feels unreachable," I explained. "Numbers aren't my thing! Sorry, but my practice hasn't changed that. I'd rather know I'm working toward it generally. That's enough for me."

"Okay," he acquiesced, "if that's what you want. I think you'll feel more comfortable with your Number once you make a little money investing."

I could see that happening. It would be more real.

"In fact," Dad went on, "you're even more ready than I expected, because you wanted to buy real shares before I planned."

"Er, yes, I suppose I did," I admitted.

"I think it's fine, though. It's obviously the culmination of the practice, so it's fitting you bought shares during our Year of Investing Practice. Now you've done everything."

"I think I have good companies to start with, and I have my buying plan for my Wishlist when those companies go on sale."

"You're set. You're ready. Are you afraid to buy when the prices get to your buy price?"

"Not in the least. I'm excited."

Having sufficiently congratulated ourselves, we could hardly move on to anything substantive, so we said our goodbyes and hung up.

My life had become so different in only a few months.

The whole is more than the sum of its parts. Somehow, I had never expected the parts of my Investing Practice to add up to such a deeply felt, life-changing, beautiful whole. How could learning about companies and the stock market make my life better? But it had.

Now I felt deeply settled. Practicing Rule #1 investing had taught me to see that the fabric of our society is woven with people who make things, provide services, are entrepreneurial in some way or another, and do good. They are hidden in plain sight. Now, as an investor, I saw them. Their companies might be too hard for me to understand, but I could see them, and I might be able to support their Missions with my investing dollars. I was thrilled to make an impact with my investments, and I had been right—investing in my Missions kept me interested when I was searching for companies to love, engaged when I felt like dropping my practice for easier pursuits, and focused when my eyes glazed over from reading a 10-K.

My goal of freedom meant, most of all, to have less stress in my life and be healthy. I wasn't there yet, but in the meantime, just by focusing on freedom and creating space for it to arrive in my life, it somehow had.

I had gone from a head-down, work-focused kind of life to unexpectedly traveling on a regular basis, to an unexpectedly exciting side gig with our *InvestED* podcast, and to making room in my life for a serious boyfriend. I would never have predicted any of it.

It didn't take oodles of money in the exact amount of my Number, whatever it is, sitting in my bank account to make me feel free, it turned out. Taking control of my finances and my financial demons made me free. Which was really the focus all along, I realized. Only once I had faced them was I open enough to even attempt investing. My feelings about money really have nothing to do with money. They have to do with a lot of other stuff in my head—my background, experiences, emotions. They have a lot to do with my family and its history with money. To someone else, the financial world offered an abundance of opportunity to create those good money feelings. But to me, it took internal work. I had come a long way with investing, finances, and how I saw myself in that world.

I'm not the only one who has observed that focusing on long-term value in companies has—poof!—manifested value in the rest of their life. Guy Spier wrote an entire book about how his education as a value investor was also an enlightenment that developed his values. Buffett and Munger regularly give advice about how to live a good life at the Berkshire Hathaway annual meeting in Omaha, and have observed that focusing on buying wonderful companies supports long-term beneficial life choices.

I was loving this practice far more than I ever thought I would. Its knowledge gave me power and control over my life that I had been sorely lacking. I was loving it more than my practice of the law.

My boyfriend lived an ocean away from me and neither of us had a flexible job. Nuno offered to give everything up and move to Boulder, but I didn't want to make him move to a strange country for a law firm–centric future I wasn't sure I wanted anymore.

I wanted to become a real investor, and I wanted to focus on my podcast with Dad. I wasn't at my Number yet, not even close, but thanks to our podcast and the housing market, I realized that I could create financial freedom for myself by quitting my law firm job and focusing on investing, and that would be more than enough for now.

What good is life if not to really live as much of it as I could? I didn't have kids, dependents, or a reason to stay. Though I would dearly miss working in the entrepreneurial community, I knew that I would return to that world again in some capacity and be able to help more effectively than I had as an exhausted, sick lawyer. I loved it too much to stay away. Most important, I was getting healthy again. I had gotten enough rest, and I no longer felt that deadly level of tired that wouldn't go away. My stomach was calmed down already and my hair had stopped falling out in clumps. I was off my medication and no longer dependent on a daily Ziploc baggie of supplements to get through the day.

I had started to feel like myself again—sturdy, strong, focused. I had started to feel like maybe I looked a bit like that image I had of myself as a successful investor.

I made the decision.

It was a rabid housing market. I sold my condo for a profit, paid off my student loans, and took the leap: I quit my law firm job. I was semiterrified at such a crazy step, but mostly I was excited about the great unknown in the future.

I put all my furniture in storage and moved with a few suitcases to my mom's house in Wyoming. I was officially living with my mom. And yet, somehow, I felt like I had come up in the world. That's what freedom was to me. I didn't care what anyone else thought. I zagged, and I felt the deep peace of moving into the river current.

I felt joyful. I felt free.

I went to Zurich for a few weeks and then Nuno and I went to Lisbon to spend Christmas with his family. Nuno's parents didn't speak much English and I spoke no Portuguese, so we drank wine and Portuglished our way through the holiday. It was great.

And I started looking toward the future. I made a list of what to do going forward to support continuing my practice.

Now, when I feel freaked out and shaky and worried about putting real money into the market, a checklist is my go-to. The cold, hard facts written on it, with requirements that I need to meet, are a stabilizing force. Checklists, to state the obvious, ensure I won't forget anything important.

Ongoing Practice Checklist

❏   Wishlist status. Calendar the quarterly and annual reports for each Wishlist company, using a separate category on my calendar so I could remove them from view unless I wanted to check. Sign up for each company's investor updates on their websites, set up e-mail alerts for each company's SEC filings, and make a filter for each company so that my e-mail wouldn't get clogged with all those alerts. As with the calendar, that way I could easily check it when I wanted to, and otherwise not be bothered.

❏ Once a quarter, reread my Story and Story inversion for each company to remind myself where I started. Small changes are easy to overlook. Recalculate my three buy prices with the updated numbers from the quarterly earnings report.

❏ Watch market-wide indicators. Not all that regularly, but keep an eye on the Shiller P/E and Buffett Indicator.

❏ Read more books about the world of value investing. *Poor Charlie's Almanack,* a heavy coffee table book compendium of Uncle Charlie's sayings, stories, and biography, is a great place to start. One investor I know told me he keeps it within reach to flip through every now and then for advice, and always finds something useful. I also wanted to learn more about other value investors and the advice they give for those of us who are still learning.

❏ Research. I decided to keep paying for the *Wall Street Journal.* I used it often for my research and for the news, and it gave me great perspective on the market. I would evaluate at the beginning of next year whether I would add another expensive research source like *Barron's* or the *Financial Times* to my payroll.

My family was scattered around the globe on Christmas Day, so we all gathered in San Diego the next week and celebrated on New Year's Day. My first year of my Investing Practice was over and what we dubbed "New Year's Christmas" was the right time to celebrate all the changes that had happened during that year.

Dad and I had a moment in between the family festivities to speak our own language to each other.

He looked at me. "This has been pretty amazing."

We both nodded. "Well, I guess we won't be talking as much as we have been. You don't really need me anymore," he half joked. "You're good on your own."

What? I thought. "Are you crazy? I need to check my work with you and I need to steal ideas from you. Can we still have investing calls?"

He smiled. "Yeah, I mean, if that's what it takes to talk, then absolutely."

Then I saw what he was getting at. "No, Dad, of course we can talk about other stuff too. We can just . . . talk."

"I don't want to lose this relationship we've developed."

"We won't," I promised. "It's just up to us to keep it up. It's a good problem to have."

I was so thankful for my problems. I had to learn to trust myself. The trust I found in my dad was a bonus.

The Year of Investing Practice may have come to an end, but my practice, and my new life, was just beginning.

DECEMBER PRACTICE: You've done it: an entire year of Investing Practice. Take a few minutes to reflect on your practice over the last year. Notice how your life has changed. Have your problems changed? Develop your own plan to take charge of your Investing Practice going forward.

IN JUNE 2017, I GOT THE NEWS FROM AN E-MAIL ALERT THAT AMAZON would acquire Whole Foods for $42 per share. My phone lit up with texts from friends who knew I loved that company, and then my dad called to congratulate me. It was like my birthday.

I had gotten it right! Lots of things could have stopped Whole Foods' potential from being fully realized, so to have a home run with a great company with a great Mission felt like winning the game. All the headaches, all the time spent reading annual reports, all the research, all the emotional ups and downs, all the doubts—it made all that practice worthwhile.

It was early evening in Zurich. Nuno and I hadn't continued dating across the Atlantic much longer before I promised to marry him. To others, I knew it seemed like our relationship had moved quickly, but in our own little bubble, we felt slow, and after months unsuccessfully trying to schedule a soon-ish wedding between our busy families on different continents, we gave up and eloped. We were married in a ramshackle judge's office on a rainy day in Boulder without any stress except showing up on time. We knew we would party with our families later, and we treasure having that day in our memories, just us.

Soon afterward, I, and a shipping container full of my clothes and furniture, moved to Zurich. Moving to another country as a newlywed had plenty of its own challenges of assimilation, but I relished them. It was really a whole new life.

Sitting in my big chair that evening, I needed to know from my dad what to do with the shares of Whole Foods I owned. I called him.

"Sell Whole Foods," my dad instructed me. "Now."

The stock price was selling slightly above the deal price of $42, and my dad wanted me to grab it before the price went down. Sometimes after a deal is announced, another buyer will show up and offer a higher price. And sometimes the deal just blows up. Here, we both thought that was highly unlikely, as John Mackey clearly wanted Amazon, and no one else, to buy his baby.

My dad was right, but it was happening awfully fast. Only a few hours had passed since hearing the news, and now I had to sell this company that I loved? I felt deflated. Everything I had gone through with this company was coming to a head, and now I, unceremoniously, like dumping just *any* company, would sell? Like it had meant nothing to me at all?

Despite our desire to "never sell," selling was inexorably part of this practice.

I took a deep breath and decided to do what I had to do. I took no pleasure in it.

I typed in the sell order and guessed at what boxes to choose—I didn't remember how to sell a stock. I placed the cursor over the SELL button. Then I moved it away, to a safe place where an inadvertent click wouldn't end my relationship with a company I loved. I moved the cursor back, then away again. It was hard to click on that SELL button. These shares were *my* shares. They were how I got into investing. They were how I practiced. If I sold them, would I lose the connection to my first year of Investing Practice? Would it be like it had never happened?

No. I reminded myself that no one can take my knowledge or my practice away from me. This selling thing was just part of that practice. I had to practice selling just like I had practiced everything else.

Once I decided, the greedy part of me wanted to wait in case the price went up a few pennies. *That's speculation,* I heard my dad's voice saying in my head. *We don't act on speculative thoughts. We act on certainty.* Right then, I had a certain profit. I pressed SELL.

The screen said, "You have exceeded the time limit for placing an order." Wait, was it a sign? *Crap. Should I keep the shares after all? No, stop, just sell the damn things.*

I filled the form in again and pressed SELL. I saw "Order filled." I couldn't look at anything else. It was done.

Nuno came home while I was burying my breakup feelings in some Amazon Prime TV (ironically) while doing yoga. I told him the whole drama of my emotional roller coaster over selling some shares of stock. "It's because you fell in love with the company." He smiled, and he was right. I knew it was a victory, but it felt like a loss. I had lost my first love, and I wasn't sure I would ever find another one.

I let myself feel sad about losing Whole Foods for about a week before I felt the desire to calculate exactly what I had made. After adding up the dividends I had gotten from the company to calculate my basis, I compared it to my selling price. *Wait a second.* The return on my investment was 41 percent . . . 41 percent!

41 percent!

That was a nice little breakup present. All I could think about was that I had hit the mark: 41 percent was a good sight more than the 26 percent my dad had set as the optimal return, and I smiled inside all the way down to my toes. It was a great start. Time to get back to researching companies and looking for my next favorite company. I had fallen in love with this practice, really. I was moving on.

I WAS WATCHING THE LIVE STREAM OF WARREN BUFFETT'S ANNUAL meeting in Omaha during the time Danielle and I were working on this book. He and Charlie Munger were taking questions from the audience, and one question was what they'd like their legacy to be. Buffett answered he'd like to be thought of as a good teacher.

Warren Buffett is, of course, one of the wealthiest men in the world, a self-made man who started his investing career with $100, and a man who has given away more money to charity than anyone in the world—and yet here he was, telling us that none of that success matters to him as much as teaching us how to properly invest and be better people.

I think he chose his legacy well.

In my view, he and Charlie are among the most influential teachers in the last hundred years and, if judged by the financial impact of their teaching, perhaps the most important teachers of the modern era. Their long-term and consistently successful investing results have been one of the major anomalies for the Efficient Market Hypothesis paradigm and a spur to the efforts of the current generation of economists to dethrone EMH. They are responsible for creating not just wealth but, more important, knowledge about how to create wealth that can be passed down through family generations. This knowledge about investing to create "generational wealth" that I've tried to teach Danielle is not only about pure financial wealth, but also requires that your values be in charge of your money. And the coolest thing for me is that it was the deep connection between values and money that made this strategy of building wealth meaningful for Danielle.

This was a big deal for me; I've been trying her whole life to get her interested in investing. When she was a baby, sometimes she'd get a tummy ache in the middle of the night and I'd walk around with her in the dark and sing "Ragtime Cowboy Joe" to her. It was a song my dad told me had magic powers for lulling babies off to sleep; apparently, it had worked on me. I've gotta say, I was skeptical, but every time I'd sing it to her, she'd quiet down, and sometimes, when she was settled down and comfortable in my arms, I'd walk around with her and tell her about the companies I was investing in. That would put her dead out.

She and I were close from the very beginning of her life, but when she was young her mom and I split up, and Danielle felt I left her too, and that broke the trust she'd had in me. I never figured out how to earn it back. This book and the podcast we do together have given me another chance to be there for her, an opportunity I never expected to have. Her decision to trust in Warren and Charlie was also a decision to trust in me. I hope I've made the best of it.

The opportunity to pass down to the next generation a set of ideas that hold the potential to create generational wealth is a game changer. Mohnish Pabrai, in his fine book *The Dhando Investor*, writes about the Patel family as an example of a family with generational wealth that is more valuable than their actual wealth because, no matter what happens, the knowledge about how to create wealth can't be taken away. They knew how to own and run hotels, and when they immigrated to the United States in the 1960s with only a few thousand dollars and that knowledge, they bought a run-down motel and started over. Today, only fifty years later, the greater Patel family owns 40 percent of the hotels and motels in America. That is the power of a generational wealth strategy.

I know this much: I've done the best I know how to teach Danielle well so that she can have her own resources to live the life she wants. I think she really does own this Rule #1 strategy, maybe in a way better than I do. When I learned it, it all just seemed like what Charlie said—"It's all so easy and obvious; what would they have to do the rest of the semester?" But Danielle has had to dig deep to learn this, and I think that her efforts to understand have created a deep well of learning for all of us. It certainly has for me. There is an old saying that if you want to master something, teach it. I'd add that if you really, really, *really* want to master it, try to teach it to your really smart kid.

What Warren and Charlie have done is revolutionary; they've created a strategy that, if carefully followed, can make anyone wealthy. Just as the Patel family's generational wealth makes it possible for the family members who use it to become rich in the hospitality business, the Rule #1 investing strategy can make it possible for your family members to become rich from stock investing. Those of us who have followed that strategy owe a generational debt of gratitude to the grandfathers, Warren and Charlie, who gave us this wisdom. And I owe them a debt I can't pay for giving me my daughter back.

I love you, Danielle.

—PHIL TOWN

YOU ARE NOT DOING THIS ALONE. YOU ARE PART OF A FAMILY OF SUC-
cessful investors that goes back to 1934 when Ben Graham, Warren
Buffett's mentor, literally wrote the book on this investing strategy.
Over these eighty-something years, this investing strategy has been
responsible for creating incredible wealth, including the fortunes of
many of the richest people in the world. As a result, we have many
resources to help you begin and continue your own Investing Practice.

Start with my website, danielletown.com. Here, I have a person-
alized plan and support for your own Investing Practice, lots of additional MATH help, resources for your Investing Intensive, advice
for buying Practice Shares, ideas for building your investing office,
help with starting an investing group, reading lists, and even more
developments on the way. This site will be responsive to what you
(and I!) need as we go through our Investing Practices.

A concrete plan helps with sticking to a practice. I found it helpful
to have all the monthly practices in one place, so I could get a better
sense of what I was setting out to do. If you would like your own
chart of all the monthly practices, e-mail me at danielle@danielle
town.com or request it through danielletown.com/financialfreedom.

If you would like to receive my free monthly newsletter, which
includes insights from my own Investing Practice, information on
companies I find interesting, and the latest resources we've developed, sign up for it at danielletown.com.

To find out what companies I'm looking at in real time and what
I'm up to, follow me:

Facebook: Danielle Town
Twitter: @danielle_town
LinkedIn: Danielle Town
Instagram: danielletown
I'd love to connect with you as well—leave me a comment or

mention so I know you've read the book and are starting your own Investing Practice.

My dad's website, ruleoneinvesting.com/book, also has many investing and financial resources available to you. Here's where you can get information that is hard to get anywhere else, like who his favorite investing gurus are and what they are buying right now, as well as helpful calculators and accounting basics. If you want a shortcut to the numbers and financial statements, the Toolbox on ruleoneinvesting.com/book provides it. His Toolbox runs searches for companies and consolidates all the SEC filings into one place, calculating growth rates, the Moat and management numbers, and pricing and valuations for you. It even color codes the results so you can easily see which companies are looking up. My dad also regularly puts on a live workshop, for which you can sign up at ruleone investing.com/book—and sometimes I show up at it, too.

Our podcast, *InvestED: The Rule #1 Podcast*, is available on all the different podcast apps, including iTunes, Google Play, and SoundCloud, and at investedpodcast.com. My dad taught me this Investing Practice on the podcast, and by listening to it, you will get the same education I did. You'll also get a bit of amusement listening to me bug my dad to answer every single one of my questions, convincing him to change his mind occasionally, and often cracking each other up. We have heard from more than one person who listened to every episode from the first to the most recent, and then went back and started at the beginning a second time to make sure they understood every point. You can e-mail us with questions and comments for the podcast at questions@investedpodcast.com.

I look forward to hearing from you about your extraordinary practice of finding financial freedom, and how you have made it your own.

Warmly,
Danielle

The Rental House's Story in Numbers

FINANCIAL STATEMENT	
No Income Statement or Balance Sheet	
Cash Flow Statement	
Net Income	$28,000
Operating Cash	$28,000
Maintenance Capital Expenditures	$4,000
Growth Capital Expenditures	$0
Windage Growth Rate	3%
OWNER EARNINGS	
Owner Earnings (Net Income plus Depreciation & Amortization plus Net Change: Accounts Receivable plus Net Change: Accounts Payable plus Income Tax plus Maintenance Capital Expenditures)	$24,000
FREE CASH FLOW	
Free Cash Flow (Net cash provided by operating activities plus Purchase of Property & Equipment plus (any other capital expenditures for maintenance and growth)	$24,000

Lemonade Stand's Story in Numbers

FINANCIAL STATEMENT	
Income Statement	
Revenue/Sales	$10,000
Expenses	$8,000
Income Tax	$500
Net Income (Revenue minus Expenses)	$2,000
Balance Sheet	
Assets	$6,000
Liabilities	$1,000
Equity (Assets minus Liabilities)	$5,000
Cash Flow Statement	
Net Income (brought over from the Income Statement)	$2,000
Depreciation & Amortization (brought over from the Income Statement)	$1,000
Net Change: Accounts Receivable	($300)
Net Change: Accounts Payable	$100
Net Cash (provided by operating activities)	$2,800
Maintenance Capital Expenditures (not provided on financial statements; review Cash Flow Statement for maintenance-related capital expenditures and add them up)	($500)
Growth Capital Expenditures (not provided on financial statements; review Cash Flow Statement for capital expenditures and add them up)	($800)
Owner Earnings (Net Income plus Depreciation & Amortization plus Net Change: Accounts Receivable plus Net Change: Accounts Payable plus Income Tax plus Maintenance Capital Expenditures)	$2,800
Free Cash Flow (Net cash provided by operating activities plus Purchase of Property & Equipment plus (any other capital expenditures for maintenance and growth) (not typically provided on financial statements, but The Lemonade Stand is a very thorough company)	$1,500

MOAT: THE BIG FOUR GROWTH RATES

Net Income Growth over past 10 years	18%
Book Value/Equity Growth over past 10 years	16%
Sales Growth over past 10 years	17%
Operating Cash Growth over past 10 years	18%
Windage Growth Rate	16%

MANAGEMENT NUMBERS (LOOKING FOR 10% OR HIGHER)

Return on Equity (ROE)	40%

Return on Invested Capital (ROIC)	33%
Long-Term Debt	$1,000
Can Free Cash Flow pay off debt in less than 2 years?	yes

OWNER EARNINGS

Owner Earnings (Net Income plus Depreciation & Amortization plus Net Change: Accounts Receivable plus Net Change: Accounts Payable plus Income Tax plus Maintenance Capital Expenditures)	$2,800

FREE CASH FLOW

Free Cash Flow (Net cash provided by operating activities plus Purchase of Property & Equipment plus (any other capital expenditures for maintenance and growth)	$1,500

MARGIN OF SAFETY NUMBERS

Earnings Per Share (EPS)	$20
Windage Growth Rate	16%
Windage Price-to-Earnings (P/E) Ratio	22
Minimum Acceptable Rate of Return	15%

Whole Foods' Story in Numbers (2015)

FINANCIAL STATEMENT	
Income Statement	
Revenue/Sales (Whole Foods also adds Investment Income)	$15,406,000,000
Expenses	$14,870,000,000
Income tax	$342,000,000
Net Income	$536,000,000
Balance Sheet	
Assets	$5,741,000
Liabilities	$1,972,000,000
Net Equity (Assets minus Liabilities) (*provided on financial statements*)	$3,769,000,000
Cash Flow Statement	
Net Income	$536,000,000
Depreciation & Amortization	$439,000,000
Net Change: Accounts receivable	($21,000,000)
Net Change: Accounts payable	$20,000,000
Net Cash Provided by Operating Activities/Operating Cash	$1,129,000,000
Maintenance Capital Expenditures	($335,000,000)
Growth Capital Expenditures (Development Cost of New Locations)	($516,000,000)
Total Capital Expenditures	$851,000,000
Owner Earnings (Net Income plus Depreciation & Amortization plus Net Change: Accounts Receivable plus Net Change: Accounts Payable plus Income Tax plus Maintenance Capital Expenditures) (*like The Lemonade Stand, Whole Foods is a very thorough company and provides Cash Flow numbers on p. 22 of their 2015 10-K*)	$981,000,000
Free Cash Flow (Net Cash Provided by Operating Activities minus Total Capital Expenditures) (*p. 22 of 2015 10-K*)	$278,000,000
MOAT: THE BIG FOUR GROWTH RATES	
Net Income Growth over past 10 years	20%
Book Value/Equity Growth over past 10 years	10%
Sales Growth over past 10 years	10%
Operating Cash Growth over past 10 years	5%
Windage Growth Rate	14%
MANAGEMENT NUMBERS (LOOKING FOR 10% OR HIGHER)	
Return on Equity (ROE)	15%
Return on Invested Capital (ROIC)	16%

Long-Term Debt	$62,000,000
Can Free Cash Flow pay off debt in less than 2 years?	yes

OWNER EARNINGS

Owner Earnings (Net Income plus Depreciation & Amortization plus Net Change: Accounts Receivable plus Net Change: Accounts Payable plus Income Tax plus Maintenance Capital Expenditures)	$981,000,000

FREE CASH FLOW

Free Cash Flow (Net Income plus Depreciation & Amortization minus Maintenance Capital Expenditures and Growth Capital Expenditures)	$278,000,000

MARGIN OF SAFETY NUMBERS

Earnings Per Share (EPS)	$1.48
Windage Growth Rate	14%
Windage Price-to-Earnings (P/E) Ratio	28
Minimum Acceptable Rate of Return	15%

Superinvestors with Audited Track Records

Investor	Relationship to Graham or Buffett	Investing Years	Rate of Return	Source
Ben Graham	Father of value investing and Warren Buffett's mentor	25	17%	Investopedia
Walter Schloss	Worked for Graham	28	21%	Buffett lecture at Columbia
Tom Knapp	Graham student	15	20%	Buffett lecture at Columbia
Warren Buffett	Worked for Graham	13	29%	Buffett lecture at Columbia
Bill Ruane	Graham student	13	18%	Buffett lecture at Columbia
Charles Munger	Buffett partner	13	20%	Buffett lecture at Columbia
Rick Guerin	Munger friend	19	33%	Buffett lecture at Columbia
Stan Perlmeter	Buffett friend	17	23%	Buffett lecture at Columbia
Washington Post Fund Manager #1	Buffett student	5	27%	Buffett lecture at Columbia
Washington Post Fund Manager #2	Buffett student	5	29%	Buffett lecture at Columbia
Washington Post Fund Manager #3	Buffett student	5	27%	Buffett lecture at Columbia
Washington Post Fund Manager #4	Buffett student	5	27%	Buffett lecture at Columbia
Berkshire Hathaway	Under Buffett and Munger	52	21%	Stock CAGR 14 to 275k
Julian Robertson	Graham and Buffett	20	32%	Investopedia
David Einhorn	Buffett	20	17%	Investopedia
Stanley Druckenmiller	Graham and Buffett	20	30%	Investopedia
Edward Thorpe	Buffett	20	28%	*Fortune's Formula* book
Seth Klarman	Buffett (25 Billion under mgmt)	20	21%	https://www .valuewalk .com/2017/09/seth -klarman-cash-return -time-sell/

Whole Foods' Payback Time

Year	Free Cash Flow	Growth Rate	Expected Growth in Free Cash Flow for Next Year	Cumulative Free Cash Flow During My Investment	Payback Time Buy Price
0	$278,000,000	14%	$38,920,000		
1	$316,920,000	14%	$44,368,800	$316,920,000	My 1-Year PBT
2	$361,288,800	14%	$50,580,432	$678,208,800	My 2-Year PBT
3	$411,869,232	14%	$57,661,692	$1,090,078,032	My 3-Year PBT
4	$469,530,924	14%	$65,734,329	$1,559,608,956	My 4-Year PBT
5	$535,265,254	14%	$74,937,136	$2,094,874,210	My 5-Year PBT
6	$610,202,389	14%	$85,428,335	$2,705,076,600	My 6-Year PBT
7	$695,630,724	14%	$97,388,301	$3,400,707,324	My 7-Year PBT
8	$793,019,025	14%	$111,022,664	$4,193,726,349	My 8-Year PBT

ACKNOWLEDGMENTS

WITHOUT THE QUESTIONS AND COMMENTS FROM OUR INTREPID POD-cast listeners, we would never have had the idea to write about this Investing Practice. We are continually grateful to each of you for engaging with us and sharing your own investing practices. Equally, there would be no book without the tradition of investing masters from whom we draw the wisdom of value investing. Benjamin Graham, Warren Buffett, and Charlie Munger lead that tradition, and we thank them for developing this practice and speaking and writing about what they do, so we can attempt to emulate their work.

Thank you to our extraordinary literary agents, Christy Fletcher and Sylvie Greenberg, who have guided us with deft and kind hands through every step of this process, and took us to the wonderful team at William Morrow/HarperCollins. There, we were fortunate to work with our editor, Matt Harper, and associate editor, Alieza Schvimer, whose hard work and insightful advice made this book better and turned it into the heartfelt story that it became; our acquiring editor, Amy Bendell, whose early enthusiasm was key; and the whole team led by the indomitable Lisa Sharkey, including Tavia Kowalchuk, Shelby Meizlik, Lauren Janiec, and Amelia Wood.

We're incredibly thankful to our friends and family who read drafts for their time and thoughtful comments: Kamala Nair, David Kienzler, Jessi Trujillo, Brian Hubbard, Katie Caves Gahr, Sarah Barthelow, Samantha Carney, Chris Collins, Chris Hazlitt, Alaina Town Bennett, Adam Bennett, and Nuno das Neves Cordeiro; to our family and friends who listened and gave advice along the way, especially Steve Town, Jeff Town, Lianne Childress, Alexis Lawrence, Ilana Miller, Devin Licata, Lauren Ivison, Megan Rushall, Afra Moenter, and Astrid Utrata; and to Danielle's former colleagues for being supportive at work and when she left Boulder, particularly

Chris Hazlitt, Mark Weakley, Laurel Durham, Jason Haislmaier, Adam Sher, Sean Odendahl, Jason Werner, Lorraine Torres, Joan Sherman, John Gaddis, Carlos Cruz-Abrams, David Kendall, Jennifer Rosenthal, Matt McKinney, Kyle White, and Brad Bernthal.

Guy Spier generously loaned some space in his library under a framed photograph of Charlie Munger whenever it was needed, and we're very thankful for his and Lory Spier's encouragement throughout the writing process. Thank you to Katharine Sephton for helping out with a constant smile.

Our deepest gratitude goes to our family for putting up with us during the occasionally arduous and often emotional writing and editing process, and somehow being endlessly encouraging through all of it: Melissa, Nuno, Mary, Alaina, Adam, Daniel, and Hunter. This book is for you.